SUPPORTING YOUNG ARTISTS

Related Resources From High/Scope Press

Books

Educating Young Children: Active Learning Practices for Preschool and Child Care Programs, Second Edition

A Study Guide to Educating Young Children: Exercises for Adult Learners, Second Edition

Tender Care and Early Learning: Supporting Infants and Toddlers in Child Care Settings

Training for Quality: Improving Early Childhood Programs Through Systematic Inservice Training

Other Resources

High/Scope Preschool Key Experiences: Creative Representation (booklet and video)

Supporting Young Artists: Exploring and Creating With Clay (video)

Supporting Young Artists: Exploring and Creating With Dough (video)

Supporting Young Artists: Exploring and Creating With Paper (video)

Supporting Young Artists: Exploring and Creating With Drawing and Painting (video)

Available from:
HIGH/SCOPE® PRESS

A division of the

HIGH/SCOPE EDUCATIONAL RESEARCH FOUNDATION
600 NORTH RIVER STREET
YPSILANTI, MICHIGAN 48198-2898
734/485-2000, FAX 734/485-0704
press@highscope.org

SUPPORTING YOUNG ARTISTS

ANN S. EPSTEIN

ELI TRIMIS

The Development of the Visual Arts in Young Children

HIGH/SCOPE® PRESS

Ypsilanti, Michigan

Published by

HIGH/SCOPE® PRESS

A division of the

HIGH/SCOPE EDUCATIONAL RESEARCH FOUNDATION
600 NORTH RIVER STREET
YPSILANTI, MICHIGAN 48198-2898
734/485-2000, FAX 734/485-0704
press@highscope.org

Editor: Linda Koopmann
Cover design, text design: Linda Eckel, Linda Eckel Graphic Design
Photography: Gregory Fox Photography and classroom teachers

Library of Congress Cataloging-in-Publication Data

Epstein, Ann S.

 Supporting young artists : the development of the visual arts in young children / Ann S. Epstein, Eli Trimis.

  p. cm.

Includes bibliographical references and index.

 ISBN 1-57379-171-7 (Soft cover : alk. paper)

 1. Art—Study and teaching (Early childhood)—United States. 2. Early childhood education—Activity programs—United States.   I. Trimis, Eli. II. Title.

 LB1139.5.A78 E67 2002

 372.5—dc21

                                                                      2002006126

Printed in the United States of America
10 9 8 7 6 5 4 3 2 1

Contents

PART II

An In-Depth Studio Approach to Developing Art in the Young Child 109

Acknowledgments

SUPPORTING YOUNG ARTISTS could not have been written without the support and creativity of many of our colleagues. We would like to begin by thanking the High/Scope Board of Directors, under the leadership of Founder and President Emeritus Dr. David P. Weikart and President Dr. Arthur Stellar, for its commitment to the arts as a vital part of a comprehensive educational approach. In the shifting debates between academics versus play, and child-initiated versus adult-initiated instruction in early childhood education, High/Scope holds a balanced position that values all types of learning and advocates an active role for all participants. With the support of the Foundation's leadership, we will maintain this steady course.

Our many colleagues have provided invaluable assistance in the conceptualization and completion of this book. The entire staff of the High/Scope Early Childhood Division contributed in some way to this publication. Mary Hohmann's early collaboration with Eli Trimis on a series of videotapes was the first step in integrating an overall active learning framework with the in-depth approach to visual arts education. Beth Marshall took the lead in developing a visual arts training workshop for early childhood practitioners that further synthesized the teacher-training components of these two approaches. Her work on adult support strategies was systematically validated through the efforts of the High/Scope field consultants who continue to help teachers and caregivers make the visual arts a daily program fixture.

Other early childhood staff who reviewed manuscript drafts and provided thoughtful feedback include Michelle Graves and Shannon Lockhart. Teachers Rosie Lucier and Sue Gainsley piloted many of the ideas at the High/Scope Demonstration Preschool and provided a wealth of documentation on young children's art-making and art-appreciating experiences. Eva Prince-Bey's remarkable organizational skills helped to keep the entire enterprise on track. Colleagues in other Foundation departments who deserve our thanks include Phyllis Weikart, Chris Ashley, and Chuck Wallgren, whose backgrounds in movement and music education added an important perspective on the overall role of the arts in human development. Editors Lynn Taylor and Nancy Brickman edited Ann Epstein's earlier articles on art and young children. Their contributions to those manuscripts in turn contributed to the development of this book.

Faculty and staff in the Early Childhood Education Department at Aristotle University in Thessaloniki, Greece, also provided support and assistance in the development and documentation of the in-depth studio approach. Special gratitude is extended to Dr. Christos Frangos, department head and founder of the Child Development Center, for his scientific expertise and dedication to the arts as a motivating force in human behavior. Preschool teachers Anastassia Thassiti, Yolanda Meimaroglou, Chryssoula Manavopoulou, Melania Papadopoulou, Evangelia Bakali, Elissavet Theodorou, Maria Papadopoulou, Elena Kotta, as well as former students and now preschool teachers Maria Loukovitou, Garifalia Moyisidou, Anastasia Papathanassiou, Marianthi Sarigiannidou, and Maria Troullou, studied, implemented, and documented the in-depth approach as the capstone experience of their student teaching. The young children in their classrooms today continue to benefit from their training, as do the many colleagues who learn from their example.

We extend awe and appreciation to the book's talented production team. Thank you to Linda Koopmann, our editor, whose careful and methodical review of the manuscript guaranteed a publication that would be clear and useful to the scholars and practitioners who read it. Pattie McDonald was meticulous and error-free in entering all the revisions. A book on the visual arts is necessarily dependent on visuals to illustrate the ideas and make them real to readers. In that regard, Kevin McDonnell's work on the related videotape series and Gregory Fox's photography in the classroom contributed enormously to the look and effectiveness of this book. Linda Eckel is responsible for the book's overall layout and design. We thank her for envisioning a product that delights the eye at the same time it engages the mind. The book's very appearance attests to the power of the visual arts in helping us appreciate and think about the world around us.

Finally, our most heartfelt thanks go to the teachers and children at the High/Scope Demonstration Preschool, the Aristotle University Child Development Center, and the many other early childhood programs throughout the United States and Greece whose experiences are documented in this book. Virtually all the teachers came to their positions with no specific training or background in fine art. Their successful efforts prove that any practitioner with a knowledge of child development, an openness to invention, and appropriate administrative and technical support, can make art an exciting and natural component of any early childhood program. The children's enthusiasm speaks for itself. Their boundless curiosity and creativity is all the evidence we need that supporting young artists is a valuable and enriching enterprise for people of all ages.

SUPPORTING YOUNG ARTISTS

INTRODUCTION

Supporting Young Artists is a book about the role of the visual arts in early childhood care and education. At the heart of its message is a strong conviction that art should be a vital component of young children's experiences—one of the foundations children need on the path to a complete and fulfilling adulthood. Early childhood educators have long held that art promotes children's expressive and social development. To justify budgetary allocations, art educators contend that academic achievement is also enhanced through engagement with the arts. Research bears out both beliefs. In the introduction to *Champions of Change: The Impact of the Arts on Learning* (Fiske, 1999), a compilation of seven studies on arts education, former United States Secretary of Education Richard Riley states that

> Parents and other caregivers want to equip young people for professionally and personally rewarding careers, and they recognize that to do so we must give them greatly enriched experiences. As these researchers have confirmed, young people can be better prepared for the 21st century through quality learning experiences in and through the arts. (p. vi)

Young people of all backgrounds benefit from involvement in the arts. An analysis of data on 25,000 students from the United States Department of Education's longitudinal survey found that arts education can help level the playing field for youngsters from disadvantaged circumstances (Catterall, Chapleau, & Iwanga, 1999). The arts are also important for advanced students who might otherwise become bored with school and disengaged from the learning process. Research by the National Research Center on the Gifted and Talented, for example, demonstrated that the arts offer the kinds of creative and individualized challenges that maintain student involvement (Oreck, Baum, & McCartney, 1999).

Engaging in the arts is a personal experience that can transform the individual. "When well taught, the arts provide young people with authentic learning experiences that engage their minds, hearts, and bodies. The learning experiences are real and meaningful for them" (Fiske, 1999, p. ix). Students draw on all their resources and become invested in ways that are deeper than just knowing the answer; even their attitudes toward others can be altered through the arts learning experience (Burton, Horowitz, & Abeles, 1999). A program's commitment to the arts transforms not only the children but also the adults and the educational setting itself. "When the arts become central to the learning environment, schools and other settings become places of discovery. Teachers are renewed. Even the physical appearance of a school building is transformed through the representations of learning" (Fiske, 1999, p. ix).

Demonstrating the connection between the arts and academic achievement has re-awakened public interest in art education at the elementary and secondary school level. But the importance of visual arts education for very young children should not be underestimated either. "To the extent that artistic behaviors are encouraged and supported during their early childhood years, the ability to function as adults is enhanced" (Baker, 1990, p. 21).

Supporting Young Artists showcases how the High/Scope educational approach treats art as a valuable component of early childhood programs in its own right and also demonstrates how art education supports children's development in other domains. Part I (Chapters One–Four) provides a comprehensive and detailed look at the High/Scope approach to the visual arts for young children. Chapter One explains our position on why art is important in early childhood education, while Chapter Two provides an overview of art in the High/Scope framework, including the guiding principles for incorporating visual art in early childhood programs, the relevant High/Scope key experiences, and research on the effectiveness of the High/Scope approach in promoting the visual arts. Chapter Three covers the development of art in the young child from the perspective of both making art and appreciating art. It highlights the underlying principles derived from theory, research, and practice in the field and presents the stages through which children progress. Chapter Four details how adults can foster this development by providing appropriate space and materials, planning art-based experiences throughout the day, and engaging in supportive interactions with children. These adult support strategies are also addressed from the perspectives of both making and appreciating art. In addition, a discussion is provided about the kinds of institutional support teachers need in order to support art development in young children.

Part II (Chapters Five–Nine) highlights an in-depth studio approach to developing art in the young child. It illustrates how active learning programs can go beyond superficial experiences to provide young children with rich opportunities for exploration and creativity in diverse media. Chapter Five presents an overview of the in-depth approach, one that builds on children's natural interests, extends their abilities, and enhances their awareness of how these media are used in the world of art. The remaining chapters apply the in-depth approach to working with drawing and painting (Chapter Six); found and recycled materials, both natural and manufactured (Chapter Seven); paper (Chapter Eight); and the plastic arts (meaning media capable of being shaped or formed)—dough and clay (Chapter Nine). Each of these chapters provides a brief history of the medium, its visual and technical characteristics, and a description of how young children investigate and use the materials. The bulk of each chapter is a detailed case study of two or three early childhood programs in which the medium is explored over a period of time. It follows children as they progress through the four interrelated stages of the in-depth approach: introduction, enrichment, production, and reflection.

Supporting Young Artists is illustrated with anecdotes and photographs from the High/Scope Demonstration Preschool and other active learning programs in the United States and around the world. Throughout the book, the authors have attempted to combine the scholarship of theory and research with the experience and lessons of practice. The hope is that readers will gain an understanding of how the visual arts can be an exciting adventure in every early childhood program, and why they should be. Immersion in the visual arts will enrich the lives of not only the children who explore its possibilities but also the adults who furnish them with this invaluable opportunity.

Part I

*The High/Scope Approach
to the Visual Arts for
Young Children*

1

Why Art Is Important in Early Childhood Education

Three-year-old Jared mixes a big container of paint with a flat wooden stick. He starts with blue and adds yellow, red, and black to make a thick mud-colored mixture. He carefully carries his container of paint to the easel, dips the end of a rounded brush into the paint, and rubs it on the paper. Starting in the middle of the page, Jared rubs the brush back and forth, dips, and rubs again. Sometimes he moves the brush up and down, sometimes from side to side, and other times around in a circular motion. Gradually, Jared fills the entire paper, but he keeps adding more paint until the paper begins to crease and curl. He works a spot at his eye level over and over until there is a hole in the page, then touches the tip of his finger to the hole. Jared continues to paint, moving beyond the edges of the paper to the back and legs of the easel itself. He is completely absorbed in his task. His motions are deliberate, and he watches intently as the shiny wet paint fills up every inch of the surface before him.

Art for Its Own Sake

Art is *intrinsically rewarding* for people of all ages—young children like Jared, the little boy we just read about, as well as older youth and adults. That is to say, art is important *for its own sake.* Contact with the world of art and those who create art enriches our existence. The art experience itself turns us *inward* to define personal ideals of beauty, meaning, and value, while viewing art directs us *outward* to discover the bonds and differences that mark our relationships with other people and their aesthetic ideals.

Art calls upon all our senses and simultaneously engages our minds and bodies. Making art provides individuals with a means to express ideas and emotions and represent their experiences. Through art, we can explore our own abilities and appreciate the skills of others; through the study of art "students begin to see the rich mosaic of the world from many perspectives" (Dobbs, 1998, p. 12).

A girl paints for the pure pleasure of making brush strokes on the paper.

For young children, in particular, art can provide an internal sense of efficacy and control over their lives. For this reason, as well as others, art belongs in any comprehensive early childhood care and education program. Focusing on the period from birth to age eight, the Task Force on Children's Learning and the Arts noted that

> As they engage in the artistic process, children learn that they can observe, organize, and interpret their experiences. They can make decisions, take actions, and monitor the effect of those actions. They can create form and meaning where none existed before. The arts experience becomes a source of communication and interaction for children and adults. (Arts Education Partnership, 1998, p. 2)

Social constructivists would add that children's thinking and their ability to express their thoughts through artistic media develops as a result of their interactions with the social and cultural context (New, 1998).

Making art allows children to express strong emotions.

Among the many forms of art, visual art is perhaps most valuable as a means of non-verbal expression. For young children, who are just developing their language skills, using the tools of visual art to convey thoughts and feelings greatly expands their avenues for communication. Indeed, the very process of making art can elicit strong emotions in young children (see next page, right).

High/Scope includes these non-verbal forms of expression in the *creative representation key experiences*. (The High/Scope key experiences are defined and discussed in more detail later in this chapter and in Chapter Two.) Creating representations "draws upon children's real experiences, strengthens their mental images, and makes more vivid the meaning behind the symbols they encounter in their world" (Hohmann & Weikart, 2002, p. 312). The materials and processes of visual art enable children to "represent their memories, ideas, predictions, hypotheses, observations, [and] feelings" (Katz, 1998, p. 28).

Using similar terms to underscore art's inherent role in communication, the Reggio Emilia approach refers to the visual arts as a graphic language (Edwards, Gandini, & Forman, 1998). In the words of its founder, Loris Malaguzzi (1998),

> Putting ideas into the form of graphic representation allows the children to understand that their actions can communicate. This is an extraordinary discovery because it helps them realize that in order to communicate, their graphics must be understandable to others. In our view, graphic communication is a tool of communication much simpler than words. (p. 92)

Creating visual representations also helps children clarify what they want to express.

To say that art (and art education) is important for its own sake is ultimately a statement of cultural values and priorities (Gardner, 1990). In the framework of the High/Scope educational approach, art is included not "instead of" or "in addition to" other domains of development. Rather, art is seen as integral to who young children are and how they develop. Children "take comfort and even joy in merging thought, feeling, perception, and movement in the creation of a painting, drawing, model, or make-believe play sequence" (Hohmann & Weikart, 2002, p. 312). Research shows that children's art arises naturally from children's play (Arts Education Partnership, 1998). Therefore, any early childhood model that values play will value art.

Children use art to represent their everyday experiences.

Making Art Can Be Gratifying for Young Children

Three-year-old Amir stands in front of the easel at work time. In his left hand is a plastic container filled with green paint he has mixed with lots of yellow and a bit of blue. In his right hand is a thick-handled large brush. Amir begins to fill his paper with large blobs of paint. He rhythmically dips his brush in the paint and jabs the tip on the paper. Amir pauses to look, notices some blank areas, and resumes filling in those spaces with blobs of paint. He laughs with pleasure, using his entire upper body to dip and jab.

Art to Promote Other Areas of Development

Apart from its intrinsic, or inherent, value, art is also *extrinsically valuable* in promoting other areas of development. Art education contributes to the development of many social and academic skills.

> For all children, at all ability levels, the arts play a central role in cognitive, motor, language, and social-emotional development. The arts motivate and engage children in learning, stimulate memory and facilitate under-standing, enhance symbolic communication, promote relationships, and provide an avenue for building competence. (Arts Education Partnership, 1998, p. v)

Research documents the role of art in promoting children's development from infancy to adolescence. At the youngest ages, for example, exposure to visual materials, especially those that allow children to discover patterns on their own, appears to be a crucial component of early brain development and a precursor to the development of creative problem-solving skills (Healy, 1994). A 10-year national study on after-school arts programs found that "children involved in the arts use linguistic and cognitive thinking skills that transfer readily to social and academic activities" (Heath, 1998). Former education secretary Riley summed up the latest research by saying,

> If young Americans are to succeed and to contribute to what Federal Reserve Chairman Alan Greenspan described as our "economy of ideas," they will need an education that develops imaginative, flexible, and tough-minded thinking. The arts powerfully nurture the ability to think in this manner. (Fiske, 1999, p. vi)

Art develops motor skills. A girl dances as she paints with her feet.

Despite the demonstrated potential of art education to enhance cognitive and social development, the study of art is too often dismissed as frivolous.

Art develops social skills. Children collaborate on a styrofoam sculpture.

"More than in any other country, art education in the United States has been considered an unimportant part of a child's scholastic profile" (Gardner, 1990, p. 36). Oddly enough, educators may have contributed to this perception of art as an unnecessary frill in the overall system of schooling. By advocating individual expressiveness in the production of art, some practitioners have shortchanged the scholarly components that also comprise education in the arts. Yet art is as much an intellectual activity as an intuitive one (Arnheim, 1989). The study of art requires perception, memory, and concept formation. It involves the use and transformation of symbols, the recognition of pattern, and the perception of similarities and differences in shape, size, color, and texture. "Being able to think about something not present and then find a way to express it is a major cognitive accomplishment for young children" (Seefeldt, 1995, p. 40).

Understanding the cognitive basis of art allows teachers to accord respect to art education and see children's production and

Representations in Clay Reveal Emerging Concepts in Logic and Math

Key experiences in logic and math

- Arranging materials in graduated order
- Using comparison words
- Describing sequence and time

In the art area at work time, four-year-old Alana flattens clay into round disks. She lines them up in order, from the smallest to the biggest. Alana gets a marker and adds dots to the disks. She takes a medium-sized disk over to her teacher, Becki, and says, "Wanna chip cookie? I already ate the biggest one. It was good! I'm gonna make more after we finish these."

Key experiences in logic and math

- Counting objects
- Comparing numbers of objects

At small-group time, three-year-old Andrew pinches small pieces off of a big chunk of clay. He rolls them between his hands to form balls. "One, two, three, eight, five," he says, touching the balls one at a time as he recites each number. Andrew gets some twigs and sticks one twig in each ball, saying, "It's a lollipop field." He returns the unused twigs to the science area.

Art develops cognitive skills. A boy methodically covers all his clay with balls.

analysis of visual art as serious work. Even in their most rudimentary explorations of visual arts media, young children are exploring and displaying their awareness of such concepts as size and shape, surface and ground, and one-to-one correspondence (see at left).

In the last two decades, there has been an effort to broaden the focus of visual arts education to encompass both its expressive dimensions and its intellectual components. One of the most influential movements in broadening visual arts education has

A girl makes a pattern by alternating balls and cylinders.

been discipline-based art education (DBAE), a concept introduced by Greer (1984) and developed and field-tested with support from the Getty Education Institute for the Arts. The goals statement of the National Art Education Association (1982) endorsed a comprehensive approach that included both the production and the analysis of art. A statement issued by the National Endowment for the Arts (1988) outlined broad goals for art education that included fostering creativity, promoting communication skills, making choices based on critical assessment, and learning about the significant achievements of the world's civilizations. This broad-based focus was reflected in the *National Standards for Arts Education: What Every Young American Should Know and Be Able to Do in the Arts* (U. S. Department of Education, 1994). The arts were also included in the mandated reforms of the Goals 2000: Educate America Act passed by Congress (National Education Goals Panel, 1994), which established the Task Force on Children's Learning and the Arts: Birth to Age Eight. The Task Force explicitly recognized the role of the arts in promoting language and literacy, thereby contributing to the first educational goal that "all children will start school ready to learn."

Art promotes language and literacy. Three "work-in-progress" signs carry a clear message from a young sculptor.

Art promotes numeracy skills. A boy shows his teacher he painted five dots, one for each finger on his hand.

Art Within a Comprehensive Approach to Child Development

In High/Scope programs, art is viewed as one component in an integrated approach to child development. High/Scope advocates art education for its own sake and for its facilitation of perceptual, physical, social, emotional, and intellectual development. High/Scope settings provide young children with ample opportunities to explore art materials, create works of art, and appreciate the art created by others. Some educational approaches begin with art and use it as the springboard for other areas of development. By contrast, High/Scope begins with a comprehensive approach to child development and includes art as one of its components. This is an important distinction. It says that while visual arts are explicitly addressed in the High/Scope curriculum, teachers do not divide children into a collection of discrete abilities or focus on isolated developmental tasks.

This comprehensive view of child development is reflected in the High/Scope preschool *key experiences:*

> The High/Scope preschool key experiences are a series of statements describing the social, cognitive, and physical development of children aged 2½ to 5. The key experiences describe what young children do, how they perceive their world, and the kinds of experiences that are important for their development. (Hohmann & Weikart, 2002, p. 297)

Similarly, the High/Scope key experiences for infants and toddlers "frame the content of early learning and development" (Post & Hohmann, 2000, p. 35).

High/Scope's key experiences (58 preschool key experiences and 41 infant-toddler experiences) address the following areas of early childhood development:

- *Preschool:* initiative and social relations, language and literacy, creative representation (the key experience category most relevant to the visual arts), movement, music, classification, seriation, number, space, and time

- *Infants and toddlers:* sense of self, social relations, communication and language, creative representation, movement, music, exploring objects, early quantity and number, space, and time

Underlying the High/Scope approach is the concept of *active learning,* whereby children interact with materials, people, ideas, and events to construct their knowledge and understanding of their world. By making plans, carrying out their intentions, and reflecting on what they have done (the *plan-do-review* sequence), children engage and make sense of their social and physical environment. This process applies to all the key experiences in the High/Scope framework and to young children's visual arts experiences in particular (see at right).

While stressing the importance of child choice and initiation, however, High/Scope also recognizes that adults play an active and vital role in supporting and extending children's learning in the arts as well as other areas. Support for this position comes from the National Art Education Association:

> Art making is a natural occurrence of childhood, an activity young children discover and pursue even in the absence of adult prompting. Yet it becomes more clear every day that the nature of children's experience with art depends crucially on the adults who are responsible, by design or default, for guiding the course of artistic development and learning. This is particularly true for young children, who depend upon adults for basic access to workable materials, as well as for the encouragement to use them. (Thompson, 1995, p. 1)

Visual Art Carries One Child Through Plan-Do-Review

At planning time, four-year-old Malka announces she is going to make a teacher outfit for her doll. "What will you use?" asks her teacher, Renée. Malka brings some crepe paper to the table and says, "I'm going to use this paper to make her smock. But I'll have to draw teddy bears on the pockets." "The teacher's smock has teddy bears on the pockets," acknowledges Renée. "And she needs a flashlight to put inside the pocket," adds Malka. "A flashlight?" inquires Renée. "Yes, so she can find all the children when they get lost," answers Malka. At work time, Malka wraps her doll in crepe paper and uses a marking pen to draw a figure she calls a teddy bear on each side. She takes a wooden clothespin and makes a yellow dot at the top, then clips it to the smock. When she is finished, Malka goes around the room saying to different children, "I'm the teacher and I can see you with my flashlight!" When Malka brings her flashlight to the table for recall time, Renée asks her to "shine" it at each of the children when it is their turn to talk about what they did at work time.

Adults encourage children to talk about and reflect on their art experiences.

High/Scope teachers use the High/Scope key experiences as a conceptual framework to plan activities, observe children, reflect on the day, and provide the learning opportunities that are essential to the healthy physical, intellectual, social, and emotional growth of young children.

The following chapter explores in greater depth the High/Scope approach to art and the key experiences that support artistic and overall development.

2

An Overview of the
High/Scope Approach to Art

At recall time, three-year-old Douglas shows his teacher and classmates the "spider web"—lines coming out of a small circle on the middle of the page—that he drew with a pencil.

———

At small-group time, four-year-old Jessie pats out an oval of red and blue play dough, being careful to keep the colors from blending too much. She selects a heart-shaped cookie cutter and says to her teacher, Michelle, "Let's make some cookies for people who are dead."

Michelle acknowledges Jessie's statement by repeating, "You want to make cookies for people who are dead?" Jessie replies, "Yes. When I'm done, they can put them in their mouth. Then they'll be alive again." Jessie cuts out cookies, re-forms the dough to fill in the holes with the same color and thickness of dough, and cuts out more cookies. She gently lifts the heart-shaped cookies off the table and places them on a cookie sheet so she "can bake them later."

This chapter presents an overview of the conceptual framework and practical implications of the High/Scope approach to the visual arts. It sets forth the principles that guide High/Scope's integration of the visual arts into its early childhood program and includes a summary of the High/Scope key experiences most relevant to implementing and understanding the development of art in young children. The chapter concludes with a review of the research demonstrating the effectiveness of the High/Scope educational approach in enhancing children's development in general and their creative representation skills in particular.

High/Scope Offers a Comprehensive
Approach to Visual Art

As a component of our comprehensive approach to child development, High/Scope advocates and practices a comprehensive approach to the visual arts. In the fullest sense of the word, being artistic involves developing and exercising a sense of aesthetics. It means being aware of the creative possibilities of materials and knowing how they can

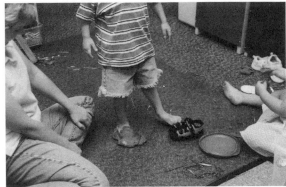

Children in High/Scope programs have many opportunities to explore art materials, including paint, paper, and clay.

be transformed to evoke feelings or stimulate ideas. Introducing young children to the visual arts gives them another way of knowing their world through direct encounters with raw materials, people, and the objects created by their interactions. By encouraging young children to explore, produce, and appreciate art, we are deepening their understanding of the environment and enriching their lives in the process. Engagement with the world of the visual arts is a skill and a pleasure they can enjoy for the rest of their lifetimes.

The High/Scope educational approach for young children is uniquely suited to incorporating these diverse components of visual arts education. Both the expressive qualities of making art and the intellectual challenges of appreciating art are encompassed in the Foundation's developmental framework.

In the realm of *making art,* the emphasis at the early childhood level should be on exploring and using materials. In the High/Scope educational approach, adults make a wide variety of art materials available. Opportunities to work with visual art materials are provided throughout the daily routine, and children are encouraged to explore

Teachers and children review artwork in a safe and accepting environment.

the materials and tools at their own developmental level, without being pressured to make an adult-designed product. For example, planning time allows children to visually represent their intentions regarding where, with what, and with whom they want to play. Work time lets children incorporate art materials in a variety of ways as they pursue their plans and interests, whether in the art area or other parts of the room. Small-group time becomes a venue for teachers to introduce new art materials and encourage children to explore their properties.

To promote *appreciating art,* High/Scope programs create a safe and nurturing environment where children's observations about art are accepted and respected. The review component of the daily routine encourages children to reflect on their activities and to observe and comment on the work of others. Conversations may center around the artwork of the children and their peers, or the work of artists whose reproductions are posted throughout the room or whose studios the children have visited. Outside time provides a setting for children to observe the aesthetic properties of the natural environment. Using children's interests and activities as the starting point, High/Scope teachers can bring in ideas from art history or contemporary art that appeal to children's inherent curiosity about the world. Art awareness

Four-year-old Michael and five-year-old Tamika are playing "race cars" at work time. They use sheets of newspaper to make a track and then they get small wooden cars from the toy area. "We need a big car for the leader," says Michael. "I know," says Tamika, "let's make one." In the art area, they collect the following scrap materials: an empty granola box, two cardboard paper towel tubes, and four plastic milk carton lids. Michael lays the cereal box flat and tapes the tubes underneath for wheels. Tamika glues the lids, two on each side, for the "door handles." They decide a racing car needs a number. Using a red marker, Tamika makes a "3" on the left side of the car. "My best number is 4," says Michael, as he writes it on the other side of the car. Tamika looks momentarily distressed. "A car has one number," she says. "Our leader car can have two," says Michael, and Tamika accepts this solution. Tamika carries the car back to the newspaper track and puts it in front of the line of toy cars. "Let's start the race," says Michael.

thus becomes part of their everyday experiences and conversations.

By maintaining this dual emphasis on making and appreciating art, the High/Scope educational approach allows young children to use the full range of their cognitive and intellectual capacities as well as their emotional and expressive ones (see at left). Including the arts as a component of a broad-based active learning curriculum also insures that experiences in the arts will generalize to other domains.

Research shows that learning in and through the arts enhances children's development when the school climate as a whole is supportive of active and productive learning (Burton et al., 1999). This description aptly characterizes the High/Scope approach. In High/Scope settings, children are actively engaged in making choices about how and what they learn. They carry out their intentions in an environment rich in materials and adult support. Finally, children reflect on their actions to maximize learning and encourage future purposeful activity. In these ways, the High/Scope approach to art accommodates the whole child in the context of the whole program.

Guiding Principles for Integrating Visual Art Into Early Childhood Programs

Integration of the visual arts into the High/Scope educational approach is guided by the set of principles listed in this section. As is true in all aspects of the curriculum model, these principles reflect child development theory and research and distill lessons learned from years of practice.

▶ **1. Art begins with exploration.** The primary goal of early art education is to promote a sense of artistic inquiry and playfulness, beginning with the exploration of materials. Art experiences for young children should focus on process, not product; it is a mistake to pressure young children to represent something with the materials before they are ready. Children first need and want to discover how the materials feel in their hands, how they look on different surfaces, and how they are transformed by their actions.

For children in the sensory-motor stage, exploring art materials with all their senses is as natural and necessary as exploring rattles, seashells, keys, and anything else that comes to hand. For children in the preoperational or concrete operational stage, artistic expression is rooted in actual experiences with objects, people, and events. To make art, children must first have a feeling, thought, or experience that they want to express. From these personal motivations, children will eventually begin to represent their ideas and experiences with art materials.

Young children are more interested in exploring a medium than in making a product.

▶ **2. Art should be integrated throughout the daily routine.**
After art materials and tools are introduced to preschool children during small-group time, these items should also be accessible during the plan-do-review portion of the daily routine. Children may choose to use various media to make and carry out their plans or to represent their activities during recall time (another name for the review part of the plan-do-review sequence).

During snack time, art objects made by children or brought in from home can engender lively conversation. During large-group time, children might use sculptural objects or banners they have created to move to music. At outside time, they might investigate the properties of the clay in the local soil or talk about the shapes and colors they observe in nature.

The principle of incorporating art throughout the curriculum in early childhood programs is equally valid in the elementary and

Art opportunities occur throughout the daily routine. At outside time, a child and teacher weave yarn through fence posts.

secondary grades. As school systems cut their budgets and eliminate art specialists from the staff, it is more important than ever for regular teachers to think about how they can include the arts as a vehicle for learning in all the subjects they teach.

▶ **3. The arts promote a broad range of skills.** The visual arts are an effective means for reaching many developmental ends. Creating and observing art promotes perceptual development as young children pay attention to the physical and tactile properties of materials and objects. Symbolic representation, the basis of reading and writing, is inherent in the use of art to convey personal experience. Manipulating art materials and tools enhances large and fine motor development.

The visual arts also encourage social cooperation as children collaborate on a project, share materials, or simply converse with one another as they work in parallel. Children demonstrate patience and persistence as they repeatedly experiment with art materials and techniques.

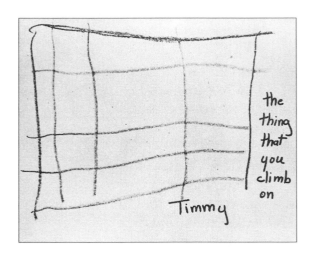

Children develop fine motor skills as they represent their experiences symbolically. A boy captures the grid of a climber in his crayon drawing.

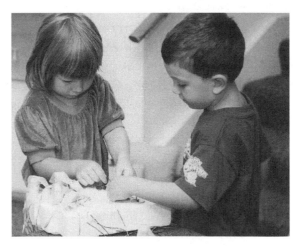

Children problem-solve together while making a collage that will be a present for their teacher.

Supporting Young Artists

They engage in problem solving as they try to achieve congruity between the mental image in their head and the concrete product of their hands.

Children can develop flexibility as they learn to see things from the perspective of other individuals and other cultures. Their language grows as they find the words to express what they see, sense, and feel while making art and viewing the art created by others.

With all these applications, it is clear that art can be incorporated into any aspect of the early childhood curriculum or any content area of elementary and secondary education.

▶ **4. The arts are also valuable in and of themselves.** The arts enrich our lives by promoting an awareness of the environment and validating individual expression. They help us create meaning out of our experiences. Society recognizes that adult artists convey their pleasures, problems, concerns, and convictions through the medium of their choice. These expressions through the visual and performing arts are treated as legitimate pursuits and accorded the dignity of professional labels. Yet the fact that young children have similar expressive needs and motivations is easily dismissed. Children are forever reminded to "use words" to express a range of emotions and needs. Introducing the visual arts into their daily lives gives children another appropriate and satisfying means of expression, as though we are also saying "use the arts—speak with images and gestures."

▶ **5. Artistic expression best occurs in a trusting, supportive, and noncompetitive environment.** Children must feel safe and secure with the people around them if they are to risk the challenge of making art and sharing their thoughts about art with others. Teachers create a safe environment by respecting students' choices and avoiding judgments about their artistic expressions. Creating this supportive environment also sets the tone for how children interact with one another. It is imperative for them to know that their aesthetic perceptions will be heard and respected. "It is important to accept a child's interpretation of what he or she sees, even if it is not the conventional view" (Hohmann & Weikart, 2002, p. 322).

Remember that making art is a public expression of a private experience. Similarly, sharing one's intellectual and emotional responses to a work of art is a highly personal statement. Children must trust the observers and listeners who surround them before they can feel comfortable revealing themselves in this way.

▶ **6. The arts can promote a sense of community.** Visual art is one of many mechanisms for bringing people together. Young children, working in parallel, can share their reactions to the materials and observe and comment on what their peers are doing. Children and adults may collaborate on an art project that grows out of some shared event or interest. Working together in a collaborative process and toward a common goal forms bonds among the group members. As we experience or create art in groups, we reveal to group members aspects of ourselves that might not emerge in other types of shared activities, such as a game or a meal.

Art promotes community. Children make puppets at small-group time and put on a puppet show for friends at outside time.

Art also builds a sense of community because it is a way of depicting common values or current social and political themes. Our reactions to these artistic statements reveal how we are alike and where we differ.

Finally, the arts are vital in linking young children to the larger community. Through exposure to local artists, museums, art fairs, and the like, children come in contact with the people and institutions who populate their communities with artistic events and expressions.

▶ **7. The arts infuse our everyday lives.** Art should not be compartmentalized. When we convey to children that art can only be done at certain times of the day, or only taught by specialists, or only practiced by people with talent, we limit their capacity to see the pervasiveness of art in ordinary existence.

Supporting Young Artists

In addition to the people and places we naturally associate with art (the artist, the studio, the museum), indoor and outdoor spaces are filled with aesthetic possibilities. Virtually every home has objects of art that adorn the furniture or the walls or the garden; young children and their families can be encouraged to share these items from home—quilts and weavings, pottery, photographs, carvings, colorful rocks and shells. Some

Art is part of everyday life. Children who have been working with clay look at ceramic figures their parents brought into the classroom.

parents may be practicing artists who can be welcomed into the classroom to share art activities with the children.

Children, as well as adults, can become aware that we bring a sense of aesthetics to everyday activities, for example, when we set the table for a dinner party, or style our hair, or landscape the yard. Art also abounds in nature. Children can experience and share their observations about light, space, color, form, and texture in the natural environment. They can learn that artists consider these same factors when they combine various elements to produce a desired aesthetic effect. In essence, the ingredients and the practice of art are everywhere if we just become attuned to them and help children become aware of them, too.

▶ **8. Feel good about yourself as an artist.** Training in the arts should help adults feel good about themselves and their own skills and abilities. Only then can they extend this sensibility and respect to children. The High/Scope visual arts training program for adults is designed to give participants, most of whom have very limited art experience, an opportunity to redefine themselves as artists. Studio and workshop sessions encourage participants to recognize the artistic touch they bring to everyday activities, to explore creative materials,

Teachers who feel confident exploring art materials share this adventurousness with young children.

to reflect on their personal sense of aesthetics, and to develop a language to talk about artistic activity, products, and perceptions. Once participants have exercised and reflected on their own artistic expression, the training provides ample opportunities for them to practice applying these lessons in developmentally appropriate ways with children. Fortified by their new-found confidence, trainers and teachers know they do not have to be professional artists or art education specialists to incorporate the visual arts into their early childhood programs.

High/Scope Key Experiences in Visual Art

OVERVIEW OF THE KEY EXPERIENCES

The High/Scope curriculum manual, *Educating Young Children: Active Learning Practices for Preschool and Child Care Programs* (Hohmann & Weikart, 2002), provides the following description of the High/Scope key experiences:

> The High/Scope preschool key experiences provide a composite picture of early childhood development, are fundamental to young children's construction of knowledge, take place repeatedly over an extended period of time, and describe the concepts and relationships young children are striving to understand. They occur in active learning settings in which children have opportunities to make choices and decisions, manipulate materials, interact with peers and adults, experience special events, reflect on ideas

and actions, use language in personally meaningful ways, and receive appropriate adult support. (p. 299)

As noted in Chapter One, the High/Scope key experiences encompass all areas of early childhood development. The visual arts fall within the key experience category named **creative representation.** Under this category, the preschool key experiences most relevant to exploring art materials and **making art** are *making models out of clay, blocks, and other materials* (working with three-dimensional materials) and *drawing and painting* (working with two-dimensional materials). The related infant-toddler key experience is *exploring building and art materials.* The preschool key experience most relevant to **appreciating art** is *relating models, pictures, and photographs to real places and things.* A precursor to art appreciation for infants and toddlers would be the key experience of *responding to and identifying pictures and photographs.* Through these key experiences, children come to recognize and appreciate the use of familiar symbols and representational techniques by others.

An overview of creative representation and the key experiences relevant to the visual arts is provided below. How children develop in these areas is described in greater detail in Chapter Three, and what adults can do to support that development is elaborated on in Chapter Four. A complete listing and discussion of all the key experiences for preschoolers appears in *Educating Young Children* (Hohmann & Weikart, 2002, Part 3) and for infants and toddlers in *Tender Care and Early Learning: Supporting Infants and Toddlers in Child Care Settings* (Post & Hohmann, 2000, Chapter 1).

CREATIVE REPRESENTATION

Infants and toddlers accumulate a critical body of knowledge through direct sensory-motor experiences. They begin to understand how an object looks, feels, sounds, tastes, and smells. With repeated experience, they gradually form a mental image of the object and can hold on to the image, even when the object is out of sight. This process of internalizing or mentally picturing something is the child's first experience with what High/Scope calls *creative representation* (Post & Hohmann, 2000, p. 41).

By preschool age, children are able to hold in mind a growing number of mental images of people, objects, and events. From these internal images they can then create external representations using

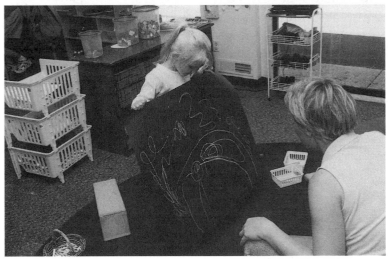

A girl represents an event with chalk. "I hid with my puppy under the widest table," she tells her teacher, "and it started to rain."

words, images, sounds, and movements. Having a mental image frees them from depending upon their immediate surroundings as the impetus for thought or the context for play. They can recall and re-create something from the past. They can imagine and build something other than what exists in front of them. Representation is intentional. That is, children consciously recognize or make something that either stands for or reminds them of something else. "Representational thought opens the door to the creativity that nurtures emerging artists, actors, writers, musicians, dancers, scientists, and diplomats" (Hohmann & Weikart, 2002, p. 312).

Representation experiences are important for young children because they lay the foundation for adult thinking skills (High/Scope, 2000). The abilities involved in representation—forming a mental image, manipulating materials and tools, anticipating the results of the transformation, and explaining the process and interpreting the results—are the same ones that adults use in solving problems. Thinking creatively and communicating with others are hallmarks of representation. When we support representation in young children, we encourage them to develop the skills they will need for expression and problem solving as students and adults.

Representation takes many forms. Children may represent things by using sound or language, imitating roles and actions, and creating things out of various materials. One of the ways in which they make things is by using art materials. Children's artwork expresses their perceptions, understanding, and feelings about what they are representing. In that sense, art serves many of the same expressive and intellectual purposes for children that it does for adults.

Children, like adult artists, choose to represent what is most salient to them. In these masks, the hair, eyes, and mouth get differential emphasis.

In their early artwork, especially if it involves a new medium, children may be expressing their perceptions and feelings about the material itself. Their focus is less on making a representational product than on experiencing the sensory-motor sensations and properties of working with that material. From this familiarity with the medium comes the realization that it can be used to represent something else, either because the material shares certain properties with what is being represented or because it can be manipulated in a way to resemble those properties.

The representation is not necessarily meant to be a literal translation of the child's internal image. "Representation does not aspire to copy the original" (Golomb, 1992, p. 3). Like adult artists, children want their artwork to capture those aspects of a person, object, or event that are most salient to them. These might be formal properties, such as color, shape, size, or texture. Or they might want to represent the functional property of something (for example, the whiskers on a mask that help them pretend to be a cat) because it best furthers their play.

> Children learn to use symbols, ranging from gestures of the hand or movements of the whole body, to pictures, figures of clay, numbers, music, and the like. And, by the age of 5 or 6, children not only can understand these various symbols but can often combine them in ways adults find striking. (Gardner, 1982, pp. 87–88)

Making models out of clay, blocks, and other materials

Among the most striking images that come to mind are the artworks children create as they use materials like paint or clay to facilitate their play and represent the work they have done. Young children make models using a variety of media. Clay and dough are typically thought of as materials that lend themselves to children's art. But there is no limit to what they can incorporate into their artistic models: paper and papier mâché; natural materials such as stones, shells, leaves, sand, seeds, nuts, and twigs; metal, wood, and rubber; cardboard boxes, tin cans, and plastic and other containers; fabric and different types of yarn; packaging materials; and string, wire, and tape. Making models lends itself to using scrap and recycled materials. (Chapter Four discusses materials for the art area.)

An initial encounter with these materials might inspire children to spontaneously recognize the similarity of certain materials to specific objects. Looking at a rounded lump of clay, a child might declare, "It's a ball." But as children become familiar with using various media, they will deliberately shape and manipulate the media to enhance the correspondence between their mental image and the model. In other words, the representational quality of their art progresses from accidental to intentional. Thus a child may say, "I'm going to make a birthday cake. I'll need pink dough because it's a strawberry cake and something tall to stick in it for candles."

As children acquire skills with art materials, they simultaneously develop a new understanding of what they are representing. They actively think about the qualities they want to convey and become increasingly aware of details. Their artwork moves from simple to complex representations. They are constantly solving problems as they attempt to manipulate the medium to better represent their images and ideas.

Children also exercise imagination when they make models, by

picturing how the raw
materials will be trans-
formed or by using what
they create in their role
play. For example, they
might make a cake out of
dough, decorate it with
scraps of fabric, and have
a birthday party. They
might cut masks out of
cereal boxes, festoon
them with strips of con-
struction paper, and pre-
tend to be animals in a
zoo. Or, the artwork they
create may simply exist
for itself and be dis-
played for other children,

A boy represents a spaceship with blocks and then represents his block structure with a drawing.

parents, and teachers to look at and comment on. Sharing their artwork allows children to inspire the creativity and imagination of others.

Drawing and painting

Drawing and painting are two of the earliest art techniques children
use to communicate what they see and think. Materials for drawing
and painting are among the materials most commonly available to
young children. One typically finds crayons, markers, pencils, chalk,
and paint in early childhood settings. But children can also paint and
draw with less conventional media, such as watery clay or thickened
glue. Young children can also use computers to draw, and they can
paint with tools other than brushes. Unconventional items, such as
shop tools, kitchen utensils, pebbles, and yarn are wonderful accom-
paniments to painting supplies. Drawing and painting also require that
programs have on hand many different types of paper that vary in
size, color, and texture. (See Chapter Four for more ideas on materials
for the art area.)

Beginning with a blank surface, children can control every component of what goes on it and how it is used. As they gain experience
with various two-dimensional formats, they can exercise even greater
control in using these art media to represent their ideas. Drawing and

Children enjoy unconventional media. A boy paints with the wheels of a toy car, and a girl draws with glue.

painting also allow children to engage in experiments with transforming materials, the most elemental of these being what happens when they mix colors.

Putting marks on paper (or sand or earth) helps children create and convey a sense of order about their environment. As they draw and paint, they focus on the basic properties of the images they want to represent. They explore shape, line, and color—the same formal properties that concern artists and critics. In the process of attending to the salient characteristics of objects, children develop their powers of observation. From rendering the broad outlines of something in recognizable form, they become increasingly concerned with capturing and depicting details. This development not only expands their inter-

Supporting Young Artists

nal mental images but also allows them to create works of artistic richness. Displaying children's drawings and paintings, and encouraging them to talk about them, further enriches the process of creation. It also gives others, both adults and peers, insights into the thinking that inspired the children to create these representations.

Relating models, pictures, and photographs to real places and things

"With their growing capacity to form mental images and express their understanding in increasingly complex language, preschoolers are beginning to see the relationship between toys, photographs, and pictures, and the objects they represent" (Hohmann & Weikart, 2002, p. 320). In fact, relating these symbolic representations to the real places and things they stand for is one of the ways that preschoolers begin to "read" pictures, posters, packages, and books. Making the connection between the symbolic and the real is also the process that draws them into understanding and appreciating the representational and expressive potential of art.

Art appreciation begins when children relate paintings, statues, illustrations, and so on to their own experiences. Initially, they are likely to notice and comment on familiar objects and subject matter. With guidance, however, they can also make observations that connect the artwork to their own emotions and opinions. Children come to recognize that colors and lines can be used to reflect feelings. They understand that an artist is depicting a theme such as "children having fun at play" or "a happy family" or "a sad little dog." With encouragement and acceptance on the part of adults and peers, they can express what they find interesting about a work of art or even venture an opinion about what they do and don't like. (See Chapter Three for a discussion of children's artistic perceptions and preferences.) As long as children are free to make their own interpretations, without being judged on their "correctness," they will enjoy the process of reflecting on artistic representations and relating them to people and events in their own lives.

Children benefit from a wide array of representational art materials in the classroom. Initially, they do not distinguish between reproductions, illustrations, and photographs. As long as it is a realistic depiction and they find something to recognize from their own experience, they will be engaged by the subject matter in the artwork. Later, children will differentiate the medium used in the representation and pay attention to stylistic differences. For example, if teachers provide them with simple cameras to photograph their friends and activities, they will move from a focus on "who" and "what" to an awareness of such factors as focus, color, and action. Later, some children may even consciously "frame" their photograph to capture specific visual elements, not just the people involved or the event taking place.

There is a similar progression with the art in children's books. For the youngest children, picture books are engaging because they find representations of people and events that are commonplace in their own lives. Somewhat later, in books that combine pictures and stories, children focus on the illustrations because they represent key ideas in the narrative. "Reading" pictures is a gateway to letter and word recognition. Once children are familiar with a book, however, they can set aside their interest in the story to focus independently on the illustrations.

With encouragement, young children can become aware of stylistic differences between books. For example, one artist may use watercolors rendered in broad brush strokes, another may use fine-detailed pencil drawings, and yet another may choose mixed-media collages to represent the characters and their world. By enriching the classroom with a variety of picture books, adults help children become aware that artists use a variety of styles and materials to convey images, emotions, and ideas. Similarly, as children encounter artwork and reproductions in a variety of media, they begin to appreciate that visual art—like music or movement—is as much a form of narrative representation as words on a page.

Research on the Effectiveness of High/Scope in Promoting the Visual Arts

To justify funding for programs in the visual and performing arts, especially during budgetary cutbacks, advocates need evidence that they promote developmental gains in children. Cost-conscious policymakers demand that in addition to acquiring the specific skills associated with each medium, students participating in arts activities also demonstrate enhanced performance in academic subjects as a whole. Before they will fund staff development in the arts, administrators require proof that such training enhances everyday teaching skills, not just specialist knowledge.

Fortunately, researchers at the elementary and secondary school level are accumulating a growing body of evidence in support of funding for the arts. For example, in a multi-year survey of 25,000 middle- and high-school students by the U.S. Department of Education, important differences emerged in the academic performance, attitudes, and behaviors of those with high versus low levels of involvement in the visual and performing arts (Catterall et al., 1999). Those students with high arts involvement, both in and out of school, outperformed their low-art-involvement peers in such areas as English, reading, mathematics, history, citizenship, and geography. They reported being less bored in school and spending less time watching television, and they were more likely to be involved in community service. Students highly involved in the arts also demonstrated more tolerance and less racial prejudice than their low-involvement peers demonstrated. These differences were true not just for children of the middle class but also for those who were economically disadvantaged.

Similar findings have been documented at the elementary level. A study of 2,000 children in different program settings

Research shows children at arts-rich schools are better able to express their thoughts and ideas. Teachers at arts-rich schools encourage children to integrate learning across disciplines.

found that those in the high-arts-involvement group outscored peers in the low-arts-involvement group on measures of creativity and overall competence (Burton et al., 1999). Students attending arts-rich schools were better able to express their thoughts and ideas, exercise their imaginations, work cooperatively with peers, and establish rapport with teachers. They saw themselves as being more competent academically, especially in language and mathematics, and their self-perceptions were validated by the researchers' classroom observations and conversations with teachers and administrators.

Support for the arts at the school level also affected teacher performance. The researchers rated teachers in arts-rich schools as being more open, flexible, knowledgable, and engaged in their own professional development, compared to their colleagues in settings that were less rich in the arts. Teachers in arts-rich schools encouraged students to integrate learning across disciplines and were themselves more aware of learning opportunities beyond their own disciplines.

High/Scope offers proof of similar effects at the early childhood level. In terms of overall development, the success of High/Scope as a comprehensive educational approach has been amply demonstrated and disseminated in a series of research and policy reports (for example, Epstein, Schweinhart, & McAdoo, 1996; Schweinhart, Barnes, & Weikart, 1993; and Schweinhart & Weikart, 1997). The same case can be made for the success of the High/Scope training model for educators. A national study found that High/Scope's staff development methods are highly effective in promoting early childhood program quality (Epstein, 1993). There is also specific evidence that High/Scope can enhance children's creative development and provide teachers with a framework for promoting arts-based activities in early childhood programs. Results from the national study, *Training for Quality: Improving Early Childhood Programs Through Systematic Inservice Training* (Epstein, 1993), showed that young children's creative representation and language skills were the two areas of development most significantly affected by program quality. Access to diverse materials and opportunities for planning and recall—hallmarks of the High/Scope educational approach—were the program characteristics that best promoted children's creative exploration and facilitated language and literacy skills. The study further showed that High/Scope programs scored higher than comparable non-High/Scope settings on these critical dimensions of quality. These results demonstrated that the High/Scope educational approach can effectively promote the development of artistic exploration and expression in young children. Moreover, High/Scope developed these artistic skills as part of a coherent framework that simultaneously supported children's overall development, including their language and literacy skills. This fact is of crucial importance to funders and policymakers.

Among early childhood models, High/Scope is the only program to date that has demonstrated an empirical relationship between an integrated approach to the arts and children's artistic and overall development. For four decades, High/Scope has conscientiously based its claims of effectiveness on demonstrated and desirable outcomes for the adults the Foundation trains and the children they teach. For art to be accepted as a legitimate component of a comprehensive education, such empirical justification must be forthcoming.

Access to diverse materials and opportunities to plan and recall—hallmarks of the High/Scope curriculum—help develop creative representation and language and literacy skills.

Funders and policymakers require firm proof that their investment in the arts will result in meaningful benefits for young children. The fact that the High/Scope approach to visual arts education also promotes language development and other critical thinking skills is further proof of its value in early childhood programs. By integrating the arts into an overall program of development, educators can insure that the arts form a partnership with other disciplines and embody the learning process with richness, complexity, and rewards.

3

The Development of Art in the Young Child

Reggie, a ten-month-old who is not yet talking, is visiting the art museum with his parents and older sister. His mother wheels him from painting to painting in his stroller. Sometimes Reggie looks at the paintings, but more often he looks at other patrons or plays with the zipper on his sweatshirt. Then his family stops in front of a huge Matisse cutout of abstract dancing figures in bright primary colors. Reggie looks at the image and beams. He chortles, waves his arms, and vigorously kicks his legs. When it is finally time to move on to the next piece, Reggie whimpers in protest. He does not want to leave the Matisse.

Art, like any area of knowledge or skill, does not develop in isolation from other abilities. In the early childhood years, the development of art is necessarily connected to perceptual, physical, cognitive, language, social, and emotional development. These connections are apparent in the questions we ask about children's artistic development: How do they differentiate lines, colors, and shapes? Can children use their muscles to build and mold with solid materials? Do they have the fine motor and eye-hand coordination needed to manipulate tools? Are they interested in or ready to collaborate on an art project with peers and adults? Can they articulate the aesthetic characteristics they encounter in their environment? Do they have labels to articulate what they perceive and words to describe how it makes them feel? When presented with different examples of visual art, can they say what they like or dislike and why?

Implied in these questions is not only a range of general developmental abilities but also two related visual arts abilities: *making art* and *appreciating art.* Most treatments of artistic development in early childhood deal only with the former ability, the creation of art. However, High/Scope finds that by encouraging children to reflect on their actions with arts media (as with all materials and activities), we are simultaneously laying the groundwork for understanding and appreciating art. This chapter discusses how children develop the skills and knowledge necessary for *both* artistic enterprises—making *and* appreciating art. Although the visual arts are best captured in the creative representation key experiences, it becomes clear throughout the chapter that visual arts also involve virtually all of the other High/Scope key experience categories.

Basic Principles in Art Development

Theory, research, and practice all point to a series of underlying principles that characterize the development of art in children (for example, Arnheim, 1989; Gardner, 1982; Hardiman & Zernich, 1980; Lowenfeld & Brittain, 1987; Parsons, 1987; Seefeldt, 1987; and Vygotsky, 1978). The most important factors may be summarized as the role of experience, the progression from simple to complex, and the quality of individuality. In *Educating Young Children*, Hohmann and Weikart (2002) elaborate these three principles of creative representation in the following way:

- *"Representation arises from children's experiences with actual objects, people, and events"* (Hohmann & Weikart 2002, p. 312)—Children first must directly experience objects or events, and the art materials they use to represent them, through their senses and actions. Representations often begin when children accidentally recognize the similarity between something in their lives and an attribute of the medium they are working with: a pipe cleaner is long and thin like a candle; glue is white like cake frosting; yarn is springy like hair. Later, the attempt to capture these similarities becomes intentional.

    The salience of an object or event, or one of its components, can also influence how children represent it. Because the child is attempting to convey something from personal experience, the creation has the intention of capturing whatever is most significant (Zurmuehlen & Kantner, 1995). For example, a child representing a mother carrying a baby may make the mother's arms longer than the rest of her body. In this case, the child is concerned with the act of carrying and does not care about proportionality. Children's creations thus reflect the range and intensity of their experiences and their opportunities to explore the artistic media used to represent them.

- *"Children's early representations consist of simple forms that gradually become more complex"* (Hohmann & Weikart, 2002, p. 313)—Visual representations evolve from elemental lines and forms to more detailed and differentiated constructions and compositions. Several factors

Exploration is an intense experience. Intrigued by the creamy paint on her brush, a girl spends work time applying it everywhere.

contribute to this increasing complexity. Through direct manipulation, children become increasingly aware of the visual attributes of the objects they are representing. With development, children can increasingly hold more of these attributes in mind. In addition, through exploration and practice they become more skillful in using various art media to represent things. While earlier creations show a great deal of repetition as they rehearse a particular movement or effect, later efforts demonstrate more variation as their skill repertoire grows (Zurmuehlen & Kantner, 1995). As a result of these developments, children's visual representations "become less accidental, less in need of supplemental verbal explanation, and more structurally detailed, integrated, and complete" (Hohmann & Weikart, 2002, p. 313).

- *"Each child's representations are unique"* (Hohmann & Weikart, 2002, p. 313)—Children vary in both their experiences and in the art media they use to represent them. They differ in whether they are attracted to the visual arts as a means of representation and in the extent to which they substitute or combine visual art with verbal, written, dramatic, musical, or other forms of representation. Children who gravitate toward the visual arts will differ regarding which art materials they find gratifying to use; they may choose different materials to satisfy different representational needs. Further, children differ in the intensity and duration they bring to their representational activities. Some explore briefly and move on; others return periodically to repeat or extend the experience; and still others remain with a set of materials and elaborate an idea over several days. As with adults, individual experiences and proclivities inevitably shape the art that children make. For these reasons, children's representations are "one-of-a-kind reflections of their specific interests and concerns" (Hohmann & Weikart, 2002, p. 314). Art, like language, opens a window to the creator's mind.

Making Art

YOUNG CHILDREN ENJOY MAKING ART

Most observation and research on the development of the visual arts in young children focuses on the making of art. This focus is understandable, given the visible joy that young children exhibit while creating art and the pleasure that adults derive from viewing these creations. In young children, artistic development begins with the exploration of materials and progresses to symbolic representation (Brittain, 1979). The importance of this exploratory stage cannot be overestimated as children learn about the properties of different media and what they can do with them (Smith, 1993).

Young children gradually move from accidental discovery with these materials to intentional representation (Golomb, 1974), for example, from recognizing that a circle they have drawn looks like a ball to deciding to draw a ball by making a circle. Because they are in the preoperational or concrete operational stage (Piaget, 1951), young children's artistic representations are rooted in their actual experiences with objects, people, and events. These representations begin with simple forms and become increasingly complex. As they become more adept at manipulating various art media, children's rep-

A child discovers the connection between movement and line.

Supporting Young Artists

resentations "become increasingly influenced by the visual attributes of the objects" (Hohmann & Weikart, 2002, p. 313).

THE IMPORTANCE OF EXPLORATION

Children need time to explore materials before they can use them to make or represent other things. For example, they need to squeeze, poke, roll, flatten, pinch, and otherwise manipulate clay before they use it to represent an animal, a vehicle, or a person. They need to feel the texture of paint with their fingers, use their hands to smear the paint, see what happens when they add a little water or a lot, use various tools to transfer paint to paper, apply paint to different surfaces, and so on—all before they even begin to mix colors (see at right).

Children also need time to explore the various tools they will use in the creative process—by cutting paper, squeezing glue, controlling a sprinkler, and so forth—before they apply these tools in a deliberate manner to achieve a special image or effect. To acquire this skill with various media, they need ample time with each. We must be careful that in our zeal to provide children with a variety of art materials and experiences, we do not shortchange their time with each one.

Chapter Five offers an overall strategy and many concrete suggestions for how adults can provide children with graduated opportunities to explore individual media in depth. Extended exploration allows children to discover the potential of each medium and technique. They develop confidence in their ability to manipulate a medium and use it to express their ideas and represent their visions.

VERBALIZATION AND NARRATIVE

Preschool children often accompany their art-making with narratives. They talk to themselves, to interested caregivers and peers, even to imaginary audiences.

A Developmental Progression of Early Explorations With Paint

Two-year-old Jackson takes a piece of white paper to the table. He fills a tray with red, blue, black, and white paint and also gets a long-handled brush. He dips the brush in the blue paint and spreads it on the paper, then dips it in the blue paint again and spreads more paint. Next, Jackson dips the brush in all the other colors until it is dripping with paint, holds the brush in the air, and watches the paint drip on the table. He puts the tip of the brush on his paper and moves it in a small circle, then spreads the blob of paint on the paper. Jackson loads up the brush again, dipping it into three colors and spreads it on the paper. He then mixes together all the paints in his tray and tips the tray onto the paper. He spreads the puddle of paint all over the paper with his brush, alternately moving the brush sideways, up and down, and in circles.

At small-group time, three-year-old Gregory paints a large, irregular red shape in the upper lefthand corner of his paper. He takes another brush, dips it in blue paint, and makes an irregular shape in the bottom lefthand corner. Gregory sets his paper aside and reaches for another piece. Throughout small-group time, Gregory continues making two or three shapes per page. Meanwhile, Alberto, almost five, works on one

(continued on next page)

painting the entire small-group time. He begins by making two lines of red circles, six across the top and five on the bottom of the page. He carefully puts a yellow dot in the middle of each circle. With black paint, Alberto begins to draw a line between pairs of circles at the top and bottom of the page. When he gets to the sixth circle at the top, he sees he is one circle short at the bottom. Alberto squeezes in one more circle and connects the top and bottom with a black line. A look of satisfaction crosses his face. He pauses, as if studying his composition, and begins to elaborate the design with dots between the lines and other patterns, each new element carefully and systematically added.

Sitting at the table in the art area, four-year-old Brianna uses the watercolors to cover most of her paper with twirly brush strokes. She keeps adding water to the paint so that her marks become fainter and fainter on the page. Her friend Deola, who is also four, mixes three colors of paint together and then covers her entire paper with paint dots, applying the paint in thick blobs.

Children explore the thick texture of finger paint and the watery texture of tempera paint with their hands.

Their comments may be denotative, naming the representations they are creating (see next page, right). Or they may be action-oriented, describing the child's actions and directing succeeding steps. Finally, the narrative may evolve into a "poetic transformation" that fluidly changes as the child creates images and attaches words and fantasies to the symbols (Zurmuehlen & Kantner, 1995, p. 7).

Using language to extend the images may happen at any point in the child's development. However, sometimes the simpler the repre-

Supporting Young Artists

sentation, the more the child embellishes (Hohmann & Weikart, 2002). That is, children verbally fill in what is not there visually. They may thus begin by telling an adult more about what is *not* there, as a way of supplementing their representational capability. Eventually, as more planning and detail go into the creation, they will be able to talk more about what is there or how they created it. In either case, adults should focus on what the child has modeled or drawn and not on what the child has left out. Whatever is in the representation reflects what is salient to the child and what the child is able to reproduce with the materials and skills at hand. As additional attributes are held in memory and through further practice with the medium, children will become more adept at letting their visual representations speak for themselves. If adults show interest in what children have done, rather than pointing out omissions, they will be encouraged to continue exploring and creating.

DEVELOPMENTAL PROGRESSIONS IN MAKING ART

Many of the principles set forth above become apparent as one examines the progression of children's art. As we observe children working with different media, we can readily see how they progress from pure exploration to accidental or spontaneous representation, and then to intentional representation. We also see how their mastery of a medium and its tools is reflected in the variety and complexity of their art. At the same time, children's increasing ability to hold the attributes of objects and events in mind can be seen in the growing detail that fills their artwork. Key features in this developmental progression are summarized on the next page (see also Hohmann & Weikart, 2002, pp. 332–336). Some progressions are more evident with one type of medium than another, for example, with two-dimensional work compared to three-dimensional. In most cases, however, these changes can be observed as children work across all artistic media and with different tools.

▶ *From accidental or spontaneous representation to intentional representation*—Initially, when an object or medium resembles something in their experience, children use that object as a stand-in for the

Making and Labeling Snow

At small-group time, four-year-old Audie takes a slab of clay and tears off bits until he has a pile of pieces. He takes another slab of clay and also tears that one into bits, which he adds to his pile. Audie arranges all the bits of clay on his clay mat and says to his teacher, "Look, Beth. It's a horrible snowstorm."

At work time, five-year-old Kristen carries several pieces of paper from the art area to the big picture windows. She sits down and folds the papers, then cuts slashes and holes in them. Kristen tapes the papers to the windows. She then tells Sam, her teacher, "Look, Sam. It's snowing outside! Now I get to wear my new boots."

Early Childhood Developmental Progressions in Making Art

From accidental or spontaneous representation to intentional representation

1. The child accidentally creates a line or form, then decides it looks like something else.

   • The line or form is associated with something familiar from personal experience.

   • One or two matching structural properties are sufficient. Further embellishment is not needed.

   • Representation may be embellished with verbal description or narration.

2. The child decides to intentionally create an object or event and finds materials to represent it.

   • Visual characteristics of the object or event are held in mind.

   • Materials are purposefully found and manipulated to match the mental image.

   • The object may not need verbal embellishment or clarification.

From simple to elaborated models

1. The child holds one or two salient characteristics in mind.

   • Crude representations suffice for the child's representational needs.

   • Skills with manipulating materials and tools are minimal.

2. The child holds more visual attributes in mind.

   • Persistence is shown in adding details to representation.

   • Skills in manipulating materials and tools are more advanced.

   • Verbal embellishment may spur further creative elaboration.

From marks and lines to shapes and figures

1. Motion and manipulation are the end point.

   • Marks and lines are on surfaces.

   • Concern is with process, not product.

   • Joy is in the repetitive motion or its effects.

2. Lines and textures are controlled.

   • Exploration of effects is deliberate.

   • Experimentation with the actions of one's body and tools on various media occurs.

3. Production of shapes and figures is deliberate.

   • Simple closed shapes and figures are formed.

   • Details are added to shapes and figures.

From random marks to relationships

1. Marks or shapes are unrelated to one another.

   • Marks appear wherever motion and experimentation produce them.

   • Representational accuracy of parts is not a concern.

2. Marks and shapes are deliberately related to one another.

   • Intention to create representational accuracy is increased.

   • Awareness of spatial relationships is increased.

   • Relationships may serve functional and/or aesthetic intentions.

real thing. That is, first they find or create a form, then they decide it looks like something else. For example, when children pat a wedge of clay into a rectangular shape, they may decide it is a car. Or, seeing a flattened piece of dough, they may call it a pancake. Although these media were not manipulated for the purpose of representing these familiar objects, children see connections in the visual characteristics. As long as the essential structural features are similar enough, children in the early stages do not need to embellish the model further. This order is generally reversed at a later stage; that is, children will first decide to create a specific object and then find or make something to represent it. In this later stage, the visual characteristics of the model are held in the child's mind, enabling the child to purposefully find objects or manipulate materials to match that mental image. Bear in mind, however, that regardless of the creator's age, found or accidentally made objects will always inspire intentional creativity and vice versa.

▶ *From simple to elaborated models*—Initially, children hold only one or two salient characteristics in mind and intentionally recreate these features in their models or drawings. Crude representations suffice for their needs, especially when they are not yet skillful in manipulating the materials. Later, as children hold more visual attributes in mind and become more adept with materials, their two- and three-dimensional representations become more detailed. Adults are sometimes amazed at children's persistence in adding details to their artistic representations. The very act of adding details—for example, sticking strands of yarn on a ball of dough to simulate hair—may in and of itself be a satisfying action for the child. Or the detailing may in turn trigger fantasies or story ideas that lead to further elaborations.

▶ *From marks and lines to shapes and figures*—When children first begin to use painting and drawing media, they are fascinated by the simple process of making marks on a surface. The sheer joy of the motions and the marks they make is sufficient; there is no concern with how the final product looks, whether it covers all or just a corner of the surface, or even if it leaves a hole in the paper. As Golomb (1974) notes, "in the pure scribble stage, motor joy rules supreme and the child is unconcerned with the looks of the final product, though he is generally pleased that his vigorous motions leave visible marks on the paper" (p. 3). The same is true of the marks children leave on the surface of dough or clay, whether by poking with their fist or pounding with a textured tool. Once they have had experience exploring exuberant motions with a medium, children will begin to explore making more controlled lines and textures on the surface. Experimentation with different effects becomes deliberate.

From lines, children progress to making shapes and forms. Forming an enclosed shape—making a line that changes direction and ends back at the point of origin—requires a great deal of visual-motor control and intentionality. In keeping with the progressions described above, children may first accidentally draw a shape and decide it looks like something familiar. Later, they will progress to intentionally drawing shapes and figures to represent specific objects and people they have in mind. Similarly, such figures will initially be simple and unadorned. With growing observational awareness and experience with the artistic media, the shapes and figures children create will become more elaborated and detailed.

▶ *From random marks to relationships*—In addition to progressing in the types of marks they make on the page, children become increasingly aware of where those marks (or shapes or figures) are in relation to one another. At first, marks may seem random, appearing on the surface wherever an exuberant hand places them. Later, the placement of the impressions left by the medium become intentional, bearing a deliberate spatial relationship to other lines and shapes. This progression happens because development is proceeding along several lines. In part, children are striving for greater representational accuracy. Thus the parts of an object, or where an object stands in relation to other objects around it, become something that children want to convey with greater faithfulness to reality. As their sense of space in general develops, this awareness will be reflected in their artwork as it is in other activities. But there also may be a factor unique to artistic representation—an emerging sense of aesthetic considerations. Children will begin to intentionally place lines, shapes, or colors in relationship because "those colors look nice next to one another" or "this dark area needed something light next to it." When this reflective process occurs, the developmental lines of making art and appreciating art converge.

Appreciating Art

YOUNG CHILDREN CAN APPRECIATE ART

Research in developmental psychology suggests that in addition to creating art, young children are more capable of appreciating art than previously acknowledged. Studies (summarized in Gardner, 1990) show that young children are highly motivated to explore their own capacity to create art. They are also intellectually capable of observing and reflecting on the artwork around them if adults engage them in meaningful conversation about it. Assessing a museum-based art appreciation program for preschoolers and their parents, Piscitelli (1988) concluded that young children not only enjoy looking at art but also like to share their observations with others.

> Young students are eager to talk about works of art, even if their vocabularies are limited. They engage with artworks at a level of observation and analysis that can be quite striking. Visitors to classrooms where students are talking about art may be surprised at how penetrating children's perceptions and observations about visual imagery can be when their attention is carefully directed and their skills of analysis and response are put into play. (Dobbs, 1998, pp. 64–65)

Untutored children do not show a natural tendency to focus on the aesthetics of art. They are more likely to focus on subject matter, judging artistic merit by size or cost and rarely connecting their own artistic activities with the art on display in museums or reproduced in books. Yet, if given help and support, young children can begin to display sensitivity to the qualities of art. If asked open-ended questions, rather than being taught didactically, they can move from a purely idiosyncratic orientation toward simple analyses of what they think the artist is trying to say or how the artwork makes them feel. Preschoolers can even sort artwork on the basis of style rather than content, provided they are encouraged and interested in doing so. Schiller (1995), for example, posted reproductions of fine artworks and made art books available to her preschool students. After giving the children time to explore these additions to the classroom, she engaged them in a discussion of what they saw and thought about the paintings. The children were fascinated to learn that Michelangelo painted on the ceiling. They noticed the "cracks" in the reproductions of old paintings, understood why Georgia O'Keefe was interested in painting dead flowers like those in their science area, and were surprised to learn that the names of the Ninja Turtle characters were once the names of real artists. "What was interesting was that the children instantly recognized that Matisse had a very different style than the realism of Michelangelo and da Vinci" (Schiller, 1995, p. 37). These observations, while often more anecdotal than systematic, suggest that there is no inherent contradiction between developmentally appropriate practice and the activities associated with art criticism, art history, and aesthetics.

ART APPRECIATION IS MISSING IN EARLY CHILDHOOD PROGRAMS

Despite mounting evidence of children's ability to appreciate art, little effort has been put into broadening early art education to include the study and appreciation of art as well as the making of art. In a briefing paper for the National Art Education Association, Colbert and Taunton (1992) identified three components of high quality early art education: creating art, looking at and talking about art, and becoming aware of art in one's everyday life. They note that while the first component is plentiful in early childhood programs, the second and third are neglected. There is universal agreement that it is appropriate and essential for young children to explore various art media and create art. Yet art appreciation, the critical understanding and knowledge-based awareness of the meaning and aesthetics of art, is generally absent in the early childhood curriculum. Why? Are young children really incapable of engaging in art appreciation? Do teachers misguidedly believe that young children can manipulate art materials but not art ideas? Or, as was indicated in Chapter Two, do early childhood teachers, like teachers at other grade levels, simply lack confidence in their own ability to view art and discourse about it knowledgably?

Unfortunately, the truth is that most adults *do* lack confidence when it comes to art appreciation and criticism. Yet, teachers must feel good about their own artistic sensibilities before they can comfortably introduce art appreciation to their students. For this reason, experiential training that gives early childhood teachers the vocabulary and a set of strategies for implementing art appreciation activities is the first step toward helping them expand the arts in this direction.

The following section summarizes theory and research relevant to the questions posed above about children's abilities: Are young children capable of engaging in art appreciation, and do teachers believe children can manipulate art materials, but not art ideas? If teachers understand and recognize children's emerging ability to appreciate art, perhaps they will be more receptive to introducing art ideas as well as art materials in their early childhood arts programs.

Supporting Young Artists

DEVELOPMENTAL PROGRESSIONS IN APPRECIATING ART

Stages of aesthetic development

One guiding framework in understanding art appreciation is Parsons's (1987) theory of aesthetic development. Parsons posits five stages in the development of aesthetic responses:

- *Stage one, concrete,* is characterized by an interest in color favorites, pictorial representation, a personal connection to the subject, and an enjoyment of paintings.

- *Stage two, beauty and realism,* is characterized by the viewer's fondness for a painting because it is beautiful and represents reality. The subject of the art is judged for its realistic qualities.

- *Stage three, emotion,* is characterized by the observer's notice of the kinds of feelings the work of art produces, regardless of the subject's beauty or realistic qualities.

- *Stage four, style and form,* is characterized as the viewer's awareness of his or her ability to interpret a painting from a personal perspective.

- *Stage five, autonomy,* is characterized by individual judgment combined with that individual's need to discuss and arrive at understanding with others.

According to this model, preschool children are at stage one because (a) they do not see and feel what others see and feel; (b) they have a strong attraction to color—the bolder and brighter the better—and tend to like a painting if it includes their favorite color; and (c) they respond to the subject matter and take pleasure in looking at art that relates to their interests.

While empirical research tends to support Parsons's general progression, there is evidence that young children are capable of higher level responses than those predicted by this model. For example, Warash and Saab (1999) found that with appropriate encouragement, young children can exceed stage one behavior. They created an art exploration project based on Vygotsky's theory that education should provide children with experiences in their zone of proximal development, that is, areas where they are likely to grow next with appropriate challenges. Teachers were trained to expose young children to works of fine art and to focus their observations with specific questions.

Beginning with an open-ended question—"Tell me one thing you see in this print"—teachers then asked probing questions to help children connect their ideas and provide more detail about what they saw.

The researchers found that children's comments about color and content often revealed deeper insights about ideas the artist was trying to convey. Contrary to Parsons's theory about stage one behavior, young children were clearly able to consider the work from the subject's perspective. For example, they spoke about what they thought Rodin's sculpture *The Thinker* was thinking about. Finally, when teachers used guiding questions in response to children's interests, the investigators found that children became aware of how distinct elements in a work of art were related to one another. The researchers concluded that young children can be encouraged and challenged to be more observant of and conversant about works of art than acknowledged by Parsons's developmental framework.

Relationship between cognitive and aesthetic development

Another attempt to conceptualize how children view works of art examined how children's artistic conceptions relate to cognitive stages of development, similar to those of Piaget. Using this model, Kerlavage (1995) summarizes three stages that comprise the early childhood period:

- *Sensorial*—The youngest children like abstract, nonobjective images (for example, see the vignette that opens this chapter). They respond intuitively to works which please the senses. They are not yet into symbols; therefore, color and pattern are the dominant influences. Because they respond viscerally to a work of art, they may have difficulty explaining the reasons for their choices. Often, one object or event will catch their attention to the exclusion of other aspects of the work. They may not differentiate between alternative forms of a work of art, for example, between a painting and a sculpture or between a reproduction and a photograph.

- *Concrete*—As children develop a sense for symbols, their choices depend more on subject matter or theme. While color and pattern are still important, subject matter and symbol identification become dominant considerations in their preferences. They prefer subject matter they can relate to portrayed in a simple and realistic manner.

Children in this middle stage also develop an initial concept of beauty, again related to the realism of the subject matter. They can articulate their preferences based on the concrete qualities of the work. The "story" of the artwork is most relevant and they see the purpose of art as representing or recording a real person, object, or event. They are also able to sort art objects according to the form of representation, for example, differentiating a photograph from a reproduction of a painting. Time is also relevant. They can identify whether the artwork depicts something from long ago, now, or in the future.

- *Expressive*—This third stage appears toward the end of the early childhood years. Children begin to perceive and appreciate the expressive and stylistic aspects of the work. While they still prefer realism, they become more interested in subtle colors, complicated compositions, and the feelings behind the message. The expressive qualities of different media also enter into their evaluation of the artwork. Because they are less egocentric and can appreciate other points of view, children in this stage also become more aware of different artistic styles. Realism is seen as just one of several means of artistic expression. As they develop a more sophisticated sense of time, they begin to distinguish different periods in the creation of art. Being able to take different perspectives also attunes them to cultural influences and other influences that affect the making of art. Taking all these factors into account, children at this stage will defend their preferences in terms of artistic style, expressive qualities, and aesthetic principles.

Empirical research conducted over the past twenty years supports this cognitive model of young children's aesthetic development. Noted researchers include Feeney and Moravcik (1987), Gardner (1970, 1978), Hardiman and Zernich (1980, 1985), and Lowenfeld and Brittain (1987). Their cumulative findings with regard to children's overall aesthetic development and their awareness of color and pattern, content, simplicity-complexity, and artistic style are briefly discussed below and summarized on the next page.

    Studies show that the youngest children initially respond to the sensory qualities of a work of art, especially color but also shape and movement. Their preferences are for bright, contrasting colors. They also respond positively to patterns. Just as simplicity characterizes the

Early Childhood Developmental Progressions in Appreciating Art

Overall aesthetic development

- Preferences in the early childhood years do not appear to be influenced by race or gender.
- Age and maturation are the deciding factors for changes in response and perception.
- Children frequently have difficulty verbalizing exact reasons for their choices. When they do begin to verbalize, they focus on content (subject matter) rather than style.
- Children invent stories about the shapes, colors, and images found in art, whether the work is realistic or abstract.

Color and pattern

- Children are strongly attracted to bright, highly saturated, intense, and contrasting colors.
- Children tend to dislike muted or dark tones.
- Young children respond more positively to patterned, brightly colored, and nonobjective pieces than they do to dark-toned realistic works.
- Children under eight have difficulty perceiving the contours of shapes and patterns within shapes.

Content (subject matter)

- Children in the early childhood years react positively to artworks that depict favorite or familiar subject matter.

- Young children do not consistently prefer abstract or realistic pictures. Their choices seem to depend on perceived themes. However, an attraction for realism increases with age through the elementary years.
- Children identify content in both abstract and realistic works and base their discussion of content on their immediate world.
- Children under eight prefer (a) still life over figure groups and portraits and (b) low realism with few objects in the image.

Simplicity versus complexity

- Young children like artworks that are simple in composition and contain unambiguous spatial relations.
- A preference for complexity and detail in a composition increases with age.

- Younger children have difficulty relating parts within a complex painting. They respond to part of a work without giving much attention to the whole work.
- Children perceive more detail about a shape in the artwork when the shape is isolated from competing surroundings.

Artistic style

- Young children give limited attention to the style of the painting. With age, children become increasingly sensitive to individual artistic style, media use, and artistic principles.
- Children tend to group paintings by subject matter even when they are asked to order artworks by style or artist.
- Young children's preferences are more related to what is pictured than how it is portrayed.
- Young children do not differentiate between photographs and reproductions. With age, they can discriminate alternative forms of representation.

artwork they make themselves, young children prefer simplicity in the artwork of others. If a work is complex, they will focus on one part and not be concerned about how it relates to the piece as a whole.

In the middle of the preschool period, children begin to pay attention to the subject matter, responding most favorably to works that depict familiar objects and events. Interestingly, it does not matter at first if the work is abstract or realistic, as long as they find a recognizable personal connection. A preference for realism does begin to emerge later, however, and increases through the elementary years. As children begin to include more detail in their own art, they begin to pay corresponding attention to the details included by the artist. However, young children still prefer works with a limited number of objects portrayed in high contrast to one another.

Toward the end of the early childhood years, the expressive qualities of the artwork affect preferences. Children also begin to pay attention to individual artistic style and become more aware of differences in media and techniques. Their earlier preferences related more to *what* was portrayed, but now they become interested in *how* it is portrayed. Their verbalizations still tend to focus on subject matter rather than style, but they are increasingly able to articulate basic aesthetic principles and describe what they think the artist is trying to convey and how it makes them feel. Their preferences may change rapidly, but they are strongly held and defended.

Stages in the Development of Visual Arts in the Young Child

In its report on promoting the arts in young children, the Arts Education Partnership (1998) lists the stages of artistic development and what young children typically do from infancy through the early elementary years. The report cautions that it is impossible to develop a precise list of stages that applies to all children and all settings.

> Studies...show that stages of artistic development are no more than approximations or informed predictions of what most children will do at a certain age, given the quantity and quality of arts experiences that are available to children in the cultures of their homes, communities, and schools. (p. 2)

The reason for listing stages, therefore, is not to categorize or judge children along a continuum of ability. Rather, the value of adopting a developmental paradigm is to understand the course of artistic progress and generate strategies that adults can use to support children's growth.

The stages of artistic growth in young children summarized on the next page draw to a large extent on the visual arts components listed in the Arts Education Partnership publication. However, the summary of stages also provides supplementary data from the studies mentioned earlier in this chapter and includes observations based on High/Scope practice and research. Moreover, the summary integrates information about the development of young children's ability to both make art and appreciate art. The next chapter describes how adults can support all these areas of artistic development by arranging and equipping the early childhood classroom with appropriate materials, providing visual arts experiences throughout the daily routine, and, perhaps most important, engaging in adult-child interaction strategies that support exploration and appreciation of the arts.

Stages in the Development of Visual Arts in the Young Child

What children can do relevant to visual arts

Younger infants (birth to 8 months)

- Discriminate contrasting images in black & white or colored objects
- Become aware they can change what they see by changing their head or body position
- Become aware that names are associated with objects and actions

Older infants (8 to 18 months)

- Hold large writing tools (crayons, chalk) and move them between their hands
- Make marks and lines on paper
- Stack blocks
- Express positive and negative feelings
- Associate names with art materials, tools, actions, and products; learn their functions and properties

Younger toddlers (18 months to 2 years)

- Build thoughts, mental pictures, and verbal labels
- Match and sort objects
- Use words to express feelings
- Squeeze, pat, roll, and otherwise explore play dough and other non-toxic plastic materials
- Make aesthetic choices such as what colors to use in their paintings
- Understand feelings expressed through pictures, photographs, songs, poems, and stories

Older toddlers (2 to 3 years)

- Develop symbolic thought and build mental concepts
- Recognize "accidental" representations or similarities
- Make simple representational drawings
- Draw simple forms and shapes
- Paint with a large brush
- Tear paper
- Mold simple objects with clay or play dough

Younger preschoolers (3 to 4 years)

- Represent with greater intentionality
- Draw and print with crayons and pencils
- Cut figures and shapes with scissors
- Match shapes, colors, and patterns
- Draw faces with some detail
- Sculpt figures with some detail
- Construct collages with paper, small objects, glue, tape, and scissors
- Exaggerate most salient aspects of representation
- Focus on one aspect or area rather than an entire work of art
- Express aesthetic preferences based on color, pattern, or movement

Older preschoolers (4 to 5 years)

- Copy simple geometric figures
- Use increasingly complex tools and media combinations
- Add greater detail to representations

- Strive for greater spatial accuracy in representations
- Express feelings when listening to stories
- Use imagination to create and elaborate representations
- Enjoy humor and exaggeration
- Identify what is missing from a picture
- Identify basic colors
- Attend to several areas or the overall work of art
- Express aesthetic preferences based on subject matter
- Differentiate forms of representation (for example, photograph versus reproduction)
- Recognize time depicted in a representation (past, present, future)

School age (5 to 8 years)

- Build inventive models from cardboard and other materials
- Enjoy creating and telling stories about visual representations
- Perceive and appreciate expressive and stylistic features of art
- Deliberately create aesthetic effects with media and tools
- Begin to see art from the artist's perspective
- Articulate simple aesthetic principles
- Differentiate cultural and other influences that affect art
- Become increasingly deliberate and opinionated in aesthetic choices

4

How Adults Support Art in Young Children

Elena, a four-year-old, has been painting at the easel. Elena's teacher Rosie kneels next to her and stays there as Elena continues to work on her painting.

Rosie: This part is interesting. *(Rosie points to an area of the painting.)*

Elena: That's my mom and this is her mouth. *(Elena dips her brush in the paint and adds two long vertical loops.)* These are her legs. Now I'm painting the grass. *(She dips her brush in green paint and adds a squiggly line along the bottom of the page.)*

Rosie: You're adding grass.

Elena: I need to paint the sidewalk. *(Elena dips her brush in yellow paint and makes a straight line, carefully connecting it to the grass.)*

Rosie: I see you changed colors for the sidewalk.

Elena: Now I'm going to make a sun up here. *(Elena dips her brush in yellow-green paint and makes a small circle in the upper left corner.)*

Elena: *(Elena adds a series of black dots across the top of the page, to the right of the sun, then makes a long dark line coming down from each dot.)* That's the rain.

Rosie: Now it's raining. I wonder what's going to happen to your mom?

Elena: She's gonna get wet! *(Elena laughs.)*

Rosie: She'll get really wet. *(Rosie laughs with Elena.)*

Elena: This is her hair. *(Elena carefully paints the hair on top of her mom's head.)* These are her shoes. *(She adds black half-circles at the bottom of each leg.)*

Rosie: She's going to need some shoes if it's raining.

Elena: We should have a rainbow up here. *(Elena points to the space above the sun and clouds.)*

Rosie: That would be lovely—in the sky, a rainbow.

Elena: *(Elena dips her brush in three colors, one at a time, and makes horizontal lines to form a rainbow.)* A rainbow!

Elena: *(Elena adds more dots at the top in the row of clouds.)*

Rosie: These remind me of the other clouds but they're a different color.

Elena: *(Elena adds more vertical stripes—rain—coming down from each cloud.)*

Elena: *(She stops abruptly.)* I'm finished now!

Rosie: You're finished.

Elena takes off her smock and carries her painting to the drying rack.

In a survey conducted by Baker (1992), preschool teachers estimated that young children spent 30 to 50 percent of their day engaged in "art-like" activities. While this acceptance of art as a regular feature of the school day is heartening, it is important to acknowledge that most early childhood teachers have little training in art education (Thompson, 1995). Lacking an art degree does not prohibit regular classroom teachers from effectively supporting art development in young children, but it does suggest that agencies and individuals should take several steps to strengthen teaching ability in this area. As we discussed in Chapter Two, if first given studio time to explore art materials and recognize their own artistic and aesthetic sensibilities, teachers will have the confidence to apply their experience to supporting children in their development as young artists. Confidence alone is not enough, however. Preschool teachers must also understand the growth of children's artistic abilities, as detailed in Chapter Three. Finally, they must know how to apply their personal experience and knowledge of child development to creating a supportive arts environment in the classroom.

In this chapter, adult support for young artists is approached from the perspective of three basic components of the High/Scope educational approach: setting up the learning environment, providing time for art experiences throughout the daily routine, and interacting with children in ways that support and extend their artistic explorations. A final section emphasizes that adults require support from their institutions so that they can, in turn, support young children in the pursuit of art. Strategies that adults and institutions can implement to support artistic development in the early childhood years are summarized in the margins on pp. 62–63.

The Role of Adults in Arts Education

The role that adults play in visual arts education should conform to the basic principles of sound developmental practice in general. That is why the Arts Education Partnership (1998) prefaces its arts recommendations with the statement that "children need interested adults and others to listen to their plans, respond to their ideas, and offer assistance and support for their explorations.... Planning must first be child-centered, then content relevant" (pp. 2–3). Using these principles of good early childhood practice, the Arts Education Partnership says adults can best support children's artistic development if they plan experiences that:

- Allow for child-initiated choices

- Emphasize process over product

- Engage children in exploring, creating, and reflecting on their own art experiences

- Foster imagination that has its origins in child play

- Connect to children's own experiences and knowledge

- Initiate children into age-appropriate artistic experiences (performances, exhibitions)

- Provide links to real life

- Evolve from and encourage children's interest in literature

- Support children's language and literacy development

If approached in this child-initiated manner, making and appreciating art will be consistent with good early childhood practices. Similarly, Colbert (1995) notes that a child-centered approach to visual arts education should emphasize playful and concrete experiences that are related to children's interests and meaningful to their lives and needs. Colbert takes the guidelines advocated by the National Association for the Education of Young Children (Bredekamp, 1987; Bredekamp & Copple, 1997) and connects them to visual arts education in the following ways:

- *Addressing all areas of development*—By supporting children as they make and describe art, adults help them integrate all areas of development, including

Daily routine

- Incorporate other sensory experiences to enhance children's understanding of visual art.

- Use art to establish a connection between home and school.

- Connect children to art and the creative process in their communities.

Adult-child interaction

- Begin with children's own experiences and interests.

- Make sure children feel safe and secure expressing themselves about art.

- Develop a language to talk about art.

- Help children develop a sense of aesthetic appreciation.

Institutional strategies to support adults

- Adopt written policies that value the arts equally with other school subjects.

- Develop a plan to include the arts and allocate resources towards them.

- Consider the artistic qualities of buildings and facilities; include arts education programs during development and renovations.

- Work with community volunteers who can serve as mentors and partners.

- Provide ongoing professional development for arts specialists and classroom teachers.

spatial relationships, language, perception, memory, reading, mathematics, and social skills. Making art helps children understand such concepts as near and far, up and down, in front of and behind. They acquire a language for talking about their own art and art created by artists. Viewing and discussing art encourages children to share their ideas and learn how others perceive things.

- *Providing learning materials that are concrete and related to children's lives*—Visual arts education is essentially concrete because it involves manipulating materials to create two- and three-dimensional forms. When art instruction involves talking about art, children can see and touch real objects or faithful reproductions. They can represent people and events in their own lives, and observe how others use art materials to stand for shared experiences.

- *Promoting active involvement by providing choices and time to explore*—Art materials are inherently attractive to children, and they are eager to experience different art media with all their senses. Art experiences should not be dominated by teachers. Coloring sheets and copying adult-made models discourage active engagement. Rather, children should be introduced to a variety of materials and given time to explore and reflect on their activities.

- *Planning based on child observation, individual interests, and developmental levels*—Art teachers tend to work in this manner naturally. They distribute open-ended materials and then circulate as children work. They provide materials that gradually enrich and extend children's independent explorations. Through systematic planning, adults can build on children's natural abilities to perceive, create, and appreciate the visual arts.

In sum, regular classroom teachers can be effective arts educators if they are flexible in their use of materials and space, open to incorporating art throughout the day, and responsive to children's interests and abilities. By following these practices, teachers can provide opportunities for the class as a whole to explore the joys of making and appreciating art. They can also individualize the arts education experience for every young artist.

The rest of this chapter presents the specific adult support strategies advocated by High/Scope to help art flourish in early childhood settings.

Supporting Young Artists

Adult Strategies to Support Young Children Making Art

LEARNING ENVIRONMENT

Set up an attractive and permanent art area

This first strategy should be obvious, yet it is striking how many classrooms do not have a permanent and well-defined art area. Too often, teachers will use a table or corner of the room to set out a limited number of materials for that day's art activities. This temporary art setup may displace another activity or have to be dismantled to make room for something else in the middle of work or choice time. Setting aside and labeling an inviting area for art sends young children the message that art is a vital part of their everyday experience. An art area also conveys the message that its materials and activities constitute a category of learning, just as books are used to learn to read or puzzles are used to develop eye-hand coordination. Finally, the presence of an art area helps adults remember to provide materials and plan experiences that promote children's representational thinking and skills.

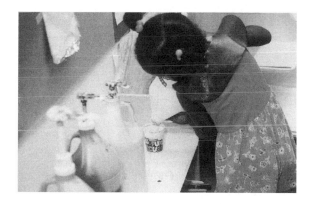 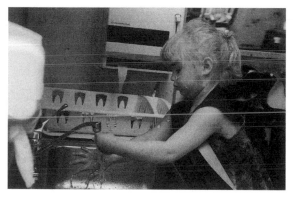

The art area should be near a sink so children can prepare materials and clean up on their own.

Provide a wide and abundant variety of tools and materials

Most early childhood programs offer basic art supplies such as crayons, paints and brushes, and play dough and modeling clay. Yet few settings provide young children with the *variety* they need to explore the properties and representational potential of diverse media. Children can use many everyday and inexpensive materials and tools

An attractive and well-stocked art area is an invitation to children.

for art, but a supply of good quality art items for their use is also important. Authentic materials and tools allow them to experience processes and effects similar to those encountered by adult artists in their studios. Variety is essential so children can choose materials that appeal to their senses or convey the images they want to represent (Arts Education Partnership, 1998).

Take care, however, not to overwhelm children by offering too many materials at once. Introduce materials slowly and give them ample time to explore each one in depth. As they become comfortable with the properties and creative possibilities of each medium, children will be ready to explore new mediums and incorporate familiar materials into their representations.

A good example of introducing materials gradually is the matter of color. It is best to begin with primary colors (red, yellow, and blue) and white paper (Hohmann, 1996). When children are just beginning to draw and paint, they need to explore the action of moving a crayon, marker, or paintbrush against the surface and seeing the kinds of marks they make with their movements. Only after they have thoroughly explored this rhythmic motion will they be ready to systematically make lines, or even more dramatically, mix colors to create new colors.

By letting children begin with the exploration of a limited number of materials and tools, adults can maximize the eventual repertoire of skills that children will employ in using them. Giving children too many new materials at once short-circuits the discovery process and impoverishes the richness of children's creative activity in the long run.

In the rest of this section, materials and tools that can encourage children's art explorations with two- and three-dimensional media are described. A more detailed list for stocking the art area, along with suggestions for storage, work space, display space, and art appreciation is provided on pages 67–69. This list should be supplemented with items that are natural and plentiful in the area where the program is located. Programs should also provide art materials and tools that are representative of those found in children's homes, communities,

Supporting Young Artists

and cultures. Finally, adults can provide children with pictures and books about the objects they intend to represent in their artwork. "Looking at real items or pictures does not inhibit creativity, but helps children make their representations more accurate, rich, aesthetically complex, and detailed" (Warash & Saab, 1999, p. 14).

- *Two-dimensional materials*—Children can use many materials to draw and paint, including paints and paintbrushes, markers, crayons, colored pencils, chalk, and oil pastels. Some materials, such as markers, allow children to apply color smoothly with little pressure. Others, such as crayons, will respond to differences in pressure and can be used to create more diverse effects. Less conventional materials for drawing and painting include water or weak solutions of glue, starch, evaporated milk, soap flakes, and other soluble materials. The addition of coffee grounds, salt, or sand will give the solution a rough or gritty texture while the addition of sugar will create a sparkling appearance when it dries. In addition to brushes, children can use their fingers, twigs, pebbles, strings, rubber bands, buttons, kitchen utensils, hardware items, and other tools to explore these materials.

  Children also need paper in a wide variety of sizes, colors, and textures. White butcher paper or craft paper enables them to see the purest colors; construction paper tends to produce muddier colors. Paper should come not only in sheets but also on a roll, in case children want to make something big. Alternative types of paper that produce interesting effects include newsprint, grocery and gift bags, cardboard, foil, and cellophane. Also, adults should supply surfaces other than paper on which children can draw and paint, such as boxes, bark, wood, fabric, and mud. Chalkboards and pavement are also good surfaces for marks made with water and watery solutions.

Creating a Learning Environment for Visual Art[1]

Two-dimensional media— materials and tools

Drawing and printing

- **Colored markers and felt-tipped marking pens** (to enable children to apply color smoothly without much pressure)
- **Crayons** (Crayons are responsive to changes in pressure.)
- **Chalk and chalkboard** (Chalk colors blend easily.)
- **Charcoal sticks**
- **Pencils**
- **Colored pencils**
- **Oil pastels** (Pastels blend well, respond to variations in pressure, and create rich, intense colors.)
- **Ink pads and stamps**
- **Computer-based drawing programs**

Painting

- **Tempera paint in primary colors** (red, yellow, blue), white, and black (Paint should be smooth and thick, the consistency of heavy cream; it can be thinned with water for more experienced painters.)
- **Water colors**
- **Finger paints** (Thick paints can be used for finger-painting as well as brush painting.)

Continued on next page

[1]See also High/Scope Educational Research Foundation, 2000, pp. 26–27; Hohmann, 1996, pp. 4–5; Hohmann and Weikart, 2002, pp. 132–135; and Tompkins, 1996b, pp. 130–132.

- Liquid starch and soap flakes (These can be used to thicken tempera paints.)
- Brushes: sturdy brushes in a variety of widths; inexpensive brushes; a few good-quality artists' brushes; 2" and 3" household paintbrushes (The softer and fuller the bristles are, the better they will hold the paint when carried from container to surface.)
- Tools to make marks: combs, toothbrushes, sticks, feathers, leaves, cotton swabs, string, shoelaces, rubber bands, bottle caps, and so forth
- Containers: shallow cups; muffin tins; empty yogurt containers; margarine tubs; paper plates or small metal trays for finger paints and thick tempera paints; buckets (Containers should be sturdy and spill-resistant, low so they don't tip over, and sized to fit into easel slots or slip into cardboard with cut-out holes. Wide flat containers allow children to dip palms, fingers, or hands into the paint.)
- Plastic squeeze bottles
- Spray bottles
- Screening with holes of various sizes

Paper
- White drawing paper
- Large roll of white butcher paper or craft paper (can be cut or torn to desired sizes)
- Construction paper in various colors (Rough surfaces produce muddier colors than white butcher or craft paper do.)
- Lined paper, graph paper
- Finger-paint paper (coated glossy paper)
- Shelving paper
- Clear and colored cellophane
- Newsprint
- Magazines and catalogs
- Cardboard and matboard
- Paper bags: plain brown grocery bags, gift bags, shopping bags with handles
- Wrapping paper
- Gift wrap
- Tissue paper
- Foil paper
- Waxed paper
- Crepe paper
- Wallpaper samples (Interior design stores often give away outdated sample books.)
- Paper tubes
- Paper plates
- Cardboard boxes and gift boxes
- Used greeting cards, post cards, stationery
- Recycled paper of all types

Three-dimensional media— materials and tools

Modeling and sculpting
- Clay, modeling clay
- Dough made of flour and water, perhaps with salt (Dough should be malleable, but not too soft.)
- Play dough
- Moist sand
- Beeswax
- Natural dyes—coffee, cinnamon, cocoa, mustard, black and red pepper—and food color to add to dough and other materials
- Tools for molding and making impressions: bowls of various shapes and sizes; dowels (wood, metal, plastic, and heavy cardboard); tongue depressors and popsicle sticks; sticks of various widths and textures; toothpicks; kitchen utensils (rolling pins, plastic-ware and silverware, cookie cutters, garlic press, tortilla press); natural materials (shells, leaves, nuts); hardware (nails, nuts and bolts, screwdrivers, mallets); plastic letters and numbers; old toy parts (wheels, pegs); lace; buttons and beads; hair rollers and barrettes; and so forth
- Plywood boards or heavy cardboard (can be used as a portable work surface)
- Heavy plastic bags or rolls (to keep clay moist and allow work to dry slowly without cracking)

Mixed media and collage
- Boxes and cartons, all sizes and shapes
- Cardboard or plastic tubes
- Egg cartons
- Yarn, ribbon, string, and twine/rope of different materials, widths, textures, and colors
- Fabric of various materials, colors, and textures
- Pipe cleaners, shoelaces, elastic strips

- Buttons, sequins, beads, feathers
- Clothespins
- Wood scraps
- Plastic foam pieces
- Dried pasta and beans
- Cotton balls
- Old socks and stockings
- Small unbreakable mirrors
- Materials from nature: wood, sticks, leaves, grass, bark, shells, pebbles, stones, pine cones, feathers, and so forth
- Straws
- Empty thread spools
- Cutting devices: scissors, plastic knives, hole punch, and so forth
- Fastening devices: paste; liquid glue; glue sticks; staplers; paper clips of various sizes and shapes; cellophane tape (heavy duty dispenser); masking tape of various widths and colors; rubber bands; yarn and string; wire; tapestry needles with big eyes and thread; and so forth

Space and equipment

Work space and equipment

- Water: sink; outdoor spigot and hose; buckets and dishpans; pitchers (used for preparation of materials and cleanup)
- Light: natural light from windows and skylights; incandescent light (preferable to fluorescent as source of artificial light)
- Tile or linoleum flooring (easy-to-clean solid color or neutral floor pattern) covered with newspapers, bed sheets, drop

cloths, a roll of clear plastic, or tarps
- Vertical surfaces: easels (Side-by-side easels allow children to observe one another at work and share ideas.); outdoor fences (Attach paper with clips, clothespins, or string.)
- Horizontal surfaces: low tables; floors; playground pavement; picnic tables; small boards and floor tiles for working with modeling materials that can then be moved to a safe drying area (Children can control their painting on horizontal surfaces more easily than on vertical surfaces.)
- Protection for clothing: smocks and paint shirts (with hooks for hanging up)
- Cleanup: sponges, rags, newspaper, towels
- Drying space: clotheslines, folding clothes racks, shelves, tables

Storage space and equipment

- Flat racks (for paper)
- Jars with lids
- Heavy-duty plastic wrap (to keep clay moist)
- Shelves, bookcases
- Clear plastic containers (good for small loose items and scraps)
- Boxes
- Hanging shoe pockets

Display space and equipment

- Low bulletin boards
- Low shelves
- Pedestals and boxes
- Work-in-progress signs

- Spotlights
- Large appliance boxes turned on their sides (open side facing outward)
- Frames (made of wood, cardboard, construction paper)
- Labels (to indicate title, artist, and so on)
- Camera (for photographs and slides)
- Photograph albums
- Slide projector and screen (or sheet or blank wall)

Art appreciation

- Art from home (photographs, weaving, pottery, quilts, and so on)
- Storybooks illustrated in different styles and media
- Reproductions of fine art: post cards, photographs, scale models of sculptures
- Posters (depicting art shows and artwork)
- Exhibit catalogs
- Art books
- Artist biographies (illustrated for children)
- Books with art from various cultures and times in history

- *Three-dimensional materials*—Include both malleable (moldable) materials that can be used to shape something and fixed materials that can be used to build structures. The more natural the material, the more likely it will have a variety of sensory properties that add to the creative experience. Good moldable materials include clay, dough, beeswax, damp sand, paper, and mashed paper pulp. Other, more commercial malleable options are Play-Doh and Plasticine. For fixed materials, natural building options include lumber, sticks and twigs, stones, shells, yarn, and fabric. Recyclable materials, such as those made of paper, plastic, cardboard, and styrofoam, are also excellent sources for art supplies. Along with these materials, adults should provide children with the tools they need to build their creations—scissors, staplers, glue, tape of various kinds, rubber bands, and woodworking tools.

In addition to supplying variety, adults should make sure children have an *abundance* of materials to work with. If children are constantly told not to waste materials, their freedom of exploration will be curtailed severely. To comply with budget restrictions, programs can stock materials that are cheap and plentiful. For example, paper presents children with many creative possibilities. Families can bring in newspapers and magazines at no cost to the program. Empty cardboard and plastic containers can also be collected along with scraps of fabric, buttons, and other discarded household items. Additional recycled materials can be donated or obtained at low cost from industrial suppliers or resale outlets. (See Chapter Five for more ideas on using paper and other recycled materials in the art area.)

Provide ample and accessible storage space

In addition to variety and abundance, children need *easy access* to the art materials and tools in the classroom. Art supplies should be stored where children can readily see them, use them, and return unused materials to their designated space. These principles of storage and access apply to the arts in the same way they apply to all materials in a High/Scope classroom (see *Educating Young Children,* [Hohmann & Weikart, 2002, Chapter 5]). When children have ready access to art supplies, they can take the initiative in exploring materials and creating the representations that further their expressiveness and play. "By encouraging children to find, use, and return things themselves, adults foster children's independence, competence, and success" (Hohmann & Weikart, 2002, p. 123).

Art supplies, unlike many other materials in the early childhood classroom, are consumable. Once used, they cannot be used again. This feature may make adults reluctant to allow children ready access to art supplies for fear they will be wasted and resources will not be available to replenish them. However, when children are encouraged to explore materials in depth, they will spend more time investigating

Easy access to art materials, such as these paint pumps, allows children to function with confidence and independence.

the properties of each medium presented to them. By beginning with inexpensive materials and establishing an atmosphere of unrestricted exploration, adults can feel confident that children will not randomly waste the art supplies in their environment.

Provide ample work space

The classroom art area should be as spacious and open as possible, because making art is a very physical experience for young children. They move their whole bodies as they push a paintbrush across the page, put their entire weight behind shaping a piece of clay, and sway back and forth as they weave yarn through the diamonds of a chain link fence. Providing children with ample space to manipulate tools and materials enables them to enjoy the kinesthetic aspects of making art.

Similarly, even though children do enjoy working at the easel the way adult artists do, they may actually find it easier to work on a flat surface (Seefeldt, 1987). Children need room to spread out on table tops, stretch across a wall, or sprawl on the floor. Unencumbered space allows children to incorporate movement in their representational efforts without fear of bumping into other things in the environment. They can unroll large sheets of paper or build expansive constructions without encroaching on the activities of the other children in the room.

When space limitations are a problem, as they often are in early childhood settings, adults should think about how alternate space can be used flexibly to accommodate art activities. For example, tables can be moved aside during work time to create a large floor space. This flexibility is enhanced if the room is arranged so that the art area and small-group tables are contiguous. It helps if both areas have the same easily cleaned flooring material or if a temporary covering, such as large sheets of cardboard from flattened appliance boxes, can be spread under the tables. Another option for increasing space is allowing children to extend an art project into the block area or house area, where they can incorporate materials from those areas into their representations. The outdoors is also a wonderful setting for art activities. It not only provides ample and unrestricted space but also permits the sensory and aesthetic properties of nature to add new elements to children's artistic pursuits. Just as water from a nearby sink is important for the indoor art area, a spigot or hose to provide water for outdoor art activities is also helpful.

Children need room to spread out so they can use their whole bodies and work on large surfaces.

Display children's artwork

The classroom should also have space for exhibiting children's finished and unfinished artwork. The display space for finished work should be easily viewed by children at their eye level and may include walls, bulletin boards, or screens for posting two-dimensional work. There should also be shelves, boxes, pedestals, and similar structures to hold three-dimensional work. Children's unfinished work-in-progress may be rolled up, put on a special table, stored on a protected shelf, placed in a free cubby, covered with clear plastic, and so on. Having a separate display space for unfinished pieces reassures children that their artwork will be protected until they are ready to resume it.

Children may want to have their finished work labeled in the same way that museums and galleries label the works of artists. An index card or a small label made of poster board can contain the child's name and personal identifying symbol, a title or description of the work (supplied by the child), and any other information the child wants to include (such as the date or the materials used to make the artwork). Many children also like to have a "work-in-progress" sign displayed next to their unfinished work; the sign validates the importance of their undertaking and emphasizes its equivalence with the work of adult artists. Children are intrigued by the idea of a work-in-progress. Seeing the work-in-progress sign serves as a reminder when they are making their work plans on a subsequent day. Visible works-in-progress can also become focal points

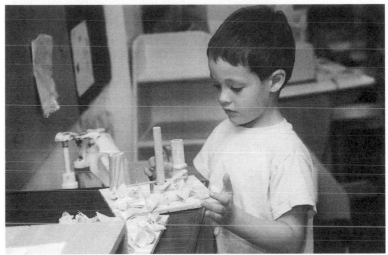

Drying racks and shelves are safe yet visible places to put finished work.

for children to share their endeavors at recall time or engage in spontaneous conversations about making art with peers and adults throughout the day.

Displaying children's artwork serves several purposes. Above all, it communicates that their activities in the visual arts are valued. Seeing their work labeled and displayed helps children identify themselves as artists, much like adult artists take pleasure in having their artwork exhibited. Putting up pictures or setting models on shelves

A "work-in-progress" sign lets others know an art project is important. It also serves as a reminder to the child during the next day's planning time.

Displaying children's art encourages reflection and sharing. Hang the work at their eye level so they can see visual images and labels.

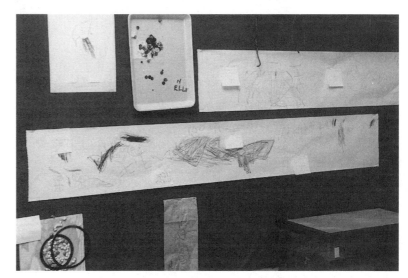

and pedestals lets the viewers, including the child artist, see the work from a new perspective. Children like to look at the work of their peers, not to copy it but to further their own ideas. Ephemeral work (such as chalk on the sidewalk) or creations that will be dismantled so the materials can be reused should be permanently recorded and displayed using alternative techniques, such as photographs and slides. Visual records and displays encourage children to share what they have done with peers, teachers, administrators, parents, and other visitors to the program. "Displaying children's art encourages them to reflect on their own work and the work of others. The classroom is an ecosystem in which children interact and learn from one another. That is how learning in the visual arts develops" (Trimis, 2000a, 2000b).

Supporting Young Artists

Send children's artwork home

Sending children's artwork home further communicates to parents that artistic activity is a vital part of a young person's development. Children and parents should also be encouraged to bring in any artwork done at home to share with adults and peers at school. Teachers can explain to parents why something that might look like no more than a glue squiggle on paper is evidence of the child's interest in and exploration of the properties of materials in the physical environment. They can also show parents how these early experiments are the necessary precursors to a child's later representational and artistic activities.

Art is serious business. It is important for parents to understand and appreciate their children's efforts.

If parents do not appreciate the educational value of the visual arts, teachers can share examples to demonstrate how artistic experiences help to promote language development, the spatial abilities needed for reading, the eye-hand coordination involved in writing, the formation of physical and relational concepts, and a range of communication and social skills. Teachers can plan a parent workshop, asking parents to bring in their children's artwork from home, and use these examples as the basis for a lively discussion of the value of visual art in children's overall development.

DAILY ROUTINE

Incorporate art activities throughout the daily routine

Teachers typically think of art as occurring during work time (choice time) or small-group time. However, the visual arts can be incorporated at virtually every other time throughout the day. Children need opportunities to apply art in different contexts and to make art in solitary as well as group settings (Colbert, 1995). For example, adults and children can talk about the illustrations in books at greeting time. Children can use art materials to indicate their intentions at planning time. Similarly, they can use two- and three-dimensional media to represent their work activities during recall time. Snacks and meals can also offer opportunities to attend to art. Children may enjoy including aesthetic elements in the table setting, such as a glassful of flowers or inventively folded napkins. Discussions at meals may also center on aesthetic concerns, for example, the shapes of the food, the colors in a reproduction hanging next to the table, or the designs on a ceramic bowl a child has brought from home.

Large-group time also lends itself to many visual arts experiences. Children can move with colorful banners or scarves. They can design simple instruments and beat or shake them to music. Moving to familiar music on one day may serve as a prelude to painting to that music on another day. Outside time is equally well-suited to art and aesthetics. Children might decorate a climbing structure, paint a large mural on a sheet of paper clipped to the fence, or draw with chalk on the playground. They can become increasingly aware of the sensory variety and beauty in nature. They can examine the clay in the local soil or the colors and forms of the native plants. Even transitions can become a time to encourage children to think about the visual arts. Ask children to recall how they moved their paintbrushes at small-group time and then suggest they move their bodies in the same way as they proceed to the next part of the day.

In addition to integrating art throughout the daily routine, art can also be the occasion for special events, such as celebrations and field trips to artists' studios and museums. Birthdays are a natural time to call attention to the colors and designs on a birthday cake or to children's handmade cards. Holiday times often involve decorative arts that are symbolic of the occasion or representative of children's diverse cultural backgrounds. Some holidays, such as Halloween or Purim, involve dressing up in costume and provide many opportunities for children to decorate themselves and others. These celebrations are wonderful times to invite families to share the visual arts that accompany their rituals and observances. Although these activities are more often undertaken with the goal of enhancing art appreciation (see the next section), seeing the art of others may also inspire children to create similar artwork on their own.

Provide time for in-depth exploration of materials, tools, and procedures

Adults should allow time for three processes in the visual arts: experimentation, repetition, and reflection. Art is a thoughtful process; it cannot be hurried. Young children need uninterrupted time to learn about the media's visual and tactile properties and to master the skills necessary to transform them into something else. Children learn best when they can work with the same basic materials and tools over and over again (Clemens, 1991). When adults create a space for works-in-progress, this allows children to revisit their art to complete their original intention or add new details to the work. Adults should also plan sufficient time for reflection and review. "In art activities, children need time to experiment, to plan, to create, to revisit, and to evaluate their work. Time for reflection and use of peer verbalization during art activities have been found to influence the evaluative processes of children" (Colbert, 1995, p. 38).

The in-depth exploratory approach to art (detailed in Chapter Five) meets all of these time-based criteria. Children can choose to explore art materials for long periods at work time. They can revisit materials as often as they like. Each time children use the same materials, they have the opportunity to discover new properties and gain confidence in how they handle and create with them. They can also work on an art project over more than one work period. Providing the same materials at multiple time points allows more children to become involved in experimentation. "Even the children who did not work [with the material] the first time might want to work with it another time. The children who worked the first time will go even further with the material the next time" (Trimis, 2000a, 2000b). Trimis notes further that the tendency in many early childhood programs is to "jump from one material to the other all the time." However, the in-depth approach is essential for children to gain an appreciation of the materials they are working with and their representational potential. This awareness of materials and their uses is cemented when adults encourage children to reflect on their artwork and that of others. In the in-depth approach, teachers take time to look at children's art, call it to the attention of other peers and adults, and help children find the language to describe their creative experiences.

ADULT-CHILD INTERACTION

Stress process over product

Although early childhood teachers generally give lip service to focusing on process rather than product, "this emphasis is routinely contradicted in practice" (Tarr, 1995, p. 25). Art educators lament that despite everything that has been written about avoiding patterns and required outcomes, early childhood teachers continue to control how children use materials and require them to make predetermined products (Szyba, 1999). What accounts for this discrepancy? Adults in the classroom are often under pressure from administrators and parents to produce child artwork that can be displayed in hallways or exhibited with pride at home. Rather than seeing this expectation as an opportunity to enlighten others about the exploratory nature of children's artwork, teachers often succumb to the demand to produce something recognizable and "pretty." Some teachers, whether responding to outer or inner expectations, create adult models for children to copy. They may even go so far as to trace or cut out forms for children to merely decorate. By offering a few colors of paper or crayons or sequins, these teachers are under the misguided impression that they are providing children with choices in their artwork.

In the High/Scope educational approach, we have moved away from this adult-directed model of art instruction because we find "it stifles creativity and reduces children's problem solving, independence, and experimentation." Our goal is "creativity, not conformity. Because the adult is less concerned with the quality of the child's product than with the process used in making it, we call this *process-oriented art.*" (Tompkins, 1996a, p. 188). To truly focus on process over product means implementing the strategies emphasized throughout this book. First, art materials should be set out for the purpose of exploration. There should be no expectation that children will have a finished piece at the end of small-group time, work time, or any other period in which art is employed. For example, young children may

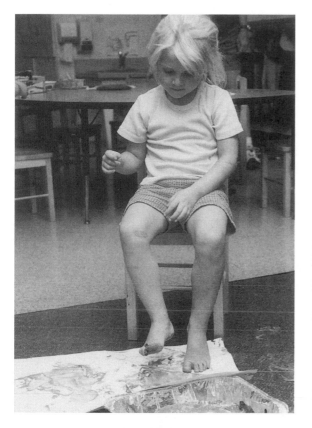

The unexpected happens when children focus on process, not product. A girl discovers new sensations by painting with her feet and fingers. Even cleanup time is fun, especially when a friend helps.

become so enamored of using a brush to apply paint that they rub a hole in the paper. Or they may become so engaged in squeezing the glue bottle that they cover a surface with glue squiggles and blobs without ever affixing something to that surface. These are all part of the creative process and should not be short-circuited. Second, teachers need to create a playful atmosphere around the use of art materials. If they show no concern with children's success in producing a work of art or failure to do so, children will feel free to just experience the joy of working with the materials and tools. Finally, adults should encourage reflection that centers on what the child is doing, not on what the child is making. This focus will call attention to the pleasure and discovery inherent in art and can lay the foundation for lifelong enjoyment in working with art's materials and tools.

Eventually, children themselves will express an interest in making a product, whether their intention is to represent something salient in their life or to create something that furthers their role play. Even children who have begun to make representational objects will need to spend time exploring when they encounter new art materials, tools, and techniques. Children in the classroom are similar to adult artists in the studio. Both need time for open-ended play and discovery. Out of this process unfolds the skill and inspiration that lead to creative production.

Accept children's individuality

We are all individuals and our exploration with art expresses that individuality. For that reason, adults should respect what children do and make with art materials and encourage them to enjoy art's sensory-motor properties as an end in itself. One way to provide this encouragement is to use art materials in the same way that children do. "By imitating, you are telling the child nonverbally that you value what she is doing" (Tompkins, 1996a, p. 190).

In addition to validating children's actions with the materials, adults should accept when children represent something that does not match the adult's idea of "reality." If adults censor, criticize, or correct what children do, it will inhibit and possibly destroy the creative process. In the process of exploration, children often use art materials in unusual ways. They may prefer to put the paint on their hands instead of the paper. They may balance balls of clay under the board instead of sculpting a shape on top of it. Similarly, when a child does create something, adults should accept what the child says it is, regardless of its resemblance to the real object. After all, viewers of adult artwork may not necessarily perceive what the artist intended, either. By taking the time to study a work of art and find the salient qualities that the artist wants to express, we enlarge our own perspective. This principle of respecting the individual's intentions applies to the art of children as well as adults.

Don't presume to know what a child has made or even that the child has made anything in particular.

Teachers gain insights into their students' thinking by being open to how they experience, express, and represent the world around them.

Listen to children talk about their art

Adults should not assume they know how children are using the materials or what children are trying to represent. (Hohmann & Weikart, 2002, p. 333) suggest, "Find out from children what they are making." For example, teachers can listen to what children say as they work or ask genuine questions to satisfy their own curiosity. Be careful not to bombard children with questions, however, even open-ended ones. Too many questions will still feel like "grilling" to the child and can stifle more spontaneous conversation. Asking "What are you making?" can become mechanical, and it assumes the child is making something when the child's art may not necessarily be representational. Tompkins (1996a, p. 191) says, "Questions work best when the children have approached you about their art and you are responding to them." The questions that emerge from a child-initiated interaction will reflect the adult's true curiosity about what the child is doing. The result becomes an authentic conversation instead of a question-and-answer session led by the adult.

Children offer many spontaneous opportunities for adults to listen and respond to their artistic intentions and actions. For example, children may announce at planning time what they intend to make. Often, they will comment on what they are doing as they work with the art materials, perhaps making up a story to go along with the actions of their hands or the images they create. When adults use materials alongside children and imitate their actions, it often prompts

When adults work quietly alongside children, conversations about art are spontaneous and natural.

children to start a conversation about their work (Tompkins, 1996a). Children can be invited to share these thoughts and experiences with their peers at recall time. Observation, listening, imitation, and dialogue around art can also take place during small- and large-group times.

Throughout the day, then, adults should be open to what children say about their art experiences. They should especially remember that it is risky for adults to interpret what the child is doing or making, because such an interpretation may be wrong. If the child feels frustrated in the act of communicating through art, the child may stop engaging in the process. Therefore, adults can best validate children's explorations by allowing them to determine the content and significance of the art themselves. Simple and factual descriptive state-

Supporting Young Artists

ments by adults work best and allow the child to decide whether to respond or elaborate on adult comments (see at right).

Balance child-initiated and adult-initiated activities

Perhaps the greatest challenge for teachers is finding the right balance between letting children discover art for themselves and helping to guide the course of their learning. In theory, most early childhood teachers believe art education is like other areas of the curriculum. That is, children thrive best if given open-ended materials and allowed to explore them. In practice, however, says Thompson (1995), teachers find this counsel "vague and insubstantial." If art education is seen as nothing more than providing materials, then "precious opportunities for immersion, reflection, and dialogue are lost, to children and their teachers" (p. 2). On the other hand, if adults discharge their educational responsibility by imposing their own ideas about what children should do and make, they can destroy children's sense of artistic adventure.

The extreme child-centered approach holds that artistic development takes care of itself. This approach results in

> Teachers who expend little effort on behalf of artistic learning. Yet life provides strong evidence that artistic learning is not the automatic result of maturation and self-guided experience. "Products" of non-interventionist approaches to art education complain of their lack of insight, understanding, and ability in the realm of artistic expression. They feel illiterate and inadequate in one of the fundamental domains of human experience. (Kindler, 1995, p. 11)

Research bears out the pitfalls of leaving young children totally on their own in the realm of art. Kindler observed that children in day care settings did not naturally spend extended periods of time in the art area. Their explorations were perfunctory and did not demonstrate the same level of engagement evident in

Keep Adult Statements Simple and Factual

At small-group time, the teacher, Michelle, is sitting at the table with six children aged three and four. Each child has a plate containing one or two colors of paint they have chosen and a large piece of white paper. On the table is an assortment of painting tools, including brushes, sponges, strings, rubber bands, and spatulas. As the children explore the paint and painting tools, Michelle occasionally makes comments describing and acknowledging what they did. When the children offer comments, Michelle repeats and extends their language.

Janelle: Look. I made spots.

Michelle: Janelle, you made red spots from the top to the bottom of the paper.

Michelle: Joshua, you used the string to make a wiggly line.

Erica: I made a yellow circle right in the middle of my page.

Michelle: That's a bright yellow circle. I see Kimmie made a yellow circle, too, with the big brush.

Michelle: Tommy is painting his hand with the spatula and the pink paint.

Tommy: That's the frosting on my handicake cupcake pattycake chop-chop.

José: Squoosh, squoosh, squoosh!

Michelle: You're squooshing the sponge with blue paint all over your paper!

Children remain in the art area longer and experiment more with the materials when adults work next to them.

the housekeeping or block area, for example. By contrast, when an adult was in the art area and became involved in dialogue about what the child was doing, the child remained there for an extended period of time and experimented with tools and materials. Kindler (1995, p. 14) asserted, "My observations clearly suggest that adult input is essential to young children's artistic explorations."

At the other extreme, art education risks becoming too adult-directed.

> The daily realities of teaching young children, amid the perceived expectations of parents and administrators, entices teachers to abandon the experiential approach to art activities. Intuitively seeking more structure and more uniform results, they gravitate toward lessons that are directive and mechanical. The use of art materials to complete designs prepared and distributed by teachers is all but universal in preschools and the primary grades. (Thompson, 1995, p. 2)

Children under this directive regime may acquire specific art skills. Their knowledge, however, is likely to be limited to the most common art materials and tools, especially those with which their classroom

Supporting Young Artists

teacher is familiar. Worse, any motivation to apply these skills in individual artistic expression will be severely compromised. Children's natural enthusiasm for exploration, their willingness to experiment, and their overall joy in artistic creativity may be lost, perhaps permanently.

In the last five to ten years, art educators have been seeking a balance between these two extremes. The theories of Vygotsky (1978) and derived practices support these efforts. Applied to art education, adult-planned experiences in the child's "zone of proximal development" provide appropriate challenges to advance exploration and learning. "In that sense, Vygotsky's theory is both child-centered and discipline-based" (Kindler, 1995, p. 2).

This approach to art education is compatible with the balance advocated by High/Scope. While the interest must stem from the child, adults do have a critical role in extending the learning and challenging children to consider aspects of the materials, interactions, and events from new perspectives. The role of adults in art education is similar to the way they can enter children's play without taking over. As in other types of play, teachers should not dominate children's art experiences. On the other hand, children should not feel abandoned when they encounter problems or want to share what they are doing and learning with an adult. As Thompson (1995) concludes,

> Art making is a natural occurrence of childhood, an activity young children discover and pursue even in the absence of adult prompting. Yet it becomes more clear every day that the nature of children's experience with art depends crucially on the adults who are responsible, by design or default, for guiding the course of artistic development and learning. This is particularly true for young children, who depend upon adults for basic access to workable materials, as well as for the encouragement to use them. (p. 1)

Adult Strategies to Support Young Children Appreciating Art

LEARNING ENVIRONMENT

Use the illustrations in children's storybooks as examples of art

Art appreciation can begin with the materials most familiar to children, such as the illustrations found in children's storybooks. That is why Post and Hohmann (2000) recommend building a library of cloth and board books beginning in infancy, and the Arts Education Partnership (1998) stresses the importance of picture books beginning in the early toddler years. Once children are familiar with the stories, adults can encourage them to look at the books for the illustrations as well as the narrative.

Mitchell (1995) offers several pointers to help teachers use children's literature as an art appreciation tool in appropriate ways. For younger children, use books with large pictures and uncomplicated illustrations. Older preschoolers and school-aged children will be able to appreciate more subtle and complicated drawings. Portraits of storybook characters are a good focus for bringing out aesthetic concepts. The teacher can help children identify the details the artist pays attention to, such as facial and bodily features or how someone dresses. Portraits done in different media can help children compare how the choice of medium affects how a particular physical characteristic is rendered. Collage books are another good medium. Adults can choose books with clear examples of how artistic techniques are used to convey different colors, shapes, and textures. Looking through storybooks is a wonderful opportunity for adults to encourage children's descriptive language. The more children look at these books, the richer the details they will begin to notice and describe.

Talking about illustrations in familiar storybooks is a good starting point for art appreciation.

Bring reproductions and illustrations of fine art into the classroom

In addition to seeing their own artwork displayed, children also benefit from viewing the work of professional artists. "Just as seeing pictures of real objects will not intimidate a child's drawing if the child is not forced to copy the work, viewing sophisticated artwork will not inhibit creativity" (Warash & Saab, 1999, p. 14). In fact, Lasky and

Supporting Young Artists

Mukerji-Bergeson (1980) claim that displaying art prints prominently in a classroom actually promotes rather than hinders children's aesthetic growth. Research supports their contention. Kerlavage (1995) reported that "preschool children who worked in media centers that included a variety of examples of adult artworks freely discussed their own work and the work of the artists represented. Additionally, their conversations were in greater depth and showed greater understanding of artistic process than a formal adult-led discussion of media and process" (pp. 59–60). Newton (1995) also found that having artwork around the classroom evoked spontaneous discussion among young children. The more familiar they became with the reproductions, the more they talked about them. New works similar to the old ones also evoked animated discussions.

Early childhood classrooms can be enriched by the prints, posters, photographs, and models available at museum gift shops, bookstores, and libraries. Magazines and brochures feature reprints of work to be shown at upcoming exhibits. The book review section of the newspaper may contain illustrations from recently published art books. There are also children's books about artists and their work. Families can save post cards they receive from friends and relatives who have visited museums. "Reproductions of the paintings, prints, and drawings of master artists are far more nourishing to children than Snoopy posters, Garfield cutouts, and cartoon-like images of objects, events, or stories" (Baker, 1990, p. 23). Viewing fine artworks can serve as sources of inspiration for young artists just as they do for adult artists.

Adults can support children's art appreciation by using these reproductions in various ways. Teachers can place them where they relate to the children's interests and activities—Mary Cassatt's paintings of mothers and children in the house area, van Gogh's paintings of sunflowers in the science area, junk auto sculptures in the block area, story quilts in the reading/writing area, or Jackson Pollack's drip paintings in the art area. The Arts Education Partnership (1998) suggests that young children can make scrapbooks or portfolios with their favorite reproductions and photographs. They can look through these picture books of their own creation in the same way in which they browse through illustrated storybooks, making up their own narrative or describing what they see.

Newton (1995) observed that children enjoyed using art reproductions in matching and sorting games. Younger preschoolers can match reproductions to verbal labels describing a literal quality of the work; older preschoolers and school-aged children can sort artwork based on its expressive quality. This game is especially effective when children choose the category or label and identify the similarities and differences in the reproductions they are sorting. Experiences like these help children acquire a range of cognitive concepts (think of the High/Scope key experiences in *classification* and *seriation)* at the same time they are building their knowledge and appreciation of fine art.

Observe art as it occurs in nature

Another way to build children's appreciation of the visual arts is to take advantage of the aesthetic properties in nature. The formal properties that art is concerned with (light, color, form, texture, and so on) all have counterparts in the natural world. Adults can help children become more aware of these properties and develop a language to talk about them. For example, teachers can talk to children about how changes in lighting (sun and clouds) affect the color of objects. They can observe and comment on shapes and textures in plants, rocks, and wildlife. Teachers can share reproductions showing how nature is depicted in art and ask children to compare their perceptions with those of the artist. Children can talk about what they, or the artist, found most interesting in a flower

A girl uses branches, twigs, and yarn to make a mixed-media tree.

Supporting Young Artists

or rock or animal. Older preschool children can explore how an artist uses formal techniques (size, color, texture) to draw attention to particular features when representing the environment. Children are natural observers. By helping them consider what they see from an aesthetic perspective, adults can promote simultaneously their appreciation of the natural environment and the artwork it inspires.

DAILY ROUTINE

Incorporate other sensory experiences to enhance children's understanding of visual art

Early art appreciation, like early development, is very sensory. That is why High/Scope's creative representation key experiences include *recognizing objects by sight, sound, touch, taste, and smell.* Young children's interactions with visual art are greatly facilitated by their total sensory involvement (Kerlavage, 1995). First, this immersion helps children respond to the work of art themselves. Second, the sensory experience gives children insight into what the artist intended in creating the work. For example, Kerlavage suggests that children will gain a greater understanding of Van Gogh's painting *Sunflowers* if they can touch and smell real sunflowers. They can more readily "see" the painting and perceive what the artist was trying to convey. Newton (1995) found that sensory-based play strategies increased children's involvement with art. For example, teachers can ask questions about the sensory qualities associated with the picture—Do you think it is warm or cold? Could you smell (hear) anything if you were there?

Art appreciation can also be enhanced by combining the visual arts with movement and music key experiences. If children move their bodies to represent or respond to works of art, their acquisition and use of descriptive words is increased. In fact, young children may be able to perceive and kinesthetically express aspects of artwork before they can verbally express it. They can use their bodies to represent lines, shapes, movement, and texture. To help develop language, adults can encourage children to describe "the position of their body, the way it moved, and the quality of the particular art element" (Newton, 1995, p. 81). These research observations directly support the validity of the movement key experience, *describing movement.* In one of our earlier strategies, we talked about providing ample space for children to move their bodies in while making art; this same consideration for the learning environment can also help young children to appreciate art.

Use art to establish a connection between home and school

Art appreciation can involve families in the life of the school and demonstrate the school's interest in family life. Because art is prevalent in both homes and schools, it is a natural way to build a bridge between the two. Regardless of whether families consciously introduce art into their homes, everyday objects and special decorative items inevitably reflect the aesthetic choices of individuals and their cultures. Teachers should make an effort to anchor school-based art experiences in children's firsthand encounters with art forms and materials at home. For example, are there family members who create art and can visit the classroom? Does the art reflect the family's culture, other cultures, or different periods in the family's history? Teachers can encourage children and their families to bring art objects from home to share with the school, perhaps mounting an exhibit of these items. It is important that items from home represent not only conventional fine arts (such as painting, printmaking, sculpture, and photography) but also feature less common media (including masks, weaving, pottery, calligraphy, beads, and baskets).

In the school setting, children naturally use art to represent the people and daily events in their family lives. The Arts Education Partnership (1998) suggests that adults encourage children to make paintings and drawings that reflect family life. It further recommends that children in late preschool and early elementary school make up stories and tell folk tales through drawing and sculpture. To encourage art appreciation, teachers can look at works of art with children and discuss how the images and feelings expressed relate to their own lives. Older preschoolers can also speculate about how the artworks might reflect the lives of the artists.

A wonderful example of such a connection is the museum workshop described by Lund and Osborne (1995). A team of art educators used the Marc Chagall painting *Birthday* to introduce preschoolers to an art museum. Because birthdays are recurring and meaningful events, children were able to relate the painting to their own experiences. Chagall made this painting to record the joy of one of his own birthday celebrations, just as children use art to represent significant

At recall time, a boy describes how he made a butterfly with paper, pipe cleaners, and tape. He shares the experience with his father at pick-up time.

events in their own lives. The workshop began with children using art materials to create their own birthday celebration. From this personal experience, they then became interested in how an artist who lived in a different culture and historical period celebrated and painted his birthday. A connection between the world of home and the world of art was mediated by this shared experience.

Appreciating art, like making art, is furthered when children share art experiences with their families. Therefore, teachers should encourage children to bring home the work of the artists they like. Families should be welcomed to participate in all the art appreciation experiences described in this chapter, including looking at book illustrations or visiting artists and art exhibits in the community. Teachers can use the information in this book to explain to parents why it is important for them to discuss the qualities and satisfactions of art with their children. Through their interest in art as a subject matter, parents communicate to children that practicing the skills involved in making and understanding art can be as valuable as mastering numbers and letters.

Connect children to art and the creative process in their communities

Art educators stress the importance of introducing young children to art and artists in the real world. Through this connection, children "get acquainted with the way artists work and use their ideas" (Trimis, 2000a, 2000b). Art appreciation can fulfill the National Association for the Education of Young Children's (NAEYC) guideline to provide young children with multicultural and nonsexist experiences, materials, and equipment. "The curriculum should extend children's experiences to include the ways of others, particularly the ways of people in the community. Reproductions of works of art are effective in introducing children to the images and ideas of people from a variety of ethnic origins, as is the study of the work of local artists, architects, craftspersons, and designers" (Colbert, 1995, p. 38).

Two types of community-based experiences can enrich children's involvement with the visual arts and enhance their aesthetic appreciation. One is interactions with artists. The other is visits to museums, exhibits, galleries, art fairs, and other venues. Teachers can make use of local resources to provide children with all of these opportunities. The program does not need to be located in a large metropolitan area to have access to individuals and organizations in the arts. Even small towns and rural settings have outlets for the arts. Any such venue, no matter how modest in scale, can be an exciting touchpoint for children, teachers, and families.

• *Interactions with artists*—"It is always much better to see artists in their own environment with their tools and materials so children realize how they work" (Trimis, 2000a, 2000b). If this is not feasible, however, teachers can invite artists to the classroom. To make the experience meaningful, adults should provide children with the kinds of materials and tools used by the artist. Let children work with these materials both before and after the visit. Children like the idea that they can do what grownups do. This delight is evident, for example, when they role play in the house area, work at the computer, or write "letters" to one another. The same principle applies to children's artistic pursuits. They want to be like adult artists and have their work with materials and tools regarded as serious work.

- *Visiting museums, galleries, art fairs, landscaped parks, monuments, and special events*—Teachers and parents can take young children on field trips to nearby museums, galleries, art fairs, landscaped parks, historical monuments, and special exhibits and art demonstrations in public spaces. The Arts Education Partnership (1998) says that even toddlers can visit children's museums and child-friendly exhibits, while young preschoolers, in small groups, are ready for interactive exhibits. Concerns that such experiences may be beyond young children are not supported by field testing and observation. "Museums and galleries are full of objects and pictures which can hold great interest" for infants and toddlers, provided adults take them to look at no more than two or three different things on any one occasion (Goldschmied & Jackson, 1994, pp. 169–170). Young children enjoy looking at art and sharing their observations with others (for example, Piscitelli, 1988; Lund & Osborne, 1995). As more museums recognize that young children can experience and respond to art, they are expanding programs for this age group (Cole & Schaefer, 1990).

To make these forays into the community meaningful, children should have many opportunities to represent their experiences afterwards. For example, children might choose to follow up field trips by creating their own exhibits in the classroom. They may re-create display cases, pedestals, and other exhibition spaces. Adults can engage children in making museum-style labels for their work that include the child's name, the artist's title, materials used, and an "artist's statement." Groups can talk about where to set up the display in terms of lighting, space, and visibility. Children might further reenact the field trip by role-playing gallery guides, setting up a museum gift shop, or erecting ropes and other barriers to protect their artwork. In all these activities, adults can help children relate their own explorations to the work of the studio artists or to the artwork they saw on display. If the children are interested, the teacher can bring in related artwork in the form of reproductions, slides, and books. These additions to the class-room extend children's understanding and begin to build a "concrete sense of history and culture in the arts" (Trimis, 2000a, 2000b).

ADULT-CHILD INTERACTION

Begin with children's own experiences and interests

Appreciating art, like making art, will remain an abstraction unless adults use children's own interests and life experiences as the starting point. To make art, children must first have a feeling, thought, or experience they want to express. Stressing the importance of experiential and psychological motivation, Seefeldt (1995) cites an example of children in two kindergarten classrooms who were asked to draw a picture of a friend. In one class, students drew stick figures indistinguishable from one another. In the other class, children began by talking to one another about their likes and dislikes, their families and homes, what made them interesting and unique as individuals. When it came time for these children to draw a friend, they carefully rendered such personal details as facial shape, eye color, length and curliness of eyelashes, and so on. Without meaningful and individual experiences, children draw stereotypical objects. Following what captures their interests, they can observe and create with an artist's eye.

The same personal motivation applies to children appreciating art. Arnheim (1989) advocates discussing artists's techniques in conjunction with a project that students have already chosen or willingly accepted. He notes that "anybody who has observed even young children spending long periods of time on some challenging piece of construction or deconstruction knows that there is no end to patience, once the goal is sufficiently attractive" (p. 33). Children will be curious about how artists achieve certain effects if they are interested in capturing similar qualities to represent their personal experiences.

The historical and cultural basis of art can also hold interest for children if it stems from their own activities. Arnheim (1989) cites a simple example: as children are drawing on paper, the teacher can introduce the idea that not everyone draws on paper. Some people draw and paint on bark. Children might then be interested in examining bark paintings (or works on clay, metal, and other media) and describing what they see. Gardner (1990) also emphasizes that art education should be grounded in student-initiated projects. "Students learn best, and most integrally, from involvement in activities that take place over a significant period of time, that are anchored in meaningful production, and that build upon natural connections to perceptual, reflective, and scholastic knowledge" (p. 46).

The Arts Education Partnership (1998) suggests several age-appropriate activities that begin with children's experiences and interests. For example:

- *Infants and toddlers*—Provide photographs of familiar people and places to see and hold.

- *Preschoolers*—Draw and describe the people, objects, and events in their world; create and illustrate stories based on children's play activities; re-create drawings from favorite books.

- *Early elementary*—Represent familiar actions and events in artistic media.

A good example of an art appreciation experience anchored in children's own lives is the Picture Museum created by preschoolers in preparation for a visit to the International Museum of Photography and Film in Rochester, New York (Kolodziej, 1995). Children from two local day care centers created the Picture Museum by bringing in their favorite photographs of themselves. They titled their pictures, which encouraged reflection and discussion about where and when the picture was taken, the events and feelings that accompanied the occasion, and why the picture was important to the child. The children also created labels for the photographs and a catalog of pictures with their descriptive comments about the images. This experience involved children in many participatory ways. In choosing a photograph for the Picture Museum, they expressed their aesthetic preferences. By describing the image and its creation to others, they engaged in the process of art criticism. While creating titles, labels, and an exhibit catalog, the children acquired a sense of how museums are organized and operate. As a result, when the children later visited the museum, they had a firsthand basis for understanding such concepts as museum, art collection, and photography as an art form.

Understanding how art appreciation develops in young children (Chapter Three) has direct implications for how adults support that development. Kerlavage (1995) summarizes these principles in the following statement and list of recommendations:

If programs that include young children's interaction with works of art are to be educationally, developmentally, and artistically meaningful, they must:

- Be based on the child's interest and knowledge of the world

- Provide opportunities for the child to engage the works from an individual point of view

- Make artworks a part of the child's everyday world

- Be based on the child's natural inclination to learn through play (p. 59)

Make sure children feel safe and secure expressing themselves about art

Brittain (1979) notes that children must feel safe and secure to risk the challenge of producing art. The same holds true for sharing observations and opinions about art. Children must know that their ideas will be received without criticism or ridicule. "It is important to accept a child's interpretation of what he or she sees, even if it is not the conventional view" (Hohmann & Weikart, 2002, p. 322). Adults can comment conversationally on children's remarks and they may add their own opinions. They must take care, however, not to correct what children say when they are interpreting a work of art or stating their opinion of what the artist intended. Just as adults may hold individual perspectives, so too will children bring their unique background and viewpoint to appreciating art. Sharing one's response to a work of art is a public revelation about something highly personal. Children must trust their listeners, and know their ideas will be respected, before they can feel comfortable revealing themselves in this way.

Develop a language to talk about art

Having a language to use when talking about art helps us focus our observations and find a common basis for articulating our thoughts. When talking to children about art, it helps if adults know what to look for and appreciate in the creative process (Engel, 1995). It also helps to remember that the language of art is not so different from the language of preschool. Both use terms like color, shape, line, and size, what Smith (1993) refers to as visual-graphic elements. Descriptive words such as empty and full, and comparison words such as lighter and darker, are used by children and art critics alike. In engendering art appreciation, teachers can help children expand the ways in which these common terms are used. Instead of focusing only on *functional* traits ("Please pass me the red cup"), adults can observe how such descriptive features also evoke an *aesthetic* response ("The bright red dress in that painting gives the dancer a lively look"). In simple words, then, teachers can make children's art experiences meaningful by having real conversations about their process and content. Adult strategies include the following (Epstein, 2001):

After small-group time, children review how they decorated their clay.

- *Use descriptive rather than judgmental terms when talking about art.* Say "I see..." or "It makes me think of..." rather than simply "I like it" or "It's pretty." Elaborating on why one likes or dislikes something helps young children build analytical skills and aesthetic judgment (Arts Education Partnership, 1998).

- *After a small-group art activity, encourage children to look at one another's work.* Ask: "Why do you think they look so different from one another even though you all made them out of the same paper and markers?" By interacting and talking with classmates, children hear others using different but similar adjectives. They acquire a much richer language to use when talking about art, which expands and clarifies their own thinking (Newton, 1995).

- *Introduce language to talk about the effect and aesthetics of the artwork.* When teachers use language rich with elaborate description, they model the process of responding to qualities in art (Newton, 1995). Use expressive as well as literal words and children will begin to do the same thing. For example, observe that "these colors look sad" or "all these little dots look busy on the page" or "this big, bright circle makes my eye keep coming back to it." Comparing two artworks with opposite qualities is another good strategy for encouraging children to expand their descriptive vocabulary. At the same time, they are exercising their logical thinking skills (see High/Scope key experiences in *classification* and *seriation)* and applying them to making aesthetic judgments.

- *Ask children to reflect on artistic intentions and feelings.* "Why do you think this artist makes little pictures but that one makes big pictures?" is a question art critics studying the minimalist and abstract expressionist movements might debate. It is also a question that young children can ponder. Guided questions can help young children go beyond merely pointing out objects in a work of art. They encourage them to think about the logical relationships between visual components and how the artist has arranged them for aesthetic purposes (Warash & Saab, 1999). When adults pose thoughtful questions, it allows young children to pursue an in-depth understanding of art and the intentions of artists.

- *Connect children's representational desires to comparable intentions of artists throughout the ages.*

  > Writing, storytelling, painting, sculpting, dancing, composing music—these are all ways adults organize and make sense of what we know. Similarly, weavers in the Middle Ages wove great tapestries that depicted their particular understanding of nature, myth, religion, and everyday court life. Preschoolers have the same need as the rest of us to remember and make sense of what they know. (Hohmann & Weikart, 2002, pp. 225–226)

  Conversations about art are important to this interpretive process. Words add another set of tools that children can use to express themselves. In art, words are a verbal complement to visual representations of actions and feelings.

Supporting Young Artists

Most adults without an art background feel inhibited talking about art. They feel that such discussions are the prerogative of those with formal training in this area and are afraid of sounding ignorant or unsophisticated if they voice their ideas. Yet we want adults to feel, and convey to children, that anyone can have an authentic and valid reaction to works of art. Adults in High/Scope art workshops have said they would feel more comfortable using the language of art with children if they could first practice talking about art among themselves. Teachers further felt that a basic familiarity with the terms used by artists and critics would enhance their knowledge and confidence. To meet this need, Marshall (1999) developed an art vocabulary list for adults. An adapted list of these terms and their definitions is provided in the Glossary (pp. 259–261). Although adults will generally use simpler terms when talking to young children, the ideas behind the words in this list are appropriate for adult-child conversations.

Feeney and Moravcik (1987, p. 13) suggest straightforward statements adults can make to talk with children about the visual elements in art. Their list is expanded on pages 100–101 with topics taken from the High/Scope adult vocabulary list found in the Glossary; examples of how adults might introduce these ideas to young children are provided. As talking about art becomes an everyday activity in the early childhood classroom, teachers may begin to use some of the adult vocabulary words in their discussions with children. Together, teachers and young children will then develop a shared language for talking about art.

Help children develop a sense of aesthetic appreciation

"The biggest role a teacher can play to foster interest in the visual arts for young children is to support their development of aesthetic appreciation and the joy and pleasure derived from the visual arts" (Warash & Saab, 1999, p. 15). Adults can help young children develop a sense of aesthetics in the following three ways:

• *Provide opportunities for children to observe high quality art.* From these examples children will "internalize beauty" (Warash & Saab, 1999). Once they have these internal images, children can create beauty on their own. As noted earlier, it is not that they will want to copy what they see. Rather, with repeated exposure to fine art, children will develop aesthetic principles. They can then apply them to

How to Talk to Young Children About Art[1]

Your use of simple and familiar language will help children become aware of the qualities in their own art and the artwork of others. Simple descriptive statements will also expand their observational and linguistic skills in general. As conversations about the elements of art become everyday occurrences, you can begin to introduce simple art words from the art vocabulary list found in the Glossary on pages 259–261. Examples of statements you can make to familiarize young children with the formal elements or properties of art are provided below.

Color
Colors abound in toys, furnishings, clothing, bodies (hair, eyes, skin), and nature, as well as in art. Variations in color provide many opportunities for adults to comment on their array. For example:

- **Hue**—*Mondrian, the artist, filled this box with blue and that box with yellow.*

- **Intensity**—*Aaron's hair is bright red. Mine is a duller shade of red.*

- **Temperature**—*The orange square in this Albers painting glows with warmth.*

- **Value**—*The leaves in this picture are dark green, just like the pine tree outside.*

- **Tint and tone**—*When you added white paint, the circle got lighter. Then you added black and it got darker.*

- **Relationship**—*The red flower really stands out next to the green leaves in the picture.*

Line
Lines appear in clothing, children's block constructions, walls and windows, and room decorations, as well as in paintings, drawings, weaving, and other art forms. Here are some examples of observations you can make about the many different properties of lines:

- **Kind**—*Jackson Pollock liked to drip squiggly lines of paint.*

- **Beginning/end**—*You started your blue line in this corner and it went clear to the other side.*

- **Direction**—*When you follow this wavy line in the painting, it makes your eyes look up.*

- **Quality**—*Mary's sneakers have wide stripes across the toe. John's have narrow ones in back.*

- **Length**—*The lines for the grass are made with short strokes. This one for the tree is longer.*

- **Relationship**—*The blue yarn goes over the red yarn and then under the yellow yarn.*

Form or shape
You can label recognizable geometric shapes, make comments about irregular forms, and describe the interrelationships among them. For example:

- **Size**—*This statue is carved from a huge rock.*

- **Name**—*You made a necklace with triangles and squares.*

- **Solidity**—*The blue square is all filled in with blue, but the red one has colored dots inside it.*

- **Relationship**—*Matisse cut out a yellow shape and put it inside the red one.*

- **Open/closed**—*Darren scooped out the clay and is sticking paper clips inside.*

Texture
Because they are so oriented to sensory impressions, children are sensitive to the physical feeling of various textures. Artwork differs not only in its actual physical texture but also in the textural effects of its visual images. You can help children become aware of how the appearance of a surface suggests the feel of the objects depicted. For example:

- **Actual/implied**—*The paint on this van Gogh sunflower is so thick your eyes can almost feel the petals.*

- **Hardness**—*Now that the clay is dry, the pot feels hard.*

- **Roughness**—*These dots in the Seurat picture make it look bumpy up close.*

- **Regularity**—*The threads in your skirt are woven tight on the pocket but loose and lacy around the trim.*

- **Reflectiveness**—*The silver crayon made such a shiny circle that it looks like a mirror.*

Space
Children develop spatial awareness in their everyday encounters with the world. Your comments

[1]Developed from an idea suggested by Feeney and Moravcik, 1987.

can help them develop a language for talking about what they see and how they move in that space. Then you can help them apply these same concepts to how artists use space. For example:

• **Distance**—*You drew the two cats close together.*

• **Location**—*Georgia O'Keefe painted a flower right in the middle of the canvas.*

• **Boundaries**—*In this painting, the woman inside the house is looking out through the window.*

• **Positive or negative**—*Keisha painted a red square and left the rest of her paper white.*

Design

As children gain experience with planning, they begin to do things by intention or design. Your comments can help them see how artists also plan so that they include different elements in their work and relate these elements to one another. For example:

• **Symmetry**—*The pattern on this side matches the pattern on the other side.*

• **Repetition**—*This basket has three stripes on the bottom and three stripes at the top.*

• **Alternation**—*Your bracelet has a blue square and then a yellow circle all the way around.*

• **Variation**—*Kandinsky used a light red up here and a darker red down there.*

• **Emphasis**—*Picasso made the mouth big so I wonder what the girl in this painting is saying.*

judging works of art and to creating their own art. Early childhood is a particularly opportune time to develop these principles. Because young children have not yet been socialized to accept only the most conventional definitions of beauty, they are open to seeing beauty in unconventional forms. Finding aesthetic value in unexpected places and unusual images is one goal of art. If children can develop this awareness early in life, their appreciation of aesthetics will be broader and more sophisticated than the narrow definitions imposed by their commercial culture.

• *Discuss visual images in paintings, sculpture, and other art forms.* Although children will naturally talk about the subject matter in images, adults can use guided questions to help them focus on the aesthetics as well. "Discussing paintings is probably the most helpful thing we can do with children other than giving them materials to paint with. Our more common failing is to demand little in understanding the arts, and to avoid discussion of them" (Parsons, 1987, p. 33). To facilitate discussion, begin with images that are based on children's concrete experiences, such as family groupings, still life arrangements, nature scenes, and holiday celebrations. Adults can employ many play strategies to encourage discussion and increase children's involvement with art. For example, Newton (1995) suggests having children pick a spot in a painting and imagine they are there. Landscapes, seascapes, and scenes of familiar interiors work well with this activity.

• *Convey a sense of the importance of art.* "Children also need to learn how and why other people create works of art, what place art holds in everyday life, and why people value art" (Colbert, 1995). Young children see adults engaged in activities such as reading on a daily basis. From this exposure, they develop the sense that reading is important. Adults can make a conscious effort to convey a similar sense of value about art. By interspersing comments about aesthetics throughout everyday conversations, teachers will communicate that an awareness of art and artistic principles can pervade and enrich daily life. They can also draw analogies between what children do and what artists do. For example, children often choose to represent family and school events with art. Similarly, artists may feel compelled to record an important historical or cultural event in a painting or sculpture. Pointing out these parallels gives a dual sense of significance to the work of children and the work of artists.

The visual arts should not be considered an "add on" to programs for young children. "Finding aesthetic pleasure in examining and reacting to representations that are based on concrete experiences is a central part of a good early childhood arts curriculum" (Warash & Saab, 1999, p. 15). When teachers integrate aesthetics into ordinary activities and conversations, they are laying the groundwork for art to become a continual and welcome presence in their students' lives.

Institutional Strategies to Support Adults

Just as adults must support children in making and appreciating art, they, in turn, need support from their institutions to make art an integral part of the program experience. While there is little direct information about how early childhood agencies provide this support, those in the field can learn lessons from art-friendly programs at public elementary and secondary schools. A study by The President's Committee on the Arts and Humanities (Longley, 2000) provides vital pointers in this regard. The committee reviewed the arts policies of 300 school districts across the country to develop recommendations for promoting the arts in grades K–12. They identified "a cluster of critical success factors shared by school districts that have created and sustained successful arts education programs" (Deasy & Fulbright, 1999, p. 32). Although some of these characteristics were unique to public school districts, five of the strategies may also be interpreted and applied to early childhood settings. These are discussed in the remainder of this chapter.

Adopt written policies that value the arts as equal to other school subjects

Increasingly, early childhood programs are under pressure to provide children with academics at the expense of arts-based experiences. Yet a report by the Committee on Early Childhood Pedagogy of the National Research Council (Bowman, Donovan, & Burns, 2000) clearly states that these are not mutually exclusive:

> What should be learned in the preschool curriculum? In addressing this question, the committee focused largely on reading, mathematics, and science because a rich research base has provided insights in these domains suggesting that more can be learned in the preschool years than was previously understood. This does not imply, however, that many of the music, arts and crafts, and physical activities that are common in quality preschool programs are of less importance. Indeed, the committee supports the notion that it is the whole child that must be developed. Moreover, these activities—important in their own right—can provide opportunities for developing language, reasoning, and social skills that support learning in more academic areas. (pp. 7–8)

To guarantee that these content areas are not pitted against one another, early childhood programs must include the arts as an explicit component of the curriculum model. This commitment should be put in writing as part of the program's mission, vision statement, and goals. According to Longley (2000), school districts that valued the arts used this formal documentation to justify funding decisions. Unlike most schools, they did not automatically eliminate art when faced with budget cutbacks. Arts-oriented districts treated art as equal with other subjects and reorganized the curriculum or made cuts across the board rather than unilaterally sacrificing arts education.

School districts that valued art also had at least one strong arts advocate on the school board. Deasy and Fulbright (1999) related the case of a district undergoing hard economic times. When the superintendent presented an annual report to repair the district's facilities, the board president responded: "All this talks about is bricks and mortar, asphalt and roofs. There's no vision in this. There's no direction. There's nothing here for kids" (p. 36). The board's challenge galvanized the entire community to develop a strategic plan in which the arts emerged as a component from the perspective of benefitting the students. Said the superintendent: "The arts surfaced from looking at the kids we serve and knowing that the light can come on for some kids through the arts" (p. 36). To apply this lesson, non-profit early childhood organizations should consider recruiting arts advocates as board members, including practicing artists and patrons of the arts. With the influence of these supporters, arts education will be guaranteed a place on the program agenda.

Develop a plan to include the arts and allocate resources toward it

Early childhood agencies, like public school districts, need to include the arts in their overall planning. There should be a broad vision and a long-term plan that includes arts education as a key component. To conserve resources, the plan can be implemented incrementally with funds apportioned steadily over time toward personnel, materials, and arts-based activities. Counter to expectations, the President's Committee on the Arts and Humanities found it was not always the districts with the biggest budgets that most successfully supported the arts (Longley, 2000). Rather, it was the consistency of their commitment that mattered. Staff cannot develop and sustain arts education programs if administrative and financial support fluctuate from year to year. Even a small level of support, provided it is dependable, allows teachers to build an arts program with the confidence that their efforts will not go to waste.

As noted earlier in this chapter, early childhood settings need not devote vast resources to include the visual arts in their curricula. Free and low-cost materials, and experiences implemented by regular teachers rather than by art specialists, can make art education feasible for virtually any program. More important than the absolute level of funding is the idea that money for art should be a standard part of the organization's annual budget plan, and that time for art should be a regular feature in teachers' daily program plans.

Include arts education programs during development and renovation of buildings and facilities

In early childhood programs, adults pay a great deal of attention to the learning environment. Typically, the setting is examined from a functional perspective. Is it safe? Do children have access to materials? Is there enough room to carry out a wide range of individual and group activities? All of these questions are important in implementing a program of arts education. However, the practice of creating and appreciating art is also influenced by the aesthetic milieu in which it takes place.

Therefore, in evaluating and creating early childhood spaces, we should look at their aesthetic as well as functional qualities.

Organizations should begin by assessing their current environment. Sometimes even a minor rearrangement of furniture or relocation of areas can create more room for carrying out art activities. Color and pattern should be used sparingly in the overall setting; too many bright colors and patterns may dominate a room and detract from the art and natural beauty that is present. Removing clutter or adding a few decorative items to the furnishings can also make the space more visually pleasing. Removing obstructions near windows can open views to the outside and let in more natural light. Changes in the type of artificial light can affect the warmth of the colors in the room, too. Such changes may require modest expenditures of time and money but they are worthwhile investments if the result is an art-friendly classroom.

At a more cost- and labor-intensive level, agencies should consider the arts when renovations, remodeling, and new construction are underway. At each step of the planning and building process, a chorus of people should be asking: How will the spatial arrangement accommodate an active arts curriculum? Does the structure provide versatile areas for solitary and cooperative creative play? Does the architecture embody principles of good design? Is the building pleasing to the senses? Will adults and children stop to reflect on the visual imagery around them? Will users and visitors be inspired to observe that the building operates efficiently and looks lovely, too?

Key features to keep in mind include work space and display space, natural and artificial lighting, color schemes, visibility of and contact with nature, the lines and angles created by dividing the space, and the visual effects of arranging furniture and other objects. These are the same basic considerations that adults apply to their home environments: Does it work? Does it look nice? It is equally important that early childhood organizations take account of these functional and aesthetic issues when creating the learning environment for young children. If aesthetic principles are conscientiously introduced into their daily work environment, then children will begin to consciously absorb these principles in their interactions with the visual world.

Work with community volunteers who can serve as mentors and partners

Teachers can work with family and community members to connect the classroom with the world of art beyond it. However, if these bridges are established at a broader level, between early education and arts organizations, the opportunities to expose young children to visual art will be greatly expanded. The President's Committee on the Arts and Humanities (Longley, 2000) commended school districts that reached out to their communities to involve interdisciplinary teams of artists and non-artists in developing the arts curriculum. Community members served as mentors for children and teachers, volunteering time to share their artistic skills and creative enthusiasm. They also partnered with administrators to defend the role of the arts in a comprehensive educational agenda. Volunteer effort not only supplemented existing funding but was also vital in rousing taxpayer support when budgets were being negotiated.

Early childhood agencies, which are often even more conscientious about community input than public schools are, can apply this participatory strategy in developing their visual arts programs. The Committee's research also documented that pro-art school districts supplemented their public budgets with private contributions of materials, services, and talent. "Personnel in these districts are entrepreneurial in their search for supplemental funds and treat that quest as a regular part of their professional responsibility" (Deasy & Fulbright, p. 32). Here, too, early childhood agencies can model themselves after art-friendly school districts. Administrative efforts to secure outside support can supplement what individual classroom teachers are able to accomplish on their own. To sustain community involvement in the arts program, agencies should invite contributors and other interested parties to visit the program and observe children's creative pursuits. Issuing these invitations is also an opportunity to educate the public to look for more than finished products or performances. Early childhood agencies can help members of the community appreciate the value of the exploratory process in early childhood arts education and the role of the arts in furthering young children's overall development.

Provide ongoing professional development for arts specialists and classroom teachers

Teachers in art-friendly school districts said that administrators encouraged them to continue developing as artists as well as teachers (Longley, 2000). Enhanced mastery of their art and growing competence in their teaching renewed their commitment to both. Although this finding applied primarily to art specialists, it was also true of the

Supporting Young Artists

professional development opportunities provided to regular classroom teachers. As described in Chapter Two, teachers without formal art training benefit from getting in touch with the artist inside them. When regular classroom teachers are given studio time to explore different media, they gain the confidence to make comparable experiences available to young children. They become aware of the many aspects of development that are furthered through firsthand exploration in the arts.

Art workshops might look like "play" to administrators, but adults, like children, learn valuable skills through play. Teachers can apply their direct experience making art to create meaningful studio experiences for young children. Similarly, engaging in art appreciation exercises allows teachers to develop their aesthetic sensibilities and bring this awareness into the classroom. Professional development workshops also provide opportunities for team planning around the arts curriculum. Regular teachers can plan with one another various strategies for including art throughout the daily routine. When art specialists are available, they can further expand the ideas generated by regular classroom teachers. Working together, these adults can serve as resources and inspiration for the children. Integration and collaboration are essential for early childhood programs to develop vital visual arts programs. They are more likely to happen when administrators include time and money for professional development as part of their arts advocacy initiatives.

"There are overwhelming reasons to integrate carefully the general classroom practices of teachers, the expertise of art specialists, and parental support for the arts in early childhood education. Of them all, the most cogent one centers on the importance of holistic learning and the investment that all of the 'art partners' have in the education of very young children" (Baker, 1990, p. 25). Achieving this worthwhile goal will require multiple levels of support in and beyond the art and early childhood fields. Institutions and communities must support teachers and parents; teachers and parents must support children. By implementing the strategies described above, adults can work together to enrich their own engagement in the visual arts at the same time they provide this vital human experience to the young children in their care.

Part II

An In-Depth Studio Approach to Developing Art in the Young Child

CHAPTER 5

An Overview of the In-Depth Studio
Approach to Art

Five-year-old Odile has chosen to work with clay nearly every day for the last two weeks. Today she begins by spreading a large sheet of waxed paper on the table. "So it won't stick," she tells her teacher Vanessa. "You're spreading waxed paper so the clay won't stick to the table," acknowledges Vanessa. Then Odile rolls out a small slab of clay with a wooden rolling pin. She sets it aside and rolls four others of about the same size. "I'm making a Munchkin house," she says. "It has to be very small." (Odile had seen the movie *The Wizard of Oz* on television earlier in the week.) Odile dips her fingers in a bowl of water and uses her moist fingers to pinch and smooth the edges of the slabs together, making a floor and four walls.

She rolls thin strands of clay with her fingers and cuts them into strips with a plastic knife, then arranges the strips into squares and attaches them to the walls of her house for windows. "I see you added windows to your house," observes Vanessa. "I need to paint it before the Munchkins move in," says Odile, "but it's too wet." "Where do you want to set it to dry?" asks Vanessa. Odile points to a counter area where other children have stored and labeled "work-in-progress." Vanessa helps her transfer the house to a square of particle board and Odile carries it to the drying shelf. "Maybe it will be dry tomorrow and I can paint it," says Odile. "My Munchkins want a red house but maybe also some green in it."

Art is one of the most important ways in which children express what they feel, see, experience, imagine, and know. "Children, like artists, play with their imagination, experimenting with materials and images" (Szekely, 1988, p. 3). That is why experiencing a preschool setting during art activities—the positive, happy atmosphere as children simultaneously create, play, and experiment—can be a revelation for adults. "Art is a goal-directed form of play. It is most difficult in practice to distinguish play from art in the activities of young children, and perhaps in those of many adults as well" (Gardner, 1982, p.166).

Art is also another type of language that children possess in the most natural way—a language expressed with their bodies, faces and hands, and actions and movements in space. "If the only means available to humans to help them understand their nature were [verbal] language, a major part of human reality would be forever closed off to comprehension" (Kiester, l985, p. 26). As children investigate their natural and human surroundings, they register the details with all their senses, collecting the material they will later use for artistic expression. For "children (like poets, writers, musicians, scientists) are fervent seekers and builders of images. Images can be used to make other images" (Malaguzzi, 1987, p. 23).

A Critique of Visual Arts Education

ALTHOUGH art is a natural language, leaving its development solely to the course of nature is not sufficient. What happens naturally in the course of artistic development is not equivalent to what can be achieved through high-quality visual arts education. Unfortunately, many organized attempts to provide young children with arts-based experiences do not meet the criteria for quality. Traditional education, though well-intentioned, often results in the drying up of children's creative abilities. Either too much emphasis is placed on free expression without adult support and guidance, or a series of repetitive adult-directed art activities is offered that is in no way authentic. "The majority of art practices in the school environment are inflexible and restricted to fixed periods of time, emphasize technique rather than vision, and constantly shift materials so children never get to know each medium and its special characteristics" (Trimis, 1996b, p.137). When art education is organized in this way, it "put[s] psychological and physical barriers in the exploratory curiosity of the child" (Szekely, l991, p. 5).

Art programs typically give children a haphazard variety of experiences with many materials. One activity follows another and often involves a different set of materials and tools each day. For example, successive days may involve blowing paints on flat papers with a straw, pasting found materials on paper, modeling with Plasticine, squeezing sparkling paints through plastic bottles, using markers on construction paper, and working at the easel with premixed paints. It is as though educators feel compelled to maintain children's involvement by providing a constantly changing assortment of materials. "Off-beat projects that will interest the students are used because it is through novelty and variety that the student's interest can be sustained" (Eisner, 1987, p. 61).

Beyond the overwhelming variety of media offered, this approach is problematic in other ways. First, the time allotted is usually predetermined and insufficient for exploration; children are pressured to finish and proceed to the next regimented activity. Second, the materials are often limited to those that are easy for adults to clean up or that result in "cute" or "pretty" products. In such a framework, children perceive art as a continuous parade of changing techniques and materials without coherence. "The danger is that students may begin to feel that art is nothing more than a series of little projects or a series of experimentations with materials, bearing little relationship to expression or creativity" (Lowenfeld & Brittain, 1987, p. 80).

Finally, children often are used as vehicles to produce works whose final forms have been predetermined by adults. "Children are deprived of making the acquaintance of the expressive or profoundly communicative functions of art. They are denied the time to investigate materials or to focus on feelings and subject matter of interest to them" (Trimis, 1996b, p.138).

In contrast to this superficial exposure to artistic media, practice and research show that "one powerful technique during the years of early schooling is for students to become involved in projects of size and scope" (Gardner, 1990, p. 40). Programs in Thessaloniki, Greece; Reggio Emilia, Italy; and High/Scope settings across the United States show that giving children sustained opportunities to explore visual arts media in depth results in remarkable skill development and satisfying personal experiences for children and adults alike. Practitioners of this in-depth studio approach believe the early childhood years are especially suitable for the discovery and control of skills inherent in each child. "At this early point in development, the provision of rich opportunities for exploration, invention, and transformation constitutes the optimal educational approach" (Gardner, 1990, p. 163).

Opportunities to investigate media in depth can result in art work of great complexity and detail.

The rest of this chapter provides an overview of the in-depth studio approach from the perspective of its philosophy and basic principles, aims, basic components, and conditions for application. The remaining chapters detail the use of the in-depth approach with specific media: painting and drawing (Chapter Six), natural and scrap found materials (Chapter Seven), paper (Chapter Eight), and plastic materials—clay and dough (Chapter Nine).

Philosophy and Principles of the
In-Depth Studio Approach

AS THE NUMBER of early childhood programs proliferates, evidence is accumulating that programs relying on a more integrated and dynamic notion of child development seem to be more successful (Epstein et al., 1996). Educational programs for young children should consider the needs and special characteristics of this age group. According to Vygotsky,

> Preschool education should offer the child neither school nor academic skills. It should offer a general idea of the world of nature and of society. Programming for preschool ages should range between the spontaneous, purely personal programming conceived by children themselves before their three years and the formal, primary school programming offered by the teacher. (Frangos, 1993, p. 48)

If given sufficient time and materials, children will produce projects of considerable size and scope.

Programs should function in what Vygotsky calls the *zone of proximal development*, that is, "the distance between the child's actual development and the level of his potential development, determined with the help of tasks solved by the child under the guidance of adults and in cooperation with his more intelligent partners" (Frangos, 1993, p. 42).

The in-depth studio approach was formulated to create a visual arts program with the "continuity and practice necessary for the development of significant forms of learning in art" (Eisner, 1987, p. 61). This approach is holistic in nature and adopts a qualitative developmental sequence of visual art activities. In more traditional ways of teaching the visual arts, reproduction and limited timing are dominant factors and emphasis is given to techniques and the final product. By contrast, the in-depth approach takes place in a more interactive environment. The major elements are play, active participation, cooperation, child initiative, and the exchange of roles. This framework emphasizes the intrinsic processes that lead to the production of a visual result.

The focus of the in-depth studio approach is first and foremost on play, not on art as an end in itself (see at right). The child, not art, is at the center. Learning takes place in real situations and is not limited to the classroom. Authentic learning about art extends to everyday life, including the neighborhood, workplaces, and museums. In general, programs that use an in-depth studio approach to art are active learning classrooms.

> Children [in these preschool settings,] are active agents who construct their own knowledge of the world as they transform their ideas and interactions into logical and intuitive sequences of thought and action, work with diverse materials to create personally meaningful experiences and outcomes, and talk about their experiences in their own words. (Hohmann & Weikart, 2002, p. 16)

Direct action on objects, reflection about actions, intrinsic motivation, invention, and problem-solving situations are important ingredients in such an approach. This developmental framework for understanding how children take an intentional and active role in their own learning forms the basis for an in-depth approach to arts education.

As a method of art instruction, the in-depth approach uses closely related experiences in similar media. Through the continuous exploration of one visual arts area or material, children's art experiences progress from the simple to the more complex. They discover things for themselves, inventing techniques through problem-solving situations. At the same time, adults provide special "scaffolding" to further the exploratory process. They may introduce one or two additional tools or ask questions to help children explore alternative solutions. Such adult initiation is particularly valuable when children appear to be stuck, that is, hesitating or giving up after constant repetition. Appropriate adult intervention at such points may encourage them to proceed with renewed interest and independence. When intrinsic motivation is supported

Play and Playfulness in Children's Art

Three-year-old Jenna pumps a dab of blue paint in one hand and yellow paint in the other. She rubs her hands together and then rubs them all over a piece of paper. Jenna explains to her teacher, who is sitting nearby, "This is a hand-washing painting." As she continues to rub her hands together and rub them on the paper, Jenna notices the blue, yellow, and now green handprints. She exclaims, "Hey! Hand-washing paintings make cool greens!"

Four-year-old Brianna uses crayons to draw a face with eyes, big eyebrows, a nose, and a wiggly line for a mouth. She takes the drawing to her teacher Becki and says, "This is you, only it's you with a silly mouth and monster eyebrows."

Five-year-old Barry rolls play dough between his hands to form a long cylinder. Then he coils the play dough in a circle and presses the edges together. He brings it to his teacher Beth and tells her it's "a yummy cinnamon roll." Barry laughs and rubs his belly as they pretend to eat it.

by adult scaffolding, children build cognitive and meta-cognitive abilities through their playful yet intentional interaction with visual arts materials (Trimis & Manavopoulos, 2001).

The multiple characteristics of the medium or its multiplicity of uses can give children the motivation to experiment further. When the program develops over an extended period of time, they have the opportunity to acquire better control of the material and more self-assurance in its use. They invent new techniques that lead them to extraordinary discoveries about the material and its potential. Almost paradoxically, the more time children spend in repeated exploration, the more spontaneous they become in the use of the medium. They also become more aware of its aesthetic possibilities.

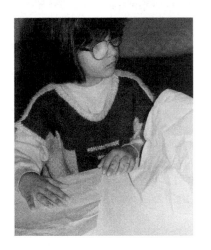

Children begin to explore paper with a simple challenge: How can we make it stand? After in-depth experiences, they create elaborate free-standing paper structures.

> Spontaneity is a product of both control and confidence. Such abilities and attitudes are more likely to develop in programs that provide for intensive work in a limited range of media than in those that shift quickly from medium to medium. It is when skill is absent that confidence diminishes and tightness and rigidity enter. (Eisner, 1972, p. 195)

The in-depth exploration lasts as long as the children's interest is sustained, from a few days to several weeks. If children lose interest, work with that material might be suspended and then reintroduced at a later point. Or a new, but related, exploration might lead children to redevelop their interest in a medium or technique they had explored earlier. "By working with a single theme for an extended period, and continuously delving deeper into that theme, the theme becomes charged with challenge, discovery and adventure. At the same time it is a means of avoiding stress, shallowness, and distraction" (Barsotti, Dahlberg,

Supporting Young Artists

Gothson, & Asen, 1993, p. 12). Exploration and experimentation with one medium allows children to focus their attention on the work being executed. Such an art program is composed of "a series of learning units, the components of which all contribute to the sense of wholeness" (Gaitskell & Hurwitz, 1975, p. 61). When art lessons proceed in this qualitative developmental sequence, children evidence a growth and satisfaction that is missing in more fragmentary approaches.

Basic Components of the In-Depth Studio Approach

The two basic components of the in-depth studio approach are thinking *in* art (doing or making art) and thinking *about* art (observing and studying art). These two components represent High/Scope's dual emphasis on making art and appreciating art. With young children, practitioners of the in-depth approach focus on the creation of art through active exploration of materials and tools. The emphasis is on process as much as, if not more than, on product. This thinking in art, however, is always accompanied by questions and experiences that encourage young children to think about the art they are creating and the art they observe around them.

Within these two components of making and observing (appreciating) art, the essential features of the in-depth studio approach can be characterized by the following statements.

▶ **Children are involved in exploration and problem solving.** Children's activities with media grow naturally out of their curiosity to explore. Questions and answers arise from their

As children explore various media, they solve technical and aesthetic problems. They often cooperate and solve social problems too.

interactions with teachers and peers and become problems for the children to solve through art. "The creative, the sensory and emotional, the imaginative and aesthetic are emphasized more than any technical excellence during the process of the program" (Trimis, 1996a, p. 111)

▶ *Children may work individually or in groups.* As in other High/Scope activities, children may choose to pursue in-depth art exploration on their own, in small groups, or in large groups. Over the course of a day or several days, these groupings may change. For example, once a material or technique has been introduced, children may initially explore its properties on their own. As they work side by side, they may discover they are solving similar problems and decide to collaborate on their investigations or create a role-playing fantasy together. Other children may join in. As the activity evolves over time, children may come and go or form new groupings.

▶ *Children are free to redefine the problem or activity.* Children follow their own interests and pace as they explore materials. A group can decide for itself whether it wants to solve a problem posed for the class as a whole or investigate its own set of questions. If a group of children is collaborating on an activity, they decide among themselves how to share the work.

▶ *Children are encouraged to make observations and express their own viewpoints.* Adults encourage children to describe the phenomena they see, express their opinions, and comment on the views of their peers and the teacher. It is expected that children will express themselves concerning their work or the work of others, and that they will learn to do it in a supportive way. Teachers introduce new vocabulary words during the discussions and children begin to use these art terms in their daily language.

▶ *The teacher's role is to encourage and support the children.* The teacher is seen as one source of information, along with children's direct experience and what they learn from peers. When a material or technique is first introduced, the teacher plays a more active role in demonstrating or modeling its basic properties. As children begin to explore on their own, however, the teacher takes cues from their interests and follows rather than leads. The teacher's visible role generally

decreases, although this will vary depending on each child's needs. Teachers observe what children do, offer commentary, pose occasional questions with genuine curiosity, and facilitate or suggest ideas when they sense children are becoming frustrated. Just the presence of the teacher, whose silent attention indicates interest, can encourage children. Adult interest, without adult control, frees them to become more adventurous in exploring and experimenting with the medium and its associated tools.

▶ *Study occurs in the classroom and the community.* Work occurs not only in the classroom but also through outreach to the broader community. The in-depth approach always begins with the students' own exploration of a material, technique, period of time, fantasy, and so on. After children have this firsthand experience, they are ready to venture beyond their four walls to see how similar art activities are carried out in the "real" world. Families are encouraged to bring in artwork from home, especially as it relates to a parent's activities or something in the family's history and culture. Teachers and parents accompany children on field trips to visit studios, museums, and galleries. They focus on artists and exhibits that feature topics directly connected to the children's classroom explorations. In these ways, the in-depth approach exploits the larger environment as a means of enriching children's involvement with the world of art.

Objectives of the In-Depth Studio Approach

THE IN-DEPTH STUDIO approach is designed to enhance children's knowledge, creative capacity, and representational ability. To achieve these overall goals, practitioners keep the following specific objectives in mind as they provide visual arts experiences for young children.

▶ *To learn about the medium in depth*—As implied by its name, the first objective of the in-depth approach is to allow children to develop detailed and firsthand knowledge of each visual arts medium. They develop this intimate relationship through ongoing experimentation that gradually reveals to them the medium's properties and its potential for representation. Only after acquiring this familiarity can children apply their experiences to creating and appreciating a body of artistic work.

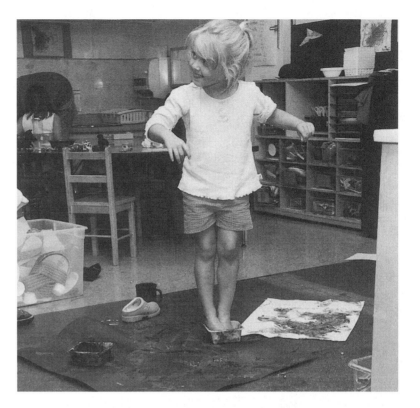

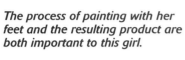

The process of painting with her feet and the resulting product are both important to this girl.

As they explore each medium in depth, children are constantly creating something with the materials and tools. Adults do not focus on a product per se, yet children inevitably see the physical result of their transformations. This is true even when maintaining a process orientation.

> Production must remain central in arts education. The heart of any arts educational process must be the capacity to handle, to use, to transform different artistic symbol systems—to think with and in the materials of an artistic medium. Such processes can occur only if artistic creation remains the cornerstone of all pedagogical efforts. (Gardner, 1988, p.164)

▶ ***To develop imagination and creative abilities***—For artists, play is an essential part of work. Artists play with their imaginations, exploring fantasies, dreams, and images. They try out new arrangements by using both familiar and unfamiliar materials. For children, too, play is intertwined with art, reflecting their world and their interests (Szekely, 1991). Playing and experimenting with art materials can lead children to unexpected and unusual visual experiences. When children have time to establish connections between their actions and the materials, they develop fluency and flexibility in their work. In an arts-enriched environment, children exhibit spontaneity and originality in their ideas. These characteristics are not nurtured in an environment where materials and methodology are changing constantly.

▶ *To involve all the senses*—The activities should afford children an opportunity to use their senses and their minds to accomplish a goal, resolve a problem, or find a solution (Eisner, 1987). The in-depth approach encourages children to perceive the world from all angles by exposing them to a wider visual and tactile environment. Children acquire new knowledge through perceptual and physical means and then apply these experiences to their creative pursuits. By enlisting all the senses in exploring art materials, the program "develops and enhances awareness of the special characteristics of the materials and [develops] visual and tactile perception" (Linderman & Herberholz, 1979, p. 11).

▶ *To connect to other areas of learning*—In addition to developing aesthetic capacities, the in-depth approach seeks to enhance children's motor, affective, perceptual, cognitive, and social growth. As children see and feel visual relationships, they connect art to other areas of learning. For example, exploring visual arts can enhance skills in such areas as language, reading and writing, number and mathematics, spatial relations, and physical and motor development.

▶ *To solve problems*—Art is a way of solving problems and representing the solutions visually. Children may discover or pose their own problems as they work with materials; adults may also challenge them with problems that grow out of the children's interests and experiments. That is why, as Eisner suggests, "we do not wait for children to learn simply by providing art materials they can manipulate but we provide supportive and encouraging instruction that guides learning" (1987, p. 15).

In the in-depth approach, art activities

Mixing dough, children develop their muscles and learn about measurement.

are problem centered in character. Adults pose problem-solving questions to introduce or extend activities. For example, adults may pose the following problems: How can we change the color of the paper? Why do you think this red is lighter than that one? What colors would you make the eyes to show this person is angry? What is the color of your breath? How can we make this paper stand? How does the color change where the sunlight falls? How does the color change where the flashlight beams? Tell me what you see when you look closely at the leaf (wood, petal, moving water, rock, tree trunk, fabric, paper, letters on the page, and so on). Who is going to find the biggest leaf (a baby leaf, a red leaf, a golden leaf, a leaf with many designs and colors, a new leaf, a dying leaf, and so on)? Let's watch the designs that the raindrops draw on our window! This problem-solving approach to exploring art materials helps young children "become flexible, confident persons through telling and saying their ideas in a visual language" (Linderman & Herberholz, 1979, p. 11).

How can we get these walls to stand? Maybe if I hold it and you push the edges together...

▶ *To develop a reflective disposition*—Reflection and recall help to enrich children's feelings and thoughts about art. Therefore, developing this reflective disposition is a very basic part of an in-depth visual arts program. "Reflection entails thinking about the process of making art and the final product. The ability to reflect about one's goals, decisions, and solutions, as well as about the influences of the works of others on one's own work, seems to be crucial to cultivate in the service of any artistic endeavor" (Rosenblatt & Winner, 1988, p.10). As discussed in earlier sections, one can think of art as having two components: thinking *in* art (doing) and thinking *about* art (studying). The in-depth studio approach encourages children to reflect during both of these activities. When children reflect during their explorations or recall these actions later, they attach words and concepts to their visual thinking. Similarly, when children examine the artwork of others, be it peers or artists, they reflect on the intentions of the individual art maker. Children then incorporate this awareness into their own intentional interactions with materials or their later observations of artworks.

▶ *To establish contact with existing art in the community and culture*—By focusing on the artwork in children's homes and communities, the program enriches the young child's sense of culture in a tangible way. Children visit galleries, museums, and artists' studios to experience works of art and the creative process firsthand. This outreach to the community is not done in a fragmentary or haphazard way. Rather, it grows organically out of the children's explorations with materials and their emerging interest in artistic products and techniques. "The wedding of the creative act with observation-reflection creates a sensitized creator-spectator who perceives and responds to the quality of forms. In the meantime [the viewer] acquires knowledge about the social-cultural parameters of the observed work" (Trimis, 2001).

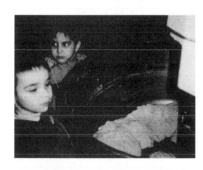

Children visit the local baker to see how dough is mixed in large batches.

▶ *To develop aesthetic judgment*—By reflecting on their own experiences and observing the work of others, children begin to develop and internalize aesthetic principles. The in-depth studio approach to art "guides a child's aesthetic judgment in relation to his environment, enriching his sense of this environment through related activities that take place in real situations" (Linderman & Herberholz, 1979, p. xvii). As described in Chapter Three, aesthetic judgment begins with the child's preferences for certain concrete properties of art (for example, color or subject matter). Through their own repeated explorations with materials and tools, young children also begin to develop a sensitivity toward techniques and artistic intention. In typical programs, with only superficial exposure to art materials, children never acquire this appreciation for the range and subtlety possible with any given medium. By contrast, the in-depth studio approach allows children to develop aesthetic principles and preferences through active and personal involvement with art and artists.

Factors to Consider When Implementing the In-Depth Studio Approach

TO IMPLEMENT the in-depth studio approach to art with young children, several factors must be taken into account. These include the *environment* (the size and organization of the art area in the classroom, related space and facilities inside the center or school, and access to art exhibits and events in the surrounding community), the *teacher's role* (modeling and demonstrating, observing, challenging, and supporting), *time* (extended time to explore, enrich, produce, and reflect), and *materials* (amount, variety, and properties). The necessary features and considerations related to each of these factors are discussed below.

ENVIRONMENT

The environmental considerations for the in-depth approach to art refer to the conditions in the classroom as well as interactions with art and nature in the surrounding community. "The classroom environment should be as playful as we can make it, as well as stimulating both visually and imaginatively" (Szekely, 1988, p. 25). Children should feel free to explore and not be afraid of making mistakes. "The mistake is not considered a factor of weakness or failure. [Mistakes are] a medium of learning and [indicate the child's] exploration of a number of alternative courses" (Frangos, 1993, p. 47). In the in-depth approach, teachers may deliberately create unusual situations to promote improvisation, discovery, and innovation.

The classroom conditions necessary to implement the in-depth studio approach are comparable to the features of the learning environment advocated in the High/Scope approach to art (see Chapter

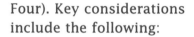

To begin their investigations, children dig, mix, and mold clay in the yard of their preschool.

Four). Key considerations include the following:

- Amount of space on the floor, tables, walls, and ceilings, as well as the capacity to extend art activities outdoors

- Organization of space to allow solitary and group activity and working from different positions (sitting, standing, and prone)

- Access to water, including indoor and outdoor sinks, basins, containers, and hoses

- Light and transparency, including the amount, focus, and changeability of natural and artificial light

- Variation in work surfaces, including orientation (horizontal tables, floors, and playgrounds; vertical easels, walls, and fences) and composition (including wood, metal, tile, cement or hardtop, sand, gravel, grass, and so on)

A general principle to keep in mind is that the classroom is the child's studio. "Creating the atmosphere of an artist's studio in the classroom means encouraging children to try different media for the primary purpose of discovering the one worth sticking with. It means using media selectively to help children achieve insights into important ideas and problems in their own work" (Barkan, 1966, pp. 429–430).

In looking at the community—the environment beyond the classroom—practitioners should pay attention to both the natural landscape and human works of art and architecture. Opportunities for implementing the in-depth approach beyond the classroom involve the following settings:

- Natural landscapes such as the play yard, parks, gardens, zoos, bodies of water, and forests

- Human works such as arts and crafts from home; artists and their studios; fairs, museums, and galleries; historic and contemporary monuments; sculptures and other art commissioned for public spaces; varied architectural styles in houses, public and private businesses, and places of worship; commercial art such as billboards and store displays

A trip to the museum and books from the library extend children's experiences with clay beyond the classroom.

TEACHER'S ROLE

Many terms can describe the role of the teacher—organizer, planner, supplier, collaborator, playmate, animator, inspirer, facilitator, assistant, co-discoverer, companion, and so on. To fulfill these roles, teachers should possess the qualities of flexibility, enthusiasm, and the joy of discovery. They should be open to learning from children—able to see the world as if for the first time, through the eyes of a child. Teachers should not be afraid to become playful explorers—to look surprised, to show excitement about the discovery process, to play and to pretend, to find expression through movement and dance, to put ideas into song. "What art teaching most requires is search, discovery, and invention" (Szekely, 1988, p. xiv). Children benefit when their teachers share their attitude of experimentation and curiosity. "Children, by nature, are curious. Adults must perhaps relearn" (Barsotti et al., 1993, p. 11).

Teachers should be aware, however, that young children's natural curiosity may have been stifled before they ever entered the program. Even at a young age, they may have encountered inhibitions against exploration in general and endured stereotypical art experiences that dampened their sense of creative adventure in particular. Therefore, another role of the teacher may be to free or release the young child to explore the world of art. In these instances, the teacher is responsible for reversing these earlier negative experiences by providing a safe and supportive environment in which children explore with increasing comfort and a growing sense of joy and confidence.

Taking these general roles into account, here are the specific things teachers do to implement the in-depth approach to the visual arts with young children:

- Arrange an environment conducive to exploring art.

- Provide materials and plan individual and group experiences; create vivid experiences.

- Demonstrate the basic properties of materials and model basic art techniques.

- Offer assistance when children seem frustrated or lost and need encouragement to continue.

- Explore materials alongside students; introduce materials (such as magnifying glasses and colored transparent paper) for exploration.

- Explore expressive as well as functional properties of everyday objects.

- Help children explore with all their senses; encourage them to explore objects from the perspective of temperature, texture, sound; recreate sensations and perceptions using the body and voice.

- Help children enhance their perceptual awareness; provide opportunities for visual discrimination through observing and comparing shape, color, line, size, pattern, texture, brightness, and so on.

- Sit silently alongside children as they work.

Teachers support children by working quietly alongside them, sharing their discoveries, and presenting interesting challenges.

- Discuss with children their intentions; comment on what they are doing; ask them their opinions and preferences; share one's own genuine observations.

- Pose open-ended questions sparingly.

- Set problems stemming from the children's interests and fantasies: What if I turned it upside down? What if we all had tails? How would it look if we were flying in the sky? How can you make it fit inside? How would you tear the paper when you are angry? What colors would you use to tell us you are sad?

- Use scaffolding to stretch the child's thinking to the next level; extend learning by introducing a new word or posing a problem.

- Develop children's awareness of different viewpoints; observe objects from different perspectives; listen to and respect different opinions.

- Help children recall their experiences; encourage them to talk about actions, feelings, and observations.

- Connect children to real objects and events in the art world.

- Encourage awareness of the natural environment, for example, the sky on a rainy day, the changing shapes of clouds, the sound of waves, the touch of the wind.

Supporting Young Artists

In sum, effective teachers encourage without interfering, giving children ample time to use the same materials and techniques repeatedly, but never overwhelming them with too many things at once. They know when to be silent so their chatter does not distract a child who is busy exploring. Well-trained teachers know when to pose questions that intrigue and challenge children. They make observations, but do not pronounce judgments. Good teachers know when to introduce something new and then turn it over to the child. They are careful not to show children too much or suggest specific ideas; they know children might copy an adult without searching and discovering on their own. "The best teacher is not the one who deals out all he knows or who withholds all he could give, but the one who, with the wisdom of a good gardener, watches, judges, and helps out when help is needed" (Arnheim, 1989, p. 58).

TIME

Perhaps the most important principle underlying the in-depth approach is the idea that children should be given sufficient time for exploration, creation, and reflection in the visual arts (see the "Structure and Sequence" section beginning on p. 134). In the in-depth approach, children's time with art materials is not limited; the length of the activity is determined by the child's interests. Children may continue with an activity for as long as they like (even the entire program day) and may come back to the same materials as often as they like. This principle is essentially compatible with the High/Scope approach in that children choose freely whether they will engage with art materials and for how long.

In the in-depth approach, however, the amount of time allocated to art activities may vary from day to day, depending on the children's level of involvement. In a High/Scope program, children follow a consistent daily routine that allows time for art in each component (see Chapter Four on including art throughout the daily routine). The length of these components is relatively stable from day to day. If they want to pursue something further when work time or small-group time comes to an end, they set aside their art to proceed to the next part of the day's routine. In both the High/Scope and in-depth approaches, however, children are free to return to those materials at a subsequent time and to do so for as many days as their interest holds. They are encouraged to make plans to extend their exploratory or creative activities. Adults make the necessary materials available and easily accessible on a constant basis, taking care to provide them with the time and continuity for in-depth investigation.

A girl carefully paints her clay house, and the figures who live there, long after the other children move on.

In addition to the principle of sufficient time is the recognition that different children need or want different amounts of time with a particular activity. Timing and sequence must follow the interests and rhythm of each child. Some children become immersed immediately; others sample materials briefly and move on to something else. Some children return daily to the art area; others show no interest for long periods of time and then unexpectedly become fascinated with a particular material or technique. For some children, art is a solitary activity that occupies them fully. For others, the social exchange draws them secondarily to

the materials. A given child may show any and all of these variations over the course of the program year. By making materials constantly available and leaving the time unpressured, children are free to engage in art in their own time and at their own pace.

MATERIALS

In implementing the in-depth studio approach, practitioners consider art materials from several perspectives, including what materials, how many, and how to use them. The issues related to each of these perspectives are explored below.

What materials to provide (types and sources)

The range of materials that can be used for art is unlimited. "Artists, seeing beauty or a message in almost any material, have given the impression that anything can be used for art expression" (Barkan,

Materials should be capable of transformation. Water added to clay makes good finger paint. A flat piece of newspaper can be folded into a bouncing strip.

1966, pp. 429–430). In the twentieth century, especially, the art world saw a vast expansion in the range of visual media that qualified as art, from natural materials to those made by humans to those manufactured by machines. We saw work in media that had been traditionally associated with the visual arts, such as pencils, crayons, clay, paints, paper, stone, marble, plaster, and metals. And we saw art made of contemporary media that originally served a different function, such as fabrics, threads, wood, found materials from nature, industrial scrap materials, broken and discarded items, and, of course, computer-designed and multi-media art.

Since young children in organized settings depend on adults to supply materials, teachers should select items that match children's developmental level and meet their expressive needs. As Arnheim (1974) suggests, materials "should be selected and employed in such a way that they challenge the student to work on tasks of visual organization at his own level of conception and make it possible for him to do so" (p. 205). At the early childhood level, teachers must take care to avoid art materials that are "cute" or "novel." Children need real materials from the natural or manufactured environment so they can acquire an awareness of the materials' aesthetic properties. Art materials should be complex enough to have color, weight, texture, plasticity, density, and so on.

In addition, art materials should be capable of transformation by the child. In other words, children should be able to change materials from one physical state into another, "a blob of paint into a line, a hunk of clay into a coil, a sheet of paper into strips" (Burton, 1980,

p. 7). Changing materials leads to an awareness that materials have properties that distinguish them from one another. For example, children learn that the plasticity of clay is different from that of dough, that the texture of wood is different from that of plastic. Transforming the physical properties of materials leads to changes in their visual appearance as well. Children's experiences manipulating materials "leads to the formation of visual concepts that are potentially extremely rich" (Burton, 1980, p. 7) and provides them with a repertoire of images they can draw on for creative representation and expression.

How many materials to provide (amount, continuity versus variety)

As emphasized throughout this book, overwhelming young children with too many materials at once or constantly changing the materials they have to work with poses several dangers. Children may become distracted and confused if asked to sample all the materials at once or sequentially in too short a time. "Constantly introducing or changing art materials may actually stand in the way of a child's mastering the material enough to express his own feelings, his own reactions to his sensory processes, and his own intellectual concepts of his environment" (Lowenfeld & Brittain, 1987, p. 178). Chandler (1973) draws an analogy to a young child who, overwhelmed by a plethora of new gifts, "retires to his bed with a well-worn stuffed animal. He is reminding us that it takes time to make something one's own" (p. 90).

Similarly, children bombarded with too many art materials in quick succession do not have time to get to know each material and make it their own. We all have seen children who are surrounded by toys but complain they have nothing to do. Likewise, children who are surrounded by an overabundance of art materials may turn off or turn away from their own creative devices. "The danger is not that they will come to prefer strong colors to subtle colors or driving rhythms to more complex musical structure, but rather that they will become unresponsive, unresourceful, bored, with nothing to do" (Chandler, 1973, p.187).

While some artists enjoy alternating between media, most immerse themselves in one medium to become an expert in its manipulation and expressive possibilities. Children, like artists, need time to explore each medium in depth and discover which ones they find most satisfying to use. As Lowenfeld & Brittain note, "no art expression is possible without self-identification with the experience expressed as well as with the art material by which it is expressed" (1987, p. 15). In addition to discovering an affinity for a particular medium, children obviously enjoy experimenting for its own sake. Just as children will practice a skill over and over to invent endless variations, so will they use the same material repeatedly to discover the many ways in which they can transform it. The material begins as an object of exploration and with repeated exposure eventually becomes a tool for expression. Children personalize the material and use it for their own purposes, gaining confidence that they can manipulate the material to achieve desired ends. "In short, materials are used by children in the way children themselves need and want to use them. The manner and style is unique to each child" (Cohen, Stern, & Balaban, 1983, p. 34).

The majority of art programs in preschool settings emphasize breadth over depth. This is as true today (for example, Katz, 1998) as it was decades ago (for example, Beittel & Mattil, 1966). Program staff typically use a wide variety of materials because they believe diversity is necessary to accommodate the different interests of the children. They overlook the fact that children can find something uniquely interesting by being allowed to explore a limited number of materials at their own pace and in their own manner. Deepening involvement permits children to choose those properties that appeal to them. In any art activity, selection, not accumulation, leads to quality in the aesthetic act. The in-depth approach helps children to see that less can be more.

How children use materials (individualizing the experience)

In addition to what materials and how many to provide, adults using the in-depth approach pay attention to *how* children use the materials. "Children approach materials as they approach life itself, with direct-ness or shyness, with attack or withdrawal, with fear and hesitancy or with courage and self-confidence" (Cohen et al., l983, p. 33). Some chil-dren become immediately engaged in art activities; others may be unsure about how to react to the sensory properties or fearful of creat-ing a mess. Teachers must be sensitive to these individual reactions, allowing children to use (or not use) the materials as they wish. With time and a lack of pressure, most children become curious about try-ing each medium. The teacher's role is to create opportunities for this direct contact whenever and as often as the child is ready. Nothing can substitute for this active and repeated engagement. "Practice in handling various materials is part of any young child's education. Observing the world is not enough. Handling materials and finding out what they do demand a different kind of thinking and the development of a variety of physical skills" (Barnes, 1987, pp. 12–13). Through the use of these materials, children will not only externalize impressions and feelings but "will develop muscles and skills, grow in powers of reasoning and logic" (Cohen et al., 1983, p. 33). In short, children will become artists.

The Structure and Sequence of an In-Depth Studio Program

When the above principles and conditions are applied, an in-depth studio program progresses through a *sequence of four stages* as children think in and about art: *introduction, enrichment, production,* and *reflection* (Trimis, 1996b, p. 142). In a sense, these stages are at the heart of the in-depth approach. They capture what the child experiences over time and the opportunities that adults consciously provide. The stages are flexible in duration and children continually cycle through them, building on what they learn in each stage as they move into the next stage. The boundaries between stages are not fixed; transitions are often seamless and movement back and forth between stages is fluid. When encountering unfamiliar materials, techniques, or ideas, children may return to an earlier stage and begin the discovery process anew. In this way, young children are like adult artists who begin with playful exploration, develop skills and knowledge, apply their abilities toward creation, and then evaluate the results with an eye toward their next undertaking. Each of these four stages is described below. Chapters Six through Nine illustrate what these stages look like when applied to working with various media in early childhood settings.

1) INTRODUCTION

Introduction is the stage in which children first encounter a material or artistic concept—a period of "getting acquainted" that is characterized by playing with materials, tools, and ideas. The length of this introductory stage depends on the children's familiarity with the medi-

During the introductory phase, children explore a medium's most basic properties, including its texture and even its smell.

um and its applications. It may be shortened or even eliminated if the material is very familiar, although children may still use this initial stage to discover new things about the medium. Exploration may be initiated with the introduction of the material itself, a visit to a workshop, or by some experience (such as a walk along the beach) that spurs the children's interests in the aesthetic properties or characteristics of certain materials or artistic concepts. The teacher may provide the materials and/or the children may collect them. For example, children may collect shells and bits of wood as they walk along the beach and bring them to the classroom for exploration. During this stage, the children's natural curiosity may be extended by the teacher posing open-ended questions ("How does the wood feel against your cheek?") or setting up games and problem-solving situations ("How can we use the shells to make music?") During open-ended introduction, children explore and discover the many properties of each material. Equally significant, they discover what it is about working with a particular material that is uniquely intriguing and satisfying to them.

2) ENRICHMENT

The enrichment stage refers to every experience that expands a child's curiosity, knowledge, skills, and aesthetic sense of a medium or artistic concept. The goal of enrichment is intimacy with a material and all its properties. This familiarity lays the groundwork for the next stage (production) in which artistic ideas emerge from the medium and/or the child grasps how to represent visual images using the medium. Enrichment is a continuous process. Although it logically follows the introduction and precedes production, enrichment in fact occurs at every stage of the encounter with artistic materials and ideas.

Enrichment happens through visual, auditory, kinesthetic, and sensory stimulation. A child's experience with a medium can be enhanced in many ways—through stories, poems, riddles, games, walks, music, sounds, dance, movement, role-playing, complementary materials, and extra tools. With concrete experiences and visual aids, teachers can help interested children learn about the physical origin of the material and its historical or cultural context. For example, visits to natural and human environments extend children's firsthand knowledge of materials and ideas—how they appear in nature and how they are used in art and architecture. Teachers also enrich the classroom environment by bringing in relevant books, pictures, posters, reproductions, and props. The direct experience with the material is further extended by relating it to other areas of the child's development, for

Related materials enrich the experience with a medium. Pictures of wheat and bread extend children's understanding of dough's many possibilities.

Supporting Young Artists

example, to language or number or temporal awareness. In these ways, children bring a wide range of knowledge and skills to bear on the use and appreciation of art materials.

3) PRODUCTION

Production is the making of art—the culmination of the child's introductory and enrichment experiences with the medium, the application of what has been learned. While production may occur at any previous point, this stage is most noteworthy for the child's intention to produce something concrete and visible. Children may produce individually or collaboratively. Ideas may originate within the child or be elicited through the child's interaction with peers or adults.

With repeated experience, production becomes an end in itself. Children build a house of paper to use in their role-play.

Ideas about what and how to produce art come from many sources. The idea may stem from the medium itself. For example, a color may elicit a feeling that reminds the child of an experience at home; the child uses that color and others to represent the event. Or the plasticity of the dough may inspire the child to create a piece that contains as many impressions with as many parts of the hand as possible. Alternatively, ideas may stem from experiences or aims outside the medium. Having internalized the properties of the medium, the child then turns to it to represent the idea or carry out a mission. For example, a child may feel sad because a playmate is ill, so the child uses dark color paint to represent his or her feelings. Or, pretending to be a dog, a child remembers having explored wrapping yarn around a piece of wire. The child then decides to make a dog's tail with these materials and use it to extend the role-play.

The desire to produce something is inherent. Most children will come to the production stage as a natural outgrowth of their artistic explorations or play intentions. Teachers also have a role in inspiring children to produce visual art. Adults can provide encouragement by bringing in examples of fine art, taking field trips to galleries and museums, and inviting artists and family members to the classroom to share their work. As long as teachers do not pressure children to produce artwork, or expect that students will make art for the purpose of pleasing parents or administrators, the products that emerge out of their in-depth experiences with art will be genuine and satisfying. They will also be pleasing to the adult, not because they are pretty or cute, but because they are evidence of the child's learning and enjoyment in the visual arts.

4) REFLECTION

To some extent, reflection takes place during each of the previous stages of the in-depth studio approach. Teachers continually help children think about what they are seeing, doing, and feeling, with regard to their own work and that of others. However, because reflection and recall involve "looking back," this component is necessarily seen as happening most deliberately in the final stage. The act of reflection entails perceiving, thinking about, sharing, and evaluating every step of the process. Reflection is the time when children make sense of what they have done, consolidate their learning, and prepare to advance to further levels of artistic expression and creative representation.

Reflection is essentially "a playing back in the mind's eye, a replay of major and minor decisions, away from the immediacy of the experience" (Susi, 1999, Introduction). During reflection, adults can encourage young children to think about their experiences and communicate about them with others with a verbal description, a visual representation, a physical reenactment, and so on. Children in High/Scope classrooms are familiar with this procedure, since they recall their work-time activities on a daily basis with their teachers and peers. In the in-depth studio approach, teachers use a variety of strategies to facilitate children's reflection about their visual arts experiences. These include:

• Asking children to recall how materials looked and felt, how they carried out various operations and practiced different techniques, and how they manipulated the materials to solve specific problems

Children enjoy looking at and talking about all the things they made with dough.

- Helping children recall or remember the steps they went through in producing their creations, how they combined materials or techniques, and how they discovered the most effective sequence for doing things

- Providing symbols and props that represent children's interactions with art, and encouraging children to reenact these experiences

- Encouraging children to look at the work of their peers and share their thoughts in supportive, nonjudgmental exchanges

- Encouraging children to examine the products and techniques of artists and compare it to their own work

Practitioners of the in-depth studio approach do not force reflection on children; reflection is spontaneous and natural in the context of sharing and discussion. As in all High/Scope activities, in the in-depth approach, children choose if and how they want to participate. Some may not be interested (especially at first); some may appear disinterested but may silently observe and listen; some may actively listen but may not talk; some may talk when it is their turn but not listen to others; some may pay attention only when their friends are talking; some may be eager to show their art and talk about the process; and some may enjoy commenting on the work of others or relating the art to other personal experiences. Adults should accept what children say and let them participate at the level where they feel comfortable. Just as adults do not judge when children explore materials or produce art, neither should they judge when children share their thoughts about their own art or the art of others. In this way, adults create a safe environment in which children can reflect on art and know that their opinions and ideas are accepted and respected.

Finally, adults should be aware that the ability to reflect develops along with other mental skills. It will take time, experience, and growth before children can participate fully in the recall process. Nevertheless, younger children will still benefit from being included in the process and will understand that art involves thinking as well as doing. Older children will be able to recall experiences that extend farther back in time and have more detailed recollections. As described in Chapter Three, the more children can retain and work with a mental image, the more they can use art materials for visual representation. Similarly, the more they can retain their art adventures with complex mental representations, the more they will be able to recall and reflect on their experiences in depth.

———

Children as artists need materials to make their ideas and experiences visual. This is the essence of creative representation in visual art.

> Just as words are important in verbal communication, and the structure of sentences and paragraphs are important in written work, in art the artist must develop skills and techniques necessary to communicate. He must have an understanding of the materials to utilize their intrinsic qualities. Important as skills and techniques may be, however, they must always remain the means to an end and never become ends in themselves. It is not the skills that are expressed, but the feelings and emotions of the artist. To concentrate only upon the materials that are used in art, or upon developing particular skills to utilize in an art expression, ignores the fundamental issue, which is that art springs from human beings and not from materials. (Lowenfeld & Brittain, 1987, p.113)

The in-depth approach recognizes that introduction, enrichment, production, and reflection are means to a greater end, namely, giving children art as one avenue for personal growth and expression.

The remaining chapters of this book describe how extensive experiences with a limited number of media can open a world of creativity for young children. Through art they discover the physical properties of the world. They learn about the qualities that make them unique, and they pursue interests and express thoughts and feelings that turn art into communication.

6

Drawing and Painting

Two-year-old Andrew sits at the table before a long piece of paper. He takes a crayon in each hand and scribbles two sets of vertical lines up and down the page. His whole body moves as he pushes the crayons up and down with equal pressure.

Robin, aged four, tears off a medium-sized piece of paper from the roll and clips it to the easel. She goes to the large paint containers and uses the plungers to serve herself one helping each of red, blue, and white paint. Then she gets three brushes and carries them to the easel, putting one brush in each container. Robin fills the entire paper with red. Then she uses the blue and white paint to make a story picture. Her teacher Sue comes over to see what she is painting.

Sue: Can you tell me about your painting?

Robin: These are the clouds. *(Robin points to a blue stripe near the top with three white dots, all the same size.)* And that's the mommy, the daddy, and the baby fish. *(She points to a blue stripe near the bottom, also with three white dots—one large, one medium, and one small.)*

Sue: What's this blue part right here? *(Sue points to the blue stripe at the bottom.)*

Robin: That's the water. *(She points to the top stripe.)* And that's the sky. *(Pointing to a large white square in the middle with blue and red dots.)* And those are the two frogs.

Sue: The two frogs. What are the two frogs doing?

Robin: They're sitting in the hole.

Sue: I see. You've got some red and some blue and some white in that frog part and some more white down here. *(Sue points to the fish.)*

Robin: The baby fish is attached to the mommy fish because she's swimming behind her. And the daddy fish is in front. I want to put this on the drying rack so I can take it home.

Robin asks Sue to hold one side of the very wet paper, and together they carry it to the rack.

Chapter Six applies the in-depth studio approach to the media of drawing and painting. Beginning with a short summary of how drawing and painting have developed as art media from ancient to modern times, the chapter continues with a review of the dimensions adults need to consider in choosing drawing and painting materials and recaps the broad developmental issues that emerge as children's interests and abilities unfold with these particular media. The majority of the chapter presents two case studies that illustrate how the in-depth approach with drawing and painting was carried out in two early childhood programs.

Drawings by children at different stages of development in the same class, from scribbles to simple patterns to detailed presentations.

A Brief History of Drawing and Painting as Art Media

Drawing and painting date back to prehistoric times when humans drew on sand, mud, rocks, wood, plaster, stone, ceramics, glass, fiber, vellum, and other surfaces. These prehistoric humans used their hands or fashioned tools, and like artists of today, they represented critical events in their daily lives. The oldest paintings, found in the caves of Lascaux in France and Altamira in Spain, depict scenes of animals and hunting. The search for food was the central preoccupation in prehistoric times. Historians speculate that people thought these paintings would bring them luck in the hunt.

Many of the paints used today have been known for thousands of years. Watercolors and oil paints, for example, have changed little since the days of the old masters. Only in the last century have new materials and processes noticeably expanded artists' choices of drawing and painting materials.

Since prehistoric times, painting and drawing materials have been made of pigments derived from minerals, rock, earth, chalk, plants (fruits and vegetables), insects, shells, and bones. For example, red, yellow, and brown pigments come from clay, while chalk produces a white pigment and black comes from soot or charcoal. The red-scaled bodies of tiny cochineal insects (found in the southwest United States and Central America) also produce red. Blue comes from the leaves of the indigo plant; ultramarine comes from a blue stone mined in Afghanistan. In early

The watercolor paints children use today are virtually the same as those used hundreds of years ago.

times, dyes from these natural sources were ground into powder and then mixed with water. Beginning in the fifteenth century, oil was used. The pigment was bound (made to adhere or stick) to the drawing and painting surface with various substances such as beeswax, egg, honey, animal fat, urine, or resins from trees.

People have painted on paper for over 2,000 years in the East but for only 500 years in the West.

In the nineteenth century, chemicals were increasingly used as the source of color. Instead of artists mixing their own pigments in the studio, commercial firms began manufacturing tubes of paint. The new artificial paints were more brilliant and came in a wider range of colors. Various fixatives also made the dyes more stable, that is, less subject to fading with time and exposure to light. More rapid changes were initiated in the 1940s and 1950s with the discovery of acrylic paints. Based on a synthetic resin, but capable of being thinned with water, acrylics thus had the advantages of both water- and oil-based paints.

The surface to which pigment is supplied is called the support. The support affects the visual appearance of the finished work of art, because along with the painting materials used, it determines how the pigment is applied and the impression it creates. Artists have always paid particular attention to the color, texture, and absorbency of the support, taking great pains to prepare it properly to receive the pigment. Water-based paints (including tempera and aquarelles) have been used since early times on various supports. In ancient Western civilizations, watercolors were applied to stone (cave walls), animal skins, bark, wood, ceramics, papyrus, and parchment. In the Far East, water-based paints were applied to other supports, including silk and vellum. Tempera, a water-based technique, was usually executed on wooden supports, with egg used to bind the pigments to the surface. In the ancient art of frescoes, pigments were mixed with water and painted on a plaster surface whose top layer was a mixture of lime with sand or marble powder. As the lime dried and the water evaporated, a hard crystal surface was formed that bound the color to the wall. Paper was discovered in China as early as 2,000 years ago, but was not used in

Europe until the sixteenth century. Since then, paper has been used extensively as a watercolor support, for example, in paintings, books and illuminated manuscripts, and maps.

Characteristics of Drawing and Painting Materials

PAINTS

When choosing and buying paints, practitioners should be aware that different brands vary in quality. Teachers should become familiar with a brand's colors and consistency before purchasing paints. Those chosen for young children should be inexpensive, but of good quality, and of course nontoxic. Begin with true primary colors (red, blue, and yellow) and black and white. Providing children with a wide range of premixed colors is not necessary; they can create and discover other colors through their own mixing.

Paints essentially come in three types—water-based, oil-based, and acrylic:

- Water-based paints are made of powdered colors bound with gum arabic. They transport easily, dry quickly, and allow for speed of application. Water-based paints are most often applied to paper.

- Oil-based paints have the greatest variety of colors. The pigments are in the form of powder mixed with oil, usually linseed or walnut. The oil absorbs oxygen from the atmosphere and forms a transpar-

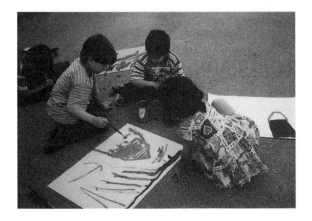 

Children can paint with many materials, from watercolors and tempera to glue and sand.

Supporting Young Artists

ent membrane that keeps the color inside. Oil paints are easily manipulated. They dry slowly so artists can alter the image, unlike frescoes or watercolors, which dry quickly. Oil-based paints can be applied in layers so the finished look ranges from transparent to opaque. They can be applied in thin coats or put on thickly to create texture (impasto). Oil-based paints are typically used on canvas, wood, or thick cardboard.

- Acrylic paints are also water soluble, but they dry to an insoluble plastic film. Like watercolors, acrylics can be applied in transparent washes or in thick opaque sheets.

For more information on types of paints, see Wright (1995).

DRAWING MATERIALS

Anything that makes a mark can be considered a drawing material— pebbles, yarn and threads, sponges, cotton swabs, bamboo, toothpicks, straws, wire, twigs, and so on, along with conventional crayons or pencils. Drawing materials, or media, are generally divided into dry and wet. Dry drawing media can be used without a brush or pen and include charcoal, graphite or lead pencils, colored pencils, chalks, pastels, and crayons. Wet drawing media require diluting before use or are suspended in a liquid medium and include felt-tipped pens, inks, and water-soluble pencils. Young children typically work with four types of drawing materials: crayons, pencils, marking pens, and pastels.

- Crayons are pigments held together by wax. They can produce images that vary in intensity from a light dusting to a "velvety" coating. Crayons are easily manipulated and can be applied to a variety of supports, including paper, wood, metal, and fabric.

- Pencils are made of graphite or lead. The lead may be plain (black or gray) or in a wide range of colors. The colors made by pencils are not very intense, although with pressure and repeated application the intensity can be increased. Pencils are easily manipulated and allow children a great deal of control over the detail of their drawings. Like crayons, pencils can be applied on a wide variety of supports.

- Marking pens are felt-tipped writing instruments that contain ink in different colors. The ink in marking pens used by young children is

Children can draw with many materials, including crayons, pastels, chalk, and markers.

water-based and must be nontoxic. The felt tips come in different thicknesses. The thinner the tip, the easier it is to add fine detail to a drawing. Like pencils, marking pens are easily handled by young children and applicable on many types of surfaces. The colors are often bright and cover a wide spectrum, making the marking pens attractive and versatile.

• Pastels are made of powdered colors with a chalk or clay base and bound with gum arabic. They may be hard or soft, depending on the binding material. Pastels are generally applied dry, but may be diluted with various liquids, including water. Pastels are manufactured in the form of sticks. Thicker pastels are easier for children to handle and less likely to break when small hands apply pressure to them. The most common support for pastels is paper, but chalks can be used on a variety of indoor and outdoor surfaces.

For more information on drawing materials, see Wright (1995).

Supporting Young Artists

PAPER

Paper is an economical support that can accept most media when prepared the right way. Today one can find an amazing array of papers in art shops and paper supply stores. Paper comes in a variety of sizes, colors, textures, and weights. It may be handmade or manufactured and may contain a variety of natural and human-made fibers. Paper made from 100 percent cotton rag does not turn brittle or yellow with age, while paper made from wood pulp (such as today's newspapers) is less durable and more sensitive to light deterioration. Paper is versatile. It serves as a support for drawing and painting and can also be a medium on its own (see Chapter Eight). Common types of paper include the following:

- All-purpose bond papers are suitable for most types of drawing and sketching. They range from lightweight to heavyweight and vary in the amount of acid they contain. The more acid-free the paper, the less it will yellow with age.

- Japanese rice paper and tissue paper are thin, lightweight papers suitable for drawing and watercolor painting. These supports tend to soak up the ink or paint, creating hazy, soft-edged shapes. Rice paper and tissue paper come in various shades of color.

- Indian papers are more robust, with a surface similar to rough watercolor paper. They are inexpensive and come in a range of tints as well as white and cream. Indian papers make an excellent support for soft drawing media.

For more information on types of paper, see Gair (1995).

BRUSHES

Purchasing brushes of good quality is worthwhile because brushes determine how well children are able to manipulate paints. Although better-quality brushes cost more at the outset, they will last longer. Many reasonably priced good-quality brushes are available for schools to purchase. Properly cleaned and stored, they will give many years of service. Affordable brushes are made of squirrel hair, ox hair, goat hair, and synthetic fibers. Sable brushes, made from the tail of the sable marten (a relative of the mink), are best for watercolors, but they are very expensive. If an early childhood program can afford to, purchasing a limited number of very high-quality brushes for children to experience would be worth the cost.

In addition to being made of different types of fiber, brushes also come in different sizes and shapes. They can be large or small, round or flat. Programs should purchase a variety of styles so children can experiment with their effects.

For more information on brushes, see Wright (1995).

Young Children and Drawing and Painting

From the earliest ages, children enjoy making marks with food spilled on the table, with sticks in the mud, with their fingers on a moist windowpane, and so on. Scribbling is so spontaneous that most two-year-olds need no encouragement from adults. For these young children, drawing is initially about energy and movement, the "dance" of the

hand and arm over the surface. "All of [the child's] body operates and the child savors the pleasure of his movement, the vivid marks that develop and live their own life, the dynamism of the lines" (Meredieu, 1981, p. 19). In some ways, this focus on movement is reminiscent of the experimentation and delight found in 1950s action painting. While exact parallels between children's explorations and the deliberate

Children need plenty of room when they paint, whether it is on the floor, or at the easel, or at the table.

Supporting Young Artists

effects created by adults are not appropriate, loose analogies help us appreciate the aesthetic qualities of the child's efforts. "With respect to certain criteria, one might contend that the works of young children are as artistic, as imaginative, or as flavorful as those of considerably older individuals...and perhaps more akin to the works of adult masters" (Gardner, 1990, p. 33).

As summarized in detail in Chapter Three, very young children begin by drawing and painting lines, dots, and simple geometric forms. By the age of three or four, they begin to draw representations of familiar objects, such as people, animals, and plants, "which are not slavish copies of the objects. Rather children at this time seek to create an equivalent in graphic form of their overall conception of the object" (Arnheim, 1974, p. 165). By the age of five or six, these objects are often given a familiar context, set against the line of the sky or the edge of a table. These early representations serve an important expressive function. Children use these images to talk to themselves (to think) and to others (to communicate).

> As the child learns to talk he also develops his visual imagery. We can get a glimpse of his view of the world if we look as well as listen. Liveliness of fantasy, dynamic spontaneity, intensity of emotional response, enthusiastic pleasure in making and doing—these are characteristics of the art as well as the speech of children up to the age of seven or so. (Lindstrom, 1974, p. 2)

Put another way, drawing and painting are parts of another language, a symbol system with its own vocabulary and syntax. Like any other language, the language of art can be further developed through interactions with different speakers in various contexts. Just as children enjoy making sounds before investing those sounds with meaning, they also enjoy making marks before attributing those marks with meaning. Adults can help children move from making marks (scribbling) to drawing and painting in the same way they encourage babies to move from babbling to speaking recognizable words to talking in sentences. "Painting and drawing should be extensions of the child's initial messing with materials, the child's original pleasure in making free scribblings, experimental lines, and in experiencing materials" (Szekely, 1988, p. 49). Children play with their voices and learn to speak; children play with art materials and learn to draw and paint.

With drawing and painting, as with verbal language, adults can best facilitate development by first attending to what children are doing and saying. Adults are accustomed to listening to a child's verbal

Children's painting progresses from blobs to simple lines and forms to representations of familiar objects.

language and adjusting their responses accordingly, but for some reason they find it harder to apply this practice to the visual arts. With art, adults are more likely to impose their interpretations immediately. For example, when looking at the artwork created by young children, adults tend to focus on the theme, by asking what the drawing or painting is about. However, for the child the form (or pattern or another aspect of the image) may be what is meaningful in and of itself. "Simple forms like the circle, the square, and the triangle are elements which, when combined, create different images of children's art vocabulary. This language

At work time, a teacher talks to a girl about her painting as other children look on with interest.

is a closed and self-contained system" (Meredieu, 1981, pp. 32–33). For young children, organizing form is an important cognitive and aesthetic development. Adults need to respect this expression of pure form instead of trying to fit children's visual language into adult-made categories of theme and content.

For young children, drawing and painting are other ways to approach the environment, to represent what is familiar and meaningful to them and to help them make sense out of what is new and strange. By creating environments that stimulate children's senses and enrich their perceptual intake, adults can support their natural motivation and stir their interests in using the visual arts to approach the known in new ways. By providing young children with in-depth

Children represent meaningful experiences such as a sleepover at a friend's house or a big snowfall.

experiences in drawing and painting, teachers can help them develop the vocabulary and syntax of this representational language.

The In-Depth Studio Approach With Drawing and Painting

The remainder of this chapter describes how the in-depth studio approach with drawing and painting was sequentially implemented in two different early childhood settings. Although each of the four stages (introduction, enrichment, production, and reflection) is described, the reader should keep in mind that these stages often overlap and cycle back on one another. Both programs began with an in-depth exploration of points and lines and led eventually to children's investigations of shapes and designs. One program focused initially on three-dimensional space; the other program focused on color and line in two-dimensional space. Both programs made use of movement and music and both incorporated a variety of natural and human-made materials. Children extended their personal investigations with visits to artists' studios, local shops, and nearby museums. For additional examples of the in-depth studio approach with this medium, see the videotape *Supporting Young Artists: Exploring and Creating With Drawing and Painting* (Trimis, 1996b).

In High/Scope programs, these kinds of explorations might begin at small- or large-group time. Depending on the level of children's interests, the explorations might continue at group times on subsequent days or weeks. Additionally, children may plan to continue and expand their investigations of the materials and the effects they produce at work time or outdoor time, where the natural environment offers unique opportunities to explore. Throughout the in-depth approach, as in High/Scope programs, children are encouraged to reflect on their activities and share their thoughts and observations with others.

PROGRAM A: THREE-DIMENSIONAL SPACE

1) Introduction

The children in Program A already had some experience drawing with markers and wax crayons, as well as painting with watercolors at the easel. To introduce a new exploratory experience, the teacher mounted a large sheet of white wrapping paper on the wall and asked the children if they wanted to play a game with finger paints. Since the children were curious and eager to try the game, she divided them into two groups and explained how it was played. A child from group one would point a finger in the air toward the hanging piece of paper. After estimating the intended spot's location on the paper, a child from group two would dip a finger in the finger paint and use the paint to mark that spot on the paper. Then, as the first child moved his or her hand around in the air, the second child would try to create the same pattern of lines on the paper, leaving a track of the movement with the finger paint.

The children enjoyed the game and remained involved for a long time, with the teacher facilitating turn-taking for those making the movements and those marking them with the paint. When the teacher asked the children if they could think of other materials they could use to make the marks, they chose pencils, crayons, and marking pens, further exploring these familiar materials in the context of

Children make dots and lines to represent movement through space.

the new game. The surface of the paper was eventually filled with a mosaic comprised of dots of different widths and lines of different lengths and directions. The markings were made in different colors and with different painting and drawing materials. Children "read" the results, describing what they saw and how they made the marks.

2) Enrichment

A series of enrichment experiences helped the children in Program A to further explore how points and lines connected to make shapes and forms. By using different materials and supports (surfaces), the children also became increasingly aware of the textures and patterns they created.

To begin, the children played a game similar to the previous game, but the new game extended the idea of connecting marks drawn on paper. First, they directed the beams of light from flashlights onto a large sheet of dark paper set in a darkened corner of the room. They used colored chalks and pastels to mark the points of light on the paper and drew lines connecting the points. Next, while some children moved the flashlight beams along the paper, others followed the movement of the lines with the drawing materials. At the end of the game, the children observed the designs they had created with the colored chalks and pastels. They compared the designs on the two sheets of paper, one made by connecting the dots and the other by following the lines made with light beams. Some children said the designs reminded them of different things: a spider, a map, a trap, or a fishnet. Others described what they saw literally as a colorful design made with many colored dots and lines.

In the next day's enrichment experience, the teacher spread sheets of paper on the floor and the walls. The children were divided into small groups, each group with its own sheet of paper. Each child chose a felt-tipped pen. Then the teacher asked the children to pretend their hands were flies. As she played a tambourine, the children "flew" their pens over the surface of the paper. When the sound of the tambourine stopped, the "flies" held their positions on the paper and left large points. This game combined movement and music and art, and the children found it to be a great deal of fun. They moved their flies eagerly across the page, creating scribbles, spirals, diagonals, zigzags, connected strokes, disconnected jumps, and many other kinds of lines. When the flies stopped moving, the dots made by the pens varied in size, intensity of color, evenness of edges, and so on. After they finished the game, children examined their papers closely and talked about what they saw. They described and labeled the different types of lines; the teacher enriched their vocabularies by naming some of the less familiar lines such as spirals or zigzags.

On the following day, the teacher spread more paper on the tables, floor, and wall. By now, the concepts of point and line had become concrete to the children and they knew what these words meant. The teacher asked them to imagine they were each a kind of line that was traveling from one point to another. They could pretend they were a quiet line or one that was bold, scared, hot, giant, and so on. The lines were to be invisible until they reached the paper. As they passed over the paper, they would become visible and leave their own special kind of mark. The line could change direction, fly away and return to the paper, or disappear completely off the edge of the paper. The children could choose to work individually or in small groups and could choose any kind of drawing or painting material to record their lines. After choosing a marking material, the children pretended to be different kinds of lines appearing and disappearing as they moved over the paper. They made marks on the paper, recording the direction and the feeling of their movements. As before, they looked at the results and described what they saw and how they felt as they made their movement and left various marks on the paper.

When the children arrived at Program A the next day, they discovered the teacher had left strips of crepe paper in the places where the paper had been the day before—on the tables, floor, and walls. Surprised, they asked the teacher why the strips were there. The teacher explained that some of the "lines" that had flown off in space the previous day had returned and fallen in these different places. The teacher asked the children what they thought they could do with all those lines. The children decided to untangle and stretch the strips of paper in all the directions in which they had moved and drawn lines on the previous day. As they filled up the classroom with colored lines, moving from walls to windows, from tables to floors, from doors to chairs, the children created a colorful mesh of lines. Some of them decided to move in the spaces between the lines; others joined this game. Examining the meshwork of crepe paper, the children became increasingly aware that the lines created shapes. They also noted that the areas inside and between the shapes were holes. These enrichment experiences had thus far led them from points and lines to shapes and holes. Those simple terms would later serve as the basis for understanding more sophisticated concepts in art, including line and form, figure and ground, positive and negative space, and so on.

With these ideas solidly established, the teacher added new studio experiences with drawing and painting. The teacher began by incorporating different kinds of music—fast, slow, soft, loud—and asking the children to draw lines and shapes that sounded like what they heard. The children moved their arms and hands to the music, letting their drawing tools create varied marks. In a different enrichment experience, children traced one another on large sheets of paper. They identified key body parts, such as facial features or fingers, as the points on the paper. Then they used different materials to connect these points and fill in the spaces with different designs, patterns, and textures. To further extend their use of materials, some children strung beads on string, dipped them in paint, and moved them in different ways on the paper (dabbing or bouncing the bead, pulling the bead by the string, and so on) to make different marks.

As a further form of enrichment, the teacher and children in Program A walked to a nearby wooded area. On their walk, they looked at the lines created by telephone poles and power lines. In the woods, the children observed how the points and lines on trees and bushes created various shapes and textures. As they walked along the muddy road, they noticed the lines left by the tire treads from trucks and automobiles. Children picked up twigs and sticks to draw their own points and lines and shapes in the soft, moist earth. They filled their shapes with pebbles and gravel to create designs and texture and collected many of these natural materials to bring back to the classroom. At school the next day, the teacher played music that was reminiscent of the sounds of the woods. The children listened to the music, chose drawing and painting materials, and recorded their impressions on the paper.

Children use crayon and paint to capture the textures and patterns in nature.

Enrichment experiences also included connecting children with the work of artists and art in the real world. The teacher brought in reproductions of paintings by the artist Miro. The children looked at the shapes this artist created and the lines between the shapes and talked about how these figures filled some of the areas and left holes or blank spaces in other areas. The teacher also put up two posters showing the paintings of Kandinsky. The children talked about the lines and shapes and textures he created with paint. When the teacher explained that Kandinsky sometimes liked to paint to music, the children looked at the paintings and said what kind of music they thought Kandinsky was listening to when he painted his pictures.

3) Production

To a certain extent, the children in Program A had already been producing art during the enrichment phase, for example, by drawing lines and creating textures in the mud. However, after repeated investigations with the media, they were now ready to apply their cumulative knowledge of drawing and painting materials to express their own ideas about line, shape, and space.

Supporting Young Artists

A boy describes to his teacher the skinny grass, round pebbles, and long worms in his painting.

After the children returned from their trip to the woods, they sorted the natural materials they had collected. Some children were very interested in making designs with the pebbles, stones, twigs, leaves, and so on. They worked individually and in groups, creating designs on the tables and floor. Many children used glue, tape, staples, and other fasteners to attach their designs to paper.

The teacher told them that some artists used materials like stones and pebbles to create a form of art called *mosaic.* The teacher explained that mosaics were created by putting colored stones, called tiles or tesserae, into a thin layer of plaster and then letting the plaster harden. She showed them pictures of mosaics from different times and cultures, some with representational images and others with abstract designs. Several children were interested in making their own mosaics. The teacher and children mixed up the plaster and poured it into shallow trays or empty plastic food containers. Children worked alone or in small groups to create their own mosaics. They learned that they had to complete their mosaics before the plaster dried; if they waited until the next day, it was too hard to embed new tiles. The children went to visit ancient archeological sites with remnants of floor mosaics, a Byzantine church, and a nearby museum with real mosaics made of pebbles and tesserae. They talked about the colors and designs they saw. After returning to the classroom, some of the children continued to make mosaics over many days. They collected more stones around the school and painted them to use as tiles. They experimented using other materials as tiles, such as beads or small plastic parts from broken toys.

Finally, the enrichment experience combining music and visual art resulted in a different type of production. As the teacher played musical selections that evoked the sounds and rhythms of their visit to the woods, the children touched and smelled the earth, sand, leaves, wood, and other materials they had collected there. Re-experiencing the sounds and smells, the children chose drawing and painting materials to record their sensory impressions. This activity was too abstract for some children, and they merely enjoyed listening to the music and/or using the materials. The visual productions of other children, however, clearly captured the moods and textures of their field trip to the woods. They represented the sensory aspects of their experience by choosing dark and cool colors, applying materials gently in the fashion of rustling leaves, heaping the paint on thickly like mud, or mixing sand with the paint to re-create the rough feel of the bark.

4) Reflection

Rather than being a final stage, reflection actually happens throughout the in-depth studio approach. Teachers not only encourage children to think about their experiences as they are happening but also build in time for sharing and recall throughout the day. Displaying the children's work also becomes an important tool in stimulating observations and discussions. In addition to these ongoing opportunities for recollection, however, helping children think back over a longer period of time has further value. Their observations can reflect the cumulative knowledge built on multiple experiences with the same set of materials.

In helping children investigate the properties of drawing and painting materials, the teachers in this program made use of both immediate recall experiences and longer-term reflection. During and after various experiences making dots and connecting them with lines, the children in Program A talked about their actions with materials and tools and their resulting visual effects. Teachers encouraged children to remember all the steps and the choices they made about how to move, what drawing materials to use, what type of paper would serve as a support, and so on. Teachers reminded children that some of the time they were making *bounded lines,* defined as the connection between points; other times they made *improvised lines* that expressed feelings or music. In their spontaneous comments, some of the children remembered many details while others could recall only a few.

Some children participated in the discussion, others listened, and still others appeared to lose interest. The teacher accepted children at the level where they chose to become involved, even if the level was uninvolvement. When children invented names for lines and shapes, the teacher acknowledged and repeated their words. If children seemed receptive,

Teachers encourage children to describe materials and motions as they explore drawing and painting.

the teacher enlarged their vocabularies by supplying additional labels for their movements and the marks they made.

The trip to the wooded area also offered many opportunities for recollection. Back at school, the children tried to remember the route they followed, what they saw along the way, and the paths through the forest. They represented this part of the experience by drawing and painting maps and illustrating them with various landmarks. Of course, they also recalled the visual design elements they saw in nature. The children re-created these by making designs on paper, impressions in plaster, and collages that combined several types of materials. They displayed their finished products, and the entire class used these visual cues as a spur to remember the trip and all the things they saw.

Similarly, after painting to music, the children exhibited their work in different ways. They hung it on the wall, spread it on the floor, and draped it on the tables. They talked about the different qualities of the lines, some long and flowing and others short and stubby. There were connections between points and there were breaks. The children saw patterns and regularities, places where someone repeated an idea. Or they saw how no two parts of a paper looked the same. In addition to reflecting on these visual elements, the children recalled the music and the pleasure of moving their bodies and hands to the different sounds. Some could recall the feelings that accompanied the music and remembered personal experiences that evoked similar feelings.

The recurring steps in this in-depth approach allowed the children to manipulate materials, learn their properties firsthand, and use them to investigate movement and express feeling. At the end of their explorations, the children had acquired a relatively sophisticated notion of line as movement. "The difference between seeing a line as a static, accomplished fact and seeing it as the movement of a point is the difference between seeing product and seeing process" (Chandler, 1973, p. 103). Without adequate time to play with points and lines, or to incorporate music and other art media into their explorations, children might not have developed this sense of line as a dynamic component of visual art. Graduated experiences planned by adults, and evolving in response to children's interests, resulted in an exciting level of aesthetic and conceptual growth.

PROGRAM B: TWO-DIMENSIONAL SPACE

1) Introduction

A drawing and painting program can start with any material that leaves marks on a surface. In Program B, children had prior drawing experiences with marking pens, crayons, and pastels. The teacher began a new phase of exploration with finger paints to allow children to approach the paint in a tactile way before working with tools and other materials. The introduction of finger paints enabled them to explore large and small movements with their arms and different parts of their hands. There was also an opportunity to explore color and discover what happens when primary colors are mixed, unintentionally or intentionally, through play activities.

The teacher prepared the tables with large sheets of white craft paper that covered most of the table's surface. Three wide-mouth jars of finger paints (one each of the primary colors of red, yellow, and blue) were placed on a nearby work table. The teacher proposed the following game. Children would each choose one color, join a table where others had chosen to use that same color, and then use their hands any way they wanted to paint their paper—fingertips, fingernails, palms, front and/or back of their hand, fists, knuckles, and so on. They could paint the whole sheet of paper, one part of the paper, or several areas. As the teacher offered possibilities, the children immediately began to work. Some explored the finger paints alone, while others experimented in groups of three or four. Some made small movements with their fingers, and others put the energy of their entire bodies behind their hand and arm motions.

Supporting Young Artists

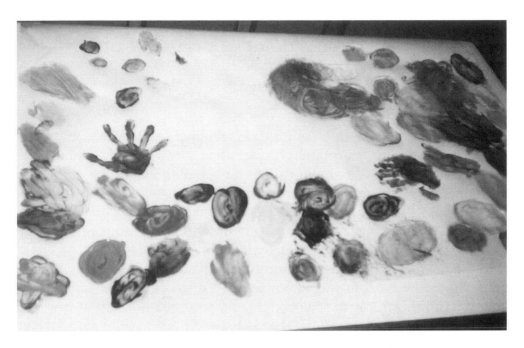

A mural results when children at small-group time explore painting with small hand movements.

The teacher circulated around the room, listening to the children talk about what they were doing. Some children covered the entire sheet of paper with one continuous coat of color. Others made dots, different kinds of lines, and various shapes. Still others printed their palms and fingers in different positions. A few children discovered that by intermingling their hands in a group effort they could create very unusual effects. And they found it was fun to smear paint on one another's hands as well as on the paper.

After a while, the teacher suggested that children could choose a second color if they wished. Some shared the colors they had with a neighbor; others went to the work table for a second color. As they added another primary color and mixed it with the first one, children were delighted to discover they had created a secondary color (green, orange, or purple). They eagerly showed their peers the new color and proceeded to mix paints, discovering more new colors. The children also continued to explore the various effects they created by using different parts of their hands to make impressions with and in the paint. Some children worked with one sheet of paper until it became saturated with finger paint, and occasionally produced a hole in the paper. Others decided to take another sheet of paper rather than cover existing work with new explorations.

2) ENRICHMENT

The enrichment phase in Program B embellished the initial paint exploration with many new experiences, including stories, additional tools and materials, music, and nature. The day after the children were introduced to finger paints, the teacher read a story about firecrackers, parrots, and lollipops. The book was illustrated with finger-paintings done in many bright colors. The children talked about other brightly colored things in their daily lives that appealed to them, such as balloons, balls, or a friend's dress. They took sheets of shiny paper from the wooden paper tray and chose one or more primary colors of finger paint to work with. The children worked individually or in groups, extending the motions they made the previous day and further investigating color mixing. As they worked, the children made firecracker sounds like the ones described in the story. Some of the children painted (represented) the brightly colored objects they had identified as their favorites.

On the following day, after the children had thoroughly explored mixing and applying the finger paints with their hands, the teacher decided they were ready for some new materials and tools. The teacher brought brushes and tempera paints outside and spread a large sheet of wrapping paper in the yard. The brushes differed in size (small to large) and shape (round and flat). Children experimented with the brushes, discovering they could achieve various effects in the same way they had used different parts of the hands. The teacher posed a question: Do you see anything else outside that you could use to paint with? The children picked up leaves, sticks, pebbles, feathers, and pieces of rope and cardboard that they found in the yard. They dipped these into the paints and found that each tool could be used to create unique visual effects. As they mixed colors and applied them with various tools, several children also compared the colors they created to those they saw around them—in their hair and eye color, on their clothes, in nature, on the school building and nearby houses, and so on.

On a subsequent day, the teacher suggested the children listen to music before beginning to paint. The teacher played different types of music—slow, fast, sad, happy—and the children used their bodies, arms, feet, hands, and heads to move according to how the music made them feel. The children walked, danced, hopped, slid along the floor, and twirled around. Then the teacher set out familiar drawing materials, including oil pastels, wax crayons, and markers. She played the music again and told them to let their hands (while holding the drawing materials) move over the surface of the paper just as their bodies had moved about the room. She suggested that children might want to draw with their eyes closed so they could feel the mood of the music even better.

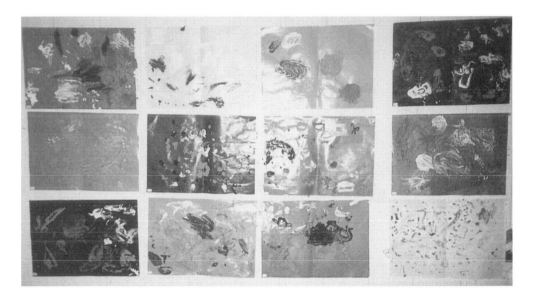

Children made these movement paintings while listening to music.

On yet another day, the teacher set out a range of drawing and painting materials and encouraged the children to use more than one medium at a time. Some children discovered they could achieve interesting effects by mixing media, for example, by covering oil pastels with a thin wash of tempera paint. The teacher explained that this technique was known as *resist painting.* Several children experimented with this technique, exploring what would happen when the different materials were the same color and when they were different colors. Mixing media and colors at the same time produced a whole new range of visual effects for the children to investigate.

Over a period of several weeks in Program B, the teacher brought in more experiences to enrich the children's work with drawing and painting materials. On one day, they read a storybook with colorful photographs of butterflies. This book had detailed close-ups of butterflies and flowers. The children discussed the dots, lines, colors, patterns, and textures in the photos. The book also led into a

"It's a caterpillar with wings and a tail."

Children represent the flowers and insects in their school yard.

discussion of where butterflies live, what they eat, and how they fly. The children went outside to collect leaves and flowers that insects like to eat. They used magnifying glasses to observe the colors and textures on the plants in greater detail. Using a variety of drawing and painting materials, and different kinds of paper, the children represented butterflies, other insects, flowers, and leaves. Several children experimented with painting on transparent cellophane paper. They taped the paper on the window to see what would happen when light shone through it.

To follow up the children's interest in insects, the class went on a trip to the zoo. They visited the insect house, as well as the other animal compounds. The teacher brought in books about animals, and several children brought in their favorite animal books from home. Children did many drawings and paintings to represent their trip to the zoo, the insects and animals they saw around the school yard,

Supporting Young Artists

and the pets and animals in and around their homes. When a local artist who specialized in drawing wildlife had an exhibit, the class went to see the show. They visited a pet store and drew the animals they saw there. Through these diverse experiences, an initial investigation with color and paint led into explorations of color and design in the natural world.

3) Production

Throughout Program B's enrichment phase, the children were already producing drawings and paintings as they explored new media and incorporated music, stories, and community visits into their art. They used drawing and painting materials to create props for role-playing. For example, for many days after the trip to the zoo, children pretended to be insects and other animals. They made masks, wings, and other costumes and moved about the room in different "animal" ways. They painted different shades of green on strips of paper and pretended they were insects crawling through the tall grass. Children playing in the house area decided to have a dinner party. They painted different kinds of foods on paper plates and invited the teacher and their friends to join them in the feast. These same children used drawing materials to "write" and illustrate their party invitations. In this way, they were using art materials to make objects that incorporated their emerging literacy skills.

Once the children were very familiar with the materials, they also became increasingly interested in drawing and painting to produce particular visual effects. In other words, they not only were representing specific experiences but also giving aesthetic expression to images inspired by the media themselves. Some children extended their color explorations by surrounding themselves with environments made of brightly painted papers and patterned fabrics. Others drew and painted on

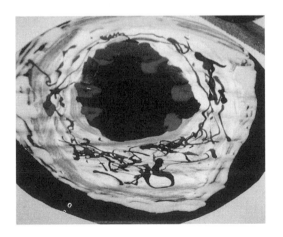

"A meatball pizza with lots of stringy cheese. Who wants to come to my party?"

crepe paper, creating elaborate designs, and then wound the colorful strips around themselves. Several children became interested in collage. They decorated large sheets of paper with paints, pastels, yarn, fabric, and natural materials such as leaves and branches. As the children placed the materials on the supporting surface, it was evident that they were considering the visual effects of their juxtapositions. The children were developing an aesthetic sense about the materials, the colors, and the combinations of shape and design.

4) Reflection

As noted in the previous program description, reflection actually occurs throughout the in-depth studio approach. It is not limited to a final phase, although looking back over several experiences at once can yield new levels of insight. During the introduction, enrichment, and production stages of Program B, teachers provided children with many opportunities to think about what they were doing. They encouraged children to share their observations with others and modeled being accepting of one another's opinions. For example, immediately after the initial exploration with the finger paints, the children displayed their work. They talked about the various visual effects and remembered how they had been produced with different parts and motions of their hands: with fingernails or fists, or by rubbing their palms or scrunching their fingers. With the teacher's help, the children labeled the kinds of dots, lines, shapes, designs, and textures on their papers. They also discussed color. Sometimes the children could name the colors; sometimes the teacher provided a label; and sometimes they enjoyed inventing a word that described how a color might feel or smell. The teacher encouraged the children to remember what colors they mixed to arrive at the final color on the paper. The children thought about the things in their environment that were the same colors as those they produced by mixing paints.

The diverse enrichment experiences provided many opportunities for reflection. After their time with paints and natural materials outdoors, the children displayed their work in the yard and eagerly showed it when their parents came to pick them up. They told their parents about where they had found the various materials they used to make their marks and how they manipulated their hands and the tools to create different effects. The children talked about the colors in the drawings and paintings, and the colors in nature. Some children

Displaying their work encourages children to talk about what they have done and to share it with peers and adults.

voiced an affinity for a particular color and used it often or even exclusively in their work. Others enjoyed experimenting with the full range of colors and were always eager to see how adding another color changed the result. By discussing their actions, the children developed a sense of their own aesthetic preferences and learned to accept and appreciate the choices of their peers.

Program A and Program B both gave children ample time and space to explore drawing and painting materials. Through repeated exposure to a limited yet varied range of materials, the children acquired a relatively sophisticated knowledge about each medium, conventional and unconventional tools, how drawing and painting could facilitate role-playing and communication, and how these media became a source of visual inspiration in themselves. The depth of the children's knowledge in making and appreciating this art form could not have been achieved without the corresponding in-depth experiences described here. In the following chapter, the same principles will be applied to children's experiences with found materials.

7

Found Materials

In the art area, three-year-old Brian shapes tin foil into a long cylinder. He wraps a pipe cleaner around the outside of the cylinder so it comes to a point at the end. Then he takes the cylinder back over to the block area and tells the other children that it is "medicine to make the alligators go to sleep."

At work time, four-year-old Tyrone finds a long cardboard box in the art area's recycling bin.

He glues pebbles in a row down the front of the box and opens both ends, saying "Now I got my own horn." Tyrone hums into one end of his "horn" and joins the other band members in the block area.

Five-year-old Douglas tapes small boxes together to make a "jet plane." He uses three soap-bar-sized boxes, taped together end-to-end, with a spaghetti box taped sideways across the top.

The in-depth studio approach with found materials, both natural and manufactured (also referred to as scrap materials or human-made materials), is described in this chapter. The chapter begins with a brief definition of found materials and an accounting of their use as an art medium throughout history and includes a review of their characteristics. This information will help teachers choose and collect appropriate found materials for young children's art experiences. The chapter concludes with two in-depth studio sequences, one with natural materials and the other with scrap materials.

A Brief History of the Use of Found Materials as an Art Medium

Found materials are ordinary and familiar objects that can be found in the natural or human environment and used to create art. They are incorporated in many types of art—folk art created by untrained artists as well as fine art produced by those with professional training. People have always used natural materials to create simple everyday utensils. Given the human propensity for decorating functional items, it was probably not long before prehistoric humans discovered the aesthetic properties inherent in the materials themselves. Natural materials that were used for artistic as well as functional purposes as early as prehistoric times include earth, sand, minerals, charcoal, wood, blood, feathers, shells, teeth, hair, eggs, and stone. Examples of artworks made with found materials include cave paintings in southern France, masks in Africa, and wall decorations in the tents and huts of the Middle East.

Today, found materials also include the plethora of human-made items often considered scrap or garbage. Manufacturers' overruns, leftovers and byproducts, empty containers, and used goods ready for the recycling bin—all can be fodder for the artistic mill. These commercial goods can be salvaged, collected, and used in unexpected ways to make an artistic statement. Artists have used found materials in their paintings, collages, assemblages, and sculptures to call attention to the unappreciated beauty in common objects or to comment on the waste in society. Among the better known artists incorporating found objects are Pablo Picasso, Georges Braque, Jean Dubuffet, Kurt Schwitters, Max Ernst, Joseph Cornell, Robert Rauschenberg, Jim Dine, Jean Tinguely, Cesar, and Dadaists such as Marcel Duchamp and Hans Arp. These artists have worked with found materials and "ready mades" ranging from sand and feathers to fabric, newsprint, canceled tickets, old tools and utensils, tires, machinery parts, and even a toilet.

Artists, liberated from the use of traditional materials, experiment with these materials that derive from our contemporary natural or urban environment. They explore worthless, cheap, temporary and ordinary materials, a variety of new techniques, and give form to new creations. [They] juxtapose new trends and stand against established ideas about art materials

Scrap materials make no-cost and low-cost art supplies. These children recycle styrofoam into a present for their teacher.

and political views. In so doing, many times they provoke speculation about the problems of a wasteful society. (Trimis & Manavopoulos, 2001)

Contemporary artists reclaim these materials and recycle them into something useful. The process of transforming garbage into art, "the ordinary into something special, is extended into a re-creation of oneself or one's environment" (Cerny & Seriff, 1996, p. 25).

Artists today are also returning to natural materials to make artistic and political statements about the environment. This ecological art emerged from the environmental art movement of the 1960s through the early 1980s (Cembalest, 1991; Blandy, Congdon, & Krug, 1998). One of its best known practitioners is Andrew Goldsworthy. By calling attention to both the beauty inherent in nature and the ugliness resulting from the earth's destruction, environmental artists hope to raise public awareness and promote activism about ecological issues. Another art movement of the late twentieth century is "land art" in which artists literally use areas of the land itself as their medium and support. Artists such as Richard Long, Robert Smithson, and Christo fit into this category. Instead of pigments and brushes, land artists use fields, forests, mountains, or bodies of water to create works of art. They may light, re-contour, wrap, and otherwise alter these vistas to make an artistic statement. The resulting artworks are deliberately subject to the natural cycles of the day or the year. They are often impermanent, which violates another traditional assumption about art.

Art long ago outgrew its definition as a framed picture on the wall or a statue in the courtyard. Traditional media and techniques have been supplemented with unconventional materials, unusual manipulations, and even unexpected locations for displaying and staging art. As a result, the fine arts have been enriched, and its practitioners and viewers provoked. The inclusion of found materials has forced the art world and the general public to re-think the definition of art, the materials we use to create it, and the impact it has on our visions, thoughts, and actions.

Characteristics of Found Materials

Found materials—natural and scrap—are often found in abundance, making them cheap as well as plentiful. (Scarce objects, such as the fallen feather of a rare bird, a stone layered by eons of erosion, or a precious jewel may also be featured in a work of art.) The no-cost or low-cost characteristic of most found art materials makes this medium an ideal choice for early childhood programs, because children are not constrained by the amount of material they can use, and programs are not constrained by the resources available for purchasing art supplies. Found materials also provide many opportunities for children, families, and communities to be actively involved in assembling art supplies. Children can collect natural materials in the school yard or on field trips. Families and local businesses can contribute recycled and scrap materials. In fact, the resale of unused industrial products and supplies, often at minimal prices, has become a new form of commercial enterprise frequented by educational programs and nonprofit social service agencies as well as artists.

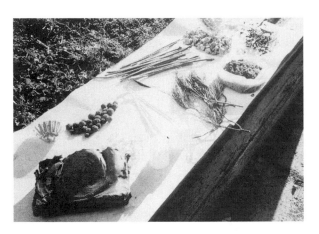
Children collect natural materials in the school yard to use in art activities.

In choosing and collecting found materials suitable for the early childhood classroom, teachers should consider safety and sanitary issues. For example, avoid items that are toxic, have sharp edges, are easily swallowed by very young children, or are likely to stain clothing, and so on. Apart from these common-sense considerations, however, the number of suitable found items is virtually unlimited, bounded only by the artistic imagination.

Natural found materials include stones, pebbles, sand, earth, mud, clay, shells, leaves, branches, sticks, grass, wood, bark, hair, feathers, nuts, and seeds. Scrap materials that can be incorporated in art include buttons, fabric, costume jewelry, shoelaces, yarn, ribbon, string, dryer lint, Velcro, boxes, beads, newspapers, computer paper, gift-wrap, greeting cards, egg cartons, packing materials, corks, plastic cups, bottle caps, plastic food containers, wire, paper plates, plastic eating utensils, hair ornaments, foam rubber, cardboard tubes, broken toy parts, and hardware. Other ideas are listed on pages 67–69 ("Creating a Learning Environment for Visual Art," Chapter Four). Ideas for using paper in all its forms are presented in Chapter Eight.

Supporting Young Artists

Young Children and Found Materials

Children naturally play with and transform materials from their environment. At the park or on the beach, for example, they spontaneously incorporate bits of nature into their constructions and fantasy play. In children's hands, everyday household items are reborn as building and role-playing materials.

Young children approach materials with an openness that surprises, delights, and sometimes shocks adults. Because they have not yet been socialized in conventional uses, children automatically employ materials in novel ways. Their imaginations are not limited by habit or narrow definitions of beauty. How did they think of that? is a common adult exclamation when marvelling at the uses children invent for familiar objects. We react this way because in contrast to artists who can suspend conventional ways of thinking to arrive at new applications and unusual combinations, most of us tend to be more rigid in our thinking about how materials should be used.

Children love "stuff." As natural collectors, they enjoy examining and sorting the things they collect as an end in itself. Many perceptual and cognitive lessons can be learned from these pursuits. With adult encouragement, however, children's collecting will take on a further purpose, that of artistic appreciation and creation. In the interests of art, we can encourage them to appreciate and deliberately exploit the aesthetic properties of the materials they assemble. For example, children can be encouraged to sort their collected items according to whatever visual properties they choose—color or shape or texture or shininess. Such an experience will raise their awareness of the aesthetic as well as functional qualities inherent in the materials. They will then begin to look at found materials with an artist's eye and mind and think

Children explore texture by using sponges as painting tools.

about how an object can be transformed and/or combined with other materials to create a particular visual experience. When children consciously employ natural and scrap found materials because of the effects they produce, they are truly creating works of visual art.

The In-Depth Studio Approach With Found Materials

The rest of this chapter describes two early childhood programs that provided young children with in-depth studio experiences with found materials. Program A focused on working with natural materials, while Program B was centered around scrap (human-made or industrial) materials. Each program is presented in terms of the four interrelated components of the in-depth approach: introduction, enrichment, production, and reflection.

PROGRAM A: NATURAL MATERIALS

1) Introduction

Program A was situated near a park and a wooded area. Although their homes and school were close to these natural surroundings, most of the children had played only occasionally with dirt, leaves, and sticks. They had not come in contact with these materials in depth and had certainly never used them in an organized way to make art. As a preliminary step to working with natural found materials, the teacher and children gathered in the school yard and its garden to describe what they saw. Then the teacher introduced a game. After asking the children to close their eyes, she gave them (or led them to) something to touch—tree bark, leaves, sand or dirt, pebbles, or stones. With the teacher's encouragement, the children described the texture of what they felt.

At snack time, as the children discussed their adventures in the yard, the teacher brought up other natural environments that she knew many of the children had experienced, such as the sea and the mountains. One child remembered playing with pebbles at the seashore. Another recalled going skiing when it snowed in the mountains. The teacher had also been skiing in the mountains, so the next day she brought in a videotape of her skiing vacation that showed her building a snowman with friends. The children talked about the color of the snow, its temperature, and its texture. The teacher asked parents if anyone had things from the sea at home, and several parents responded by bringing in shells and pebbles the children had helped to collect on family outings.

After these discussions, the teacher asked the children to collect some natural materials on their way to and from school the next day and also asked the parents to help their children find appropriate items.

At outside time, children explore natural materials collected in the school yard and on a walk in the woods.

The teacher explained that they should not pick flowers or leaves from living plants, but they could gather up things that had already fallen to the ground. In keeping with these instructions, children brought in stones, leaves, dead flowers, and grass. To add to this collection, the class went on a walk to the nearby woods, and many parents joined them. The children carried little bags and boxes to collect the materials they wanted to bring back and returned to the classroom with flower and grass bouquets, sand, earth, bark, pieces of wood, dried branches, stones and pebbles, snail shells, feathers, and pine cones.

Back in the classroom, the children sorted their treasures and began exploring their properties by working individually or in small groups. Some children created little boats with bark, sticks, and leaves. At outside time, they carried their boats to a creek that bordered the school yard and floated them on the water. Other children created human figures with the natural found materials, using leaves, sticks, stone, bark, and feathers. They made their creations on paper or carried the materials outside to work in the soil. A third group collaborated to create a stable. They used one stick to draw a rectangular shape in the earth and then planted other sticks all around to create an enclosure. They pretended pieces of bark and leaves were horses that were trapped in the stable. When some of the horses escaped, the children put stones between the sticks to create a "fence" that would keep them inside.

2) Enrichment

To proceed with enrichment, the teacher in Program A brought in additional natural materials to supplement those found by the children.

These included sea pebbles, a variety of shells, a turtle carapace, leaves of different shapes and colors, and pine cones of different sizes and shapes. The children created an exhibit with these materials, deciding to sort them by "big" and "little" items. When they came across objects of "medium" size, the children had some interesting debates and negotiations about where to place them. The teacher set out drawing tools near the exhibit, and some of the children chose to draw representations of the found materials. She also provided magnifying glasses so the children could examine the found materials more closely. Some children were intrigued by the designs and patterns they observed. Inspired, they made drawings of the veins on the leaves, the spiral on the shells, and other detailed properties.

Children sort and make collages with the natural materials they gathered.

The shapes and patterns of leaves are intriguing to young artists.

Supporting Young Artists

The teacher provided further enrichment by bringing in posters and books with pictures and photographs of nature. She included different kinds of scenery from the nearby area or from family trips they had mentioned—scenes the children would be familiar with. Parents were asked to bring in post cards and photographs from home that showed the family in these different scenic settings and highlighted the natural properties of the surroundings. Children took the books and photographs outside and looked for wildlife that had the same characteristics as those in the illustrations. They were especially interested in color and shape. One of the parents mentioned a storybook with an ecological theme, written for preschoolers. The parent loaned the book to the program, and the teacher read it to the children many times over the next couple of weeks.

The town where Program A was located had a folk-art museum with many artworks created from natural materials. The teacher called the museum and arranged a visit. The guide at the museum welcomed the children, and at the teacher's suggestion, showed them artworks made with many of the same materials the children had collected and used in their own artwork. The guide told the children stories about the lives of the artists, encouraged their observations, answered their questions, and sent them home with pamphlets that illustrated several of the works they had seen. In the gift shop, the teacher purchased post cards that featured reproductions of some of the works.

Back in the classroom over the next several days, children continued to work with the found materials, experimenting with some of the images and techniques they had seen at the folk-art museum. These experiences were further enriched when the teacher brought in slides of work by contemporary artists who employed similar materials. Some of the artists used natural materials as a way of focusing on ecological problems. The class discussed their reactions to the slides as works of art. They also talked about environmental issues at a concrete level, expressing how sad they would be if familiar plants and animals were to disappear or become sick.

The children became particularly interested in three of the natural materials used by the folk and environmental artists: clay, wood, and stone. A subsequent trip to the park further aroused the children's interest in clay. As a result of their enthusiasm, the teacher promised to do something special with this medium. After a few days, when it was clear to them that their teacher had forgotten her promise, the children reminded her! She invited a local potter to visit the program, and he showed the children how he worked with clay. The children observed him softening the clay in water and fashioning it into ropes and coils. They saw him pound and flatten harder pieces of clay and use the slabs to make a hand-built box. The potter gave each child a lump of clay and let the children try these things for themselves.

3) Production

Events happening in the children's lives led automatically to their producing artwork with the natural materials. Since it was carnival time and the children were excited about masks and disguises, the teacher showed them photographs of African masks. The children recognized that many of the materials were similar to those they had seen at the folk-art museum, and they were eager to create their own masks with natural materials. Working with familiar materials and a few new ones, they created masks using heavy paper decorated with feathers, pine needles, dried wheat, and nuts. They attached the decorations using various techniques, including poking them into the paper, stapling, taping, and glueing. When the masks were ready, the children pretended to be different creatures, and made up songs and dances. Over the next several days, they made more masks and also decorated their clothes with additional materials, such as straw and leaves.

Production activities continued with a field trip to the nearby park. The children took buckets, shovels, and the materials they had collected in the forest. They collected more materials en route to the park and also when they got there. The children then proceeded to make elaborate constructions in the park with all of these materials. They used the sticks to make drawings in the soil and decorated their drawings with leaves, grass, stones, and more sticks. Some children added water to the earth to make mud and sculpted it into mounds similar to those they had seen in the museum. They decorated these mud constructions with different materials. Other children were fascinated with the process of imprinting. They used the mud to make imprints of their hands and various textured materials on large sheets of paper the teacher had brought along.

The children were very excited about these activities and asked the teacher if they could return to the park the next day. This time the children brought more of their collected materials, including shells, sea pebbles, and pine cones. They extended their play and made even larger constructions. A great deal of spontaneous conversation occurred among the children as they described what they were doing and invited their peers to look at their constructions. Groups devised ways to join their constructions together to make larger and more elaborate structures. Before it was time to leave the park, the children collected more earth, sand, grass, twigs, and other materials and brought them back to the

Sand and pebbles embedded in glue make interesting designs.

classroom. The next day, they covered their tables and parts of the floor with newspapers and sheets of plastic. Working in pairs and small groups, the children extended the experiences from the park to art production in an indoor setting. Some children made mud and began to build more constructions, such as a fortress for pirates with hidden treasures. Others experimented with imprinting designs by moistening the sand and creating mosaic-like designs with prints from shells, stones, and other objects.

As noted earlier, the teacher had invited a potter to the classroom after their trips to the museum and park had clearly piqued the children's interest in clay and mud. The children's production flourished following their session with this local craftsman. Inspired by the potter's demonstration, the children rolled and cut the clay, made coils and spirals, designed circles, built human and animal figures, and sculpted flowers. Some children decorated their forms with additional natural materials, combining the clay with shells, leaves, and grass. Several days later, as the Easter holiday approached, a few children chose to make baskets with the clay. They also made eggs out of clay and other natural materials; some painted the eggs in different colors. The teacher read the children a story about a little town where everything was egg-shaped. Some of the children decided to create their own little town, using the full range of clay, and collected natural materials to make egg-shaped structures and creatures. As these children invented stories about what was happening in their town, more and more other children were drawn into the fantasy play. The construction stayed up and grew more elaborate, continuing to evolve even after the children returned from their holiday break.

4) Reflection

Throughout these production activities, as well as the earlier introduction and enrichment phases, the teacher encouraged the children to think about their experiences with materials in the natural world. After their initial trip to the school yard and garden, the children remembered what the different materials felt like. They talked about

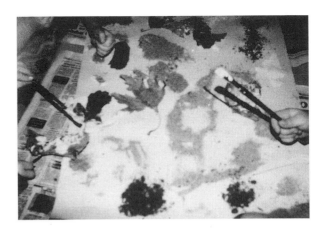

Children create a mural with natural materials from their field trips. They review the different textures, colors, and patterns.

the roughness of the bark, the smoothness of a leaf, the grittiness of the dirt, the warmth or coolness of the earth in the sun versus the shade. The teacher accepted the words and labels the children used to describe these textures. Occasionally, when the children expressed interest, she supplied new vocabulary words to label the sensations.

The children's thoughts were extended during their trip to the forest to collect natural materials. As they scouted the area, they remembered the discussions about the materials in the school yard. Referring to the earlier experience, the children began to comment on the textures they felt and the colors and shapes they saw around them. A few children even noticed footprints—their own and those of animals—and talked about an in-depth studio printmaking program they had participated in during the previous year. The trips to the park elicited similar observations and recollections about their earlier experiences in nature and working with various art materials.

Reflection was most focused after the children had completed their elaborate constructions in the classroom and were sharing them with one another. They talked eagerly about the different materials they had used and the processes and techniques they employed in creating their structures and designs. With encouragement from the teacher, the children were able to describe their intentions and how they carried them out, by making comments such as, "I wanted to make a bridge, so I put some stones here and some stones here, and then I put this stick on top of them." To further facilitate the recall

Supporting Young Artists

process, the teacher had taken slides of their trips to the forest, the museum, and the park. As the teacher projected the slides on the classroom wall, the children talked about these experiences and pointed to similarities between art objects in the pictures and those they had created in the classroom. Discussing their own artwork, and observing that created by others, inspired the children to create more artworks with found natural materials on subsequent days.

PROGRAM B: SCRAP MATERIALS

1) Introduction

Program B was located in an urban area near a major road lined with many billboards and businesses with prominent advertising signs. To capitalize on this familiar environment, the teacher used the in-depth studio approach to focus on the images and materials these signs portrayed. On the one hand, the surrounding vicinity offered an opportunity for the children to explore consumerism at a very concrete level. On the other hand, the signs were an instant museum right in the school's back yard. Their presence provided a rich context in which to explore the medium of scrap materials.

The children in Program B had worked extensively with conventional art materials and media, including marking pens, crayons, finger and brush painting, collage, dough, and Plasticine. They had never worked with any type of found materials before. Based on the fresh approach the children brought to working with more standard materials, the teacher was confident they would bring a nontraditional and creative spirit to investigating commercial products as an art medium.

In the introductory stage, the teacher mentioned the billboards and other signs across the road that the children saw every day on their way to and from class. From the glass doors of the school and then more closely from the edge of the school yard, the teacher and children observed these signs advertising consumer goods. With guidance from the teacher, and drawing on their earlier experiences, the children commented on both the content and the form of these ads. For each sign, they looked at the whole as well as its parts and described the shape, color, texture, and size of the products featured in the advertisements. These discussions served to re-introduce familiar daily objects and encouraged the children to "observe [them] carefully, in a systematic way, in order to better notice what had been observed earlier" (Perkins, 1994, p. 17).

Billboards near the school stimulate a discussion of the shape, size, color, and texture of the products advertised.

After they returned to the classroom, the children talked about other places where they had seen advertisements, such as on television, and who they thought had made the ads. As they elaborated on the specific products they had seen advertised, the discussion centered on the items their families purchased and used at home. The teacher then asked what happened when they were done with the products—what did their families do with the leftovers or the empty packaging? Some of the children said they were thrown away, some mentioned putting things in recycling bins, and others did not know what happened to unused goods. As a result of this discussion, the children decided to bring in unused and empty packaging material and create a supermarket in the classroom. The teacher asked parents to help assemble these materials from home over the next several days, reminding them to clean out any residual products left in the containers.

Families contributed a wide variety of clean, empty product containers, including soda bottles, detergent boxes, baby-powder containers, plastic shampoo bottles, egg cartons, coffee cans, cereal boxes, cardboard produce trays, paper-towel tubes, plastic fruit baskets, and so on. All the materials were collected in a corner of the room. When the pile of empty containers was large, the children were ready to decide where they wanted to construct their supermarket. They decided the best place would be in the area with shelves. Then the children had to decide how to organize the goods in the supermarket. Solving this problem led to a lively debate, but ended in a consensus that the items would be sorted according to their purpose. That is, food items would go together, as would those for personal care, household cleaning, automotive care, and so on. Drawing on their own experiences, the children also decided there should be advertisements, price signs, and other printed matter on the walls around the area of the supermarket.

Supporting Young Artists

After they arranged the supermarket, the children began to role-play. Some stocked the shelves, others were customers, and still others pretended to be cashiers. Some children wanted to play the same role each day, while others enjoyed trying out different roles. They made money out of bottle caps and cut-up pieces of construction paper with numbers (sometime real, sometimes invented) written on them. The children re-enacted familiar scenes from their home lives. For example, they pretended to be parents and children who met their neighbors at the market. They wrote up shopping lists, some scribbling letter-like forms and others writing real letters or words. The children made cars in the block area, drove their cars to the supermarket, and parked them in the parking lot.

With their parents' help, the children brought in advertisements from home that they found in magazines, newspaper circulars, mailbox flyers, and so on. They taped these written materials on the supermarket shelves and posted them on the walls. The children played a game, trying to match the pictures on the advertisements to the actual objects or class of objects on the shelves. The teacher and children invented various sorting and guessing games, figuring out where unusual items should be placed or trying to remember which shelf held certain items. Children recalled or made up funny advertising

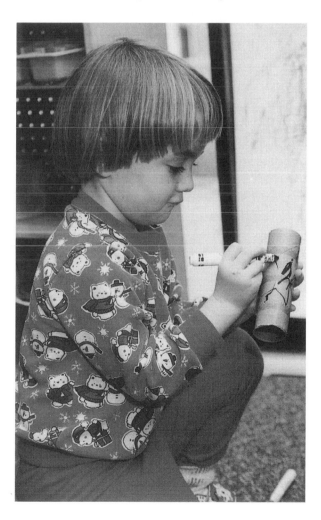

A girl turns a paper-towel tube into a roll of "chip cookie freezer dough."

songs and jingles about the products. They arranged different types of containers on the floor and made up a game in which they threw a ball and tried to hit a certain color. Then they invented a movement game and wove in and out of the rows of objects on the floor, waving or clapping little boxes in their hands as they moved.

After a few days, the teacher provided the children with familiar drawing and painting materials. The children used these materials to represent the products on the shelves of their supermarkets. They illustrated not only the items but how they were employed at home—where they were kept, which families used them, what they did with them, and how they disposed of them. Some of the children then began to make their own advertising posters for products they especially liked or found personally meaningful, such as toys and articles of clothing. They drew the products, "wrote" ad copy, and indicated prices and special sales.

Throughout the creation of the supermarket and the dramatic play it inspired, children were engaging in a multitude of key experiences. For example, clipping advertisements and making posters involved language and literacy; role-playing involved creative representation and social relations; sorting the products involved logical operations; making money and playing cashier involved numeracy; inventing jingles incorporated music; dancing around the shelves was movement; illustrating how their families used the products involved creative representation; and so on. In addition, there were multiple opportunities to involve families and reference children's homes and communities by focusing on objects and events in their everyday lives.

2) Enrichment

Only after the children had thoroughly explored and represented these materials in their conventional form did the teacher add the idea of transforming them for another purpose—making art. Building on their familiarity with single advertising posters, the teacher suggested they combine and reassemble several posters into collages. She began by providing them with a concrete and visual image. Since there were a couple of nearby billboards where several layers of advertising were visible simultaneously, the children went on a walk to observe these and talked about how interesting it was to see more than one product at the same time. The teacher also guided the discussion to help the children focus on the interesting juxtapositions of colors and shapes that came from combining materials and messages.

Back in the Program B classroom, the teacher spread large pieces of paper on the floor. Working alone or in groups, children cut shapes and objects from different kinds of advertising material. They arranged and rearranged them on the paper, and when they were pleased with the organization, they glued the pieces in place. The teacher told them they were making collages. The children talked as they worked, expressing opinions about the items they were cutting out, the designs of the advertisements, and the aesthetics of their collage arrangements. Some of the children used painting and drawing materials to add more details and flourishes to the collages. They decided their advertising billboard should hang in the large front window of the center, overlooking the other billboards in the neighborhood.

A "rocket ship" is made from empty cartons covered with newspaper. After the paste dried, the children painted it.

Next, the teacher suggested the children select some materials from the supermarket shelves and see what they could make with them. Again working individually or in small teams, the children carried packaging materials from the shelves to the tables and floor space. They began to organize the materials into different shapes and designs, transforming them through unique combinations. As the children constructed, deconstructed, and reconstructed the scrap materials, they decided to use a variety of packages to make a long train. This construction led to a more general interest in all types of vehicles.

Over the next several days, the children used more scrap materials to create boats, ships, trains, and airplanes. They transformed the materials with scissors, glue, and tape. Some chose to paint the packages, adding bright colors and details. Others used additional scrap materials to create passengers and consumer goods being transported by their vehicles. They constructed roadways, train stations, and airports using blocks and additional found materials. The children m-ade vehicle noises and moved their bodies like cars, trains, and airplanes. They invented role-plays centered on transportation, such as car chases, flights to visit grandparents, the daily drive to and from school, train wrecks, driving a new baby home from the hospital, filling up a truck to move to a new house, and sailing on the water during a big storm.

The teacher extended and enriched the children's interest in transportation by bringing in related books, photographs, and posters. The class also went on field trips to the nearby harbor, train station, and heliport. To enrich the children's awareness of using scrap materials as an art medium in general, the teacher connected them to the world of artists working with found materials. She brought in slides of work by installation artists who specialized in using scrap materials. She read about an upcoming exhibit that featured artwork made of found materials and arranged to bring the children to a special showing where they could meet the artist and hear her talk about her work. Throughout the children's investigation, the teacher was always bringing in different types of found materials and encouraging families to contribute their disposable items to the classroom.

3) Production

Some of the children in Program B became enamored with the idea of producing vehicles, and their constructions became much more detailed. They brought in additional scrap materials from home to provide further elaboration. The idea of making something very large captured the imagination of eight children. They created two core groups of four children each, with others joining and leaving from one day to the next, and collaborated to make something "really big!" The children built a complex series of vehicles and created appropriate environments for them—streets and parking lots, train tracks, bodies of water, a large harbor with ferry boats, airports, and so on. At outside time, they carried the most portable materials to the school yard and continued to create more transportation scenarios. The children invented elaborate stories and played out various roles. Every day they expanded one or more fantasies, using a wide variety of scrap materials and conventional art media (crayons, paint) for basic construction and decoration. The children used these same materials to make uniforms and props to further their dramatic play—inverting a small box to make a pilot's cap, using paper-towel tubes as oars, and drawing spokes on circular pizza cardboard to make wheels.

While these children continued to make vehicles and related props, other students became increasingly interested in the expressive qualities of the scrap materials themselves. Their constructions no longer represented vehicles or anything else recognizable as specific objects. Rather, these children were producing artworks based on the aesthetic properties inherent in the materials and their potential for transformation. Some children worked in two dimensions. They disassembled the packaging materials, laid them flat or attached them to paper, and decorated them with other found materials of different colors and textures (yarn, lace, buttons, beads, and so on). Other children chose to create three-dimensional

A roll of corrugated cardboard becomes a tower in children's re-enactment of a fairy tale.

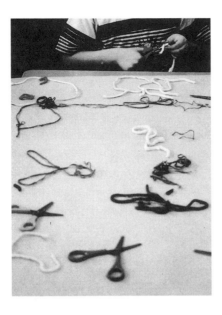

Children can create lines and forms by cutting up scrap yarn.

art forms. They used the size and shape of the found materials as the taking-off point for adding projections, creating angles, exploring light and shadow, or playing with weight and balance. Children worked individually, in pairs, or in groups to create these visual works of art that were often striking for their uncommon applications and combinations of materials. The teacher respected the nonrepresentational character of their productions. She never asked What is that? but left it to the children to describe their intentions and actions or to just let the products speak for themselves.

In other programs using the in-depth studio approach with scrap materials, children have followed their interests into completely different areas of production. For example, in one program they decided to make real and imaginary animals; a trip to the zoo inspired further production efforts in this vein. In another program, the children were interested in houses. They toured their neighborhood to see various architectural styles and decorative embellishments and visited a natural history museum to see how dwellings were constructed in different eras or by different groups of people. They later incorporated their observations into making living spaces with cardboard, wood, metal, and fabric. In other early childhood programs, young children have also used scrap materials to create toys, musical instruments, and puppets.

4) Reflection

Program B provided numerous opportunities for children to recall and reflect as they collected and used scrap materials. After they had their initial look at billboards and signs in their neighborhood, the children remembered the design features of the advertisements and products that were promoted. Back in the classroom, they talked about the purpose of these products and which ones they used at home. To lead into the idea of making scrap art, the teacher wondered aloud about

Supporting Young Artists

what happened to the leftover products and empty packaging materials. The ensuing discussion encouraged the children to think about aesthetic and ecological issues, including commercial design, consumerism, and recycling. This conversation led eventually to their actions and thoughts about how these waste materials could be used in the service of art.

Creating the supermarket involved almost continual reflection on the part of the students. The children thought about the items and their uses as they sorted them on the supermarket shelves. They had to remember the products they assembled and the corresponding advertisements they cut out so they could pair signs and products in the supermarket displays. They were obviously thinking about their shopping experiences at home so they could re-enact them in the classroom supermarket.

Constructing vehicles with the scrap materials provided similar opportunities for reflection and recall. The children's ideas immediately enriched their ongoing building and artistic endeavors. For example, as they pored over the picture books and photographs of vehicles, they discussed the vehicles' characteristics and compared them to the ones being created in the classroom. As a result, many children went back and added more detail to their own constructions. During the process, they spontaneously talked about personal travel experiences. They recounted everyday events such as traveling in the car or on the bus; they remembered special trips on less common forms of transportation, such as sailboats and airplanes. Visits to the harbor, train station, and heliport stimulated further discussion about past experiences with families; elicited recollections of television shows that featured these locations; and spurred ideas for building new vehicles and carrying out dramatic play activities.

The teacher provided ample space for children to store their works-in-progress. Completed constructions were always displayed for many days afterwards. Having their work centrally located and visible allowed the children to observe the transformation process, share their ideas with adults and peers, and get ideas from evaluating their own work and seeing the work of others. When products were eventually taken apart, the children saved and recycled whatever they could for use in subsequent art projects and dramatic play. Materials that were not reusable were sorted and recycled. Children were thus engaged in a continual process of review and reuse, which helped them to become concretely aware of both aesthetic ideals and ecological concerns.

In conclusion, the aesthetic potential of natural and scrap found materials in early childhood settings is unbounded. Their use is encouraged by the medium's abundance and low cost. Young children are not constrained by convention in how they approach these materials as a vehicle for creative expression. Found materials epitomize the value of art for its own sake. The children in Programs A and B took delight in the inherent properties of these materials and used them to create striking visual images. In-depth experiences with found materials are also the means to promote other areas of development. Children's construction activities and dramatic play allowed them to exercise skills in such key experience areas as social relations, language and literacy, numeracy, classification, seriation, and movement and music. In a sense, children's use of found materials is spontaneous. They need no invitation to discover something and bend it to their own uses. But with guidance from supportive adults, children can also become increasingly aware of the aesthetic potential of found material and come to enjoy it as another medium in the visual arts.

8

Paper

Five-year-old Rachel takes a sheet of red construction paper from the art area and places it on the table in the house area. Then she gets some sheets of newspaper, tears them in half, crumples them into balls, and carefully arranges them on the red paper. She announces to her teacher Beth, "I'm making meatball soup." "Mmmm, meatball soup! How does it taste?" asks Beth. "I don't know," says Rachel, "do you want to taste some?" "Sure," says Beth. "What should I use to eat it?" Rachel thinks a minute and goes back to the art area. She gets some bottle caps and tapes them to the ends of straws. "Here are the spoons," she says to Beth. Beth and Rachel "eat" some soup. "Oops, I spilled on me," says Rachel. "I better get a napkin." She returns to the art area and chooses two colorful sheets of magazine paper. "These are the fancy napkins because we're having a meatball soup dinner party," she announces. Then Rachel folds each sheet of magazine paper in quarters and gives one to Beth. "Now finish your soup before it gets cold," she admonishes her teacher.

Chapter Eight presents the in-depth studio approach with paper. Beginning with a short history of paper in the context of making art and a summary of paper's characteristics, the chapter continues with a brief discussion of the benefits of using paper as an art medium in early childhood programs. The bulk of Chapter Eight is a discussion of three programs that used the in-depth approach. In Program A, the children primarily used paper that was specifically intended for art activities. The other two programs emphasized recycled paper. The children in Program B delved into scrap paper (see Chapter Seven for additional ideas on using scrap materials), and the children in Program C made their own paper. In each program description, the in-depth studio components of introduction, enrichment, production, and reflection are presented.

A Brief History of the Use of Paper as an Art Medium

The American Heritage Dictionary of the English Language defines paper as "a thin sheet material made of cellulose pulp, derived mainly from wood, rags, and certain grasses, processed into flexible leaves or rolls by deposit from an aqueous suspension, and used chiefly for writing, printing, drawing, wrapping, and covering walls" (Morris, 1981, p. 949). Paper is such a common and wonderfully versatile material that we often take it for granted. "It is an ideal surface for writers as well as a surface on which lie many of the world's greatest artistic treasures" (Shannon, 1997, p. 10). Despite predictions that we will become a paperless society, and notwithstanding the proliferation of electronic newspapers, magazines, and books, we remain highly dependent on the use of paper in our everyday lives. Many of us still prefer the rough feel of a newspaper, the slick sheen of a glossy magazine, and the heft of a book to the glaring screen of a computer. Paper remains the vehicle of choice for storing and conveying history, information about everyday affairs, and plans for the future. If anything, the proliferation of personal and professional online documents may have resulted in the use of more paper in order to provide tangible proof of our thoughts and concrete evidence of their electronic transmission.

The basic process of papermaking is the same today as when papermaking techniques originated in China approximately two thousand years ago (Thompson, 1992). Plant fibers are steeped in water, drained, dried, and wrapped around a roll. According to tradition, the first papermaker was Tsai Luin, who in A.D. 105 manufactured paper from hemp, tree bark, raki, and fishing nets (Luoma, 1998, p. 159). By the seventh century A.D., papermaking had reached Japan. The Japanese perfected the art and became renowned for the excellence of their paper. The art of handmade paper, *uoshi,* survives in Japan today and is evident in mother-of-pearl leaves, umbrellas, colorful kites, and the paper-folding art of origami.

From Asia, papermaking spread westward. By the time Gutenberg printed the first Bible in the mid-fifteenth century, many European countries had paper mills. But unlike Asian paper, European papers were made almost exclusively from old cloth rags. The raw materials were macerated into pulp by mechanical means, while the remainder of the process was done by hand. Paper and papermaking techniques were introduced to the Americas by Spanish and British colonists in the late sixteenth century. Up until recently, paper was almost exclusively made from recycled cloth or other materials. Only since the middle of the twentieth century has new wood pulp been used commercially as the source of paper.

As the variety of papermaking fibers increased and techniques became more refined, the uses of paper expanded from manuscripts, books, and painting "to the making of everyday articles as varied as armor, clothing, lamps, floor and wall coverings, and umbrellas" (Bell, 1982, p. 8). Today paper is one of the world's most important industrial products, used to create items ranging from the simplest (grocery bags, money, and tickets) to the more elaborate and complex (handmade gift-wrap, jewelry, and masks). Since various additives can enhance its strength and permanence, paper is often used in place of other materials, including glass, wood, and even metal. The uses of paper appear to be unlimited.

With increased technical knowledge, paper expanded from a support for manuscripts and art to a multitude of household and industrial products.

Paper's versatility has made it a favorite material of artists for a long time. Although initially used as a surface for drawing and painting, paper has recently been explored as a medium by itself. Artists and craftspeople in the twentieth century "expanded its role as an art medium and have pushed its use far beyond the boundaries of traditional function" (Smith, 1982, Introduction). "They use paper for objects of a size and importance previously reserved for canvas, marble, or bronze...and elevate the medium from a peripheral concern to a major one" (Glaubinger, 1986, p. 1).

Perhaps the artist who did the most to revive contemporary interest in paper as a medium was Joseph Albers in the 1920s and 1930s. Albers was fascinated by the properties of materials and their artistic and architectural potential when shaped. Experimentation with sheets of paper, as well as with other materials, was a central process in the preliminary art courses Albers taught at the Bauhaus in Dessau, Germany. Whitford (1984) quotes Albers as saying, "economy of form depends on the materials we are working with...you will have more by doing less" (p. 133) and "the simplest and least likely materials could be used to teach important lessons about nature or construction that are relevant to engineering as well as to art" (p. 134).

Experimentation reveals the versatility of paper for design, construction, representation, and role-play.

Albers's teaching approach was not aimed at producing decorative or functional objects with paper. Rather, his focus was on experimentation so students would grow to respect the material and "use it in any way that makes sense, preserving its inherent characteristics" (Whitford, 1984, p. 135). This emphasis on experimentation is equally fitting for the use of paper as an art medium with young children. Rather than being limited to the service of other media, or confined to two-dimensional expression, paper can be used to create artwork of unlimited

Supporting Young Artists

magnitude and complexity. The in-depth studio approach builds children's awareness of this medium's unbounded potential and helps them unleash paper's creative possibilities.

Characteristics of Paper

Paper is plentiful and readily available; it surrounds us in our daily lives. Paper is economical. It can be reused and recycled into still more paper. As an art material, paper is easy to work with, requiring no special tools or complicated techniques to get started. Paper is also approachable. It inspires the experienced artist, but does not intimidate the beginning creator.

Among paper's many properties are color, texture, weight, flexibility, tension, tractability, compression, opacity or transparency, absorbency, porousness, weight, smell, and sound. It can be soft or rigid, smooth or rough, light or heavy, plain or colored, used to make sounds, or made to move. Paper is also a fragile substance. Yet, if folded several times or used to reinforce itself, paper can become remarkably strong and rigid. Paper lends itself readily to both two-dimensional and three-dimensional art. It can be spread flat, draped and hung, suspended, or stood on end.

Paper can be manipulated in many ways—torn, cut, folded, creased, crushed, molded, engraved, twisted, braided, coiled, wrapped,

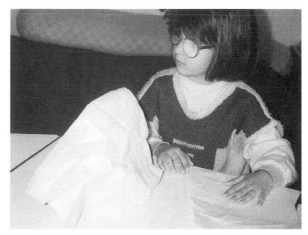

Paper can be manipulated and transformed in texture and shape.

Children use paper to represent storybooks and make their own books.

rolled, mashed, shredded, burned, or dissolved. Its versatility in everyday usage generalizes to its limitless possibilities as an art medium. Paper is a magical material that can challenge and inspire artists of all ages and all levels of training.

For use as an art medium in the classroom, paper can be divided into two types: art paper made expressly for use as an art material and scrap paper made for other purposes, but suitable for artistic manipulation. The division between art paper and scrap paper is not firm. Many types of paper easily cross the line, just as most types of paper can serve equally well as a support for other media or as a medium in itself. Nevertheless, adults should take care to supply young children with paper in its myriad forms so they can truly discover its multiple uses.

Paper made expressly or primarily for art includes watercolor paper, finger-paint paper, drawing paper, sketch pads, craft paper, construction paper, tissue paper, rice paper, crepe paper, cellophane (plain and colored), and foil. Many of these art papers come in different grades and qualities. Scrap paper that can be employed toward artistic ends includes newsprint, magazines and catalogs, cardboard, paper towels and paper-towel tubes, toilet paper, egg cartons, lined and graph paper, grocery bags, wrapping paper and gift bags, paper plates and cups, paper napkins, cartons and boxes, greetings cards, and outdated calendars. (For more ideas on the types of paper to include in the classroom, see "Creating a Learning Environment for Art," pp. 67–69).

Young Children and Paper

Most early childhood programs provide paper for children to use as a background surface, but rarely do program staff consider paper as a medium for shaping and structuring. The learning potential of paper is almost never fully exploited, even though paper's diverse properties can provide children with key experiences in multiple domains. The ease with which paper is manipulated allows children to explore paper at their own developmental level and pursue their own interests. Paper is an excellent medium for promoting small-motor development and eye-hand coordination. It can also be transformed in weight and resistance, making it a good facilitator of children's large-motor development. Because of its physical properties, working with paper also promotes perceptual and sensory development in young children. The fact that paper is inexpensive and plentiful means that adults need not inhibit children's natural inclination to experiment with materials. All these factors make young children and paper an ideal match.

Paper also serves as a vehicle for developing early literacy and numeracy skills. When paper is used as a writing surface, children intentionally create letters and numbers on it. They may also inadvertently encounter written characters when they use scrap paper for artistic ends.

Finally, the waste of paper can be the focus of simple discussions about social responsibility. Scrap paper, like other found materials, can be a concrete starting point for introducing concerns about the environment. Through these discussions, children can acquire basic concepts and establish a foundation for exploring more complex ecological issues as their thinking develops. In sum, because paper is so universal and so versatile, early childhood programs should routinely consider using it as an art medium.

The In-Depth Studio Approach With Paper

The three programs described in this chapter each offered children an in-depth studio experience with paper. In Program A, which is described at length, the main focus was on art paper, that is, paper made exclusively or primarily for use as a visual medium. Programs B and C were shorter sequences that focused on recycling, that is, paper as a found material. In Program B, the children used existing scrap paper as their medium. In Program C, the children recycled scrap paper to make their own handmade paper. Each of these programs is described in terms of the four components of the in-depth studio approach: introduction, enrichment, production, and reflection.

For additional examples of the in-depth studio approach with this versatile medium, see the videotape *Supporting Young Artists: Exploring and Creating with Paper* (Trimis, 1997).

PROGRAM A: ART PAPER

1) Introduction

Program A was a preschool setting in a small village. The aim of the in-depth approach in this instance was to acquaint children with the properties of paper and the actions and results of its transformation. The teacher began with the plainest and most familiar types of paper and gradually introduced more luxurious and exotic types. At first children worked only with their hands, experiencing the tactile qualities of paper. Later, they proceeded to using various tools.

The Children in Program A had experienced only small-sized newsprint, craft paper, and construction paper. In all these instances, the paper had been used as a surface for drawing and painting. At no point had the children worked with larger paper or papers of different qualities, and never had they used paper as a medium in its own right.

To begin the introductory process, the teacher created an exhibit with a large variety of paper and paper products, including newspapers, magazines, paper napkins, grocery bags, notebooks, paper plates and cups, small and large boxes, glazed paper, craft paper, wrapping paper, cellophane, and tissue paper. The children were intrigued by the exhibit. They commented on the material, touched it, moved the items around, and tried looking through some of the transparent paper. They talked about the use of each item, as well as the paper products they had at home, the ones they saw in the stores, and those they saw advertised on television.

At the teacher's suggestion, the children started looking around

Children explore familiar items made of paper.

to identify all the paper products in their own classroom and went outside to find things made out of paper in the schoolyard and the neighborhood. The teacher explained that paper came from trees and talked about how paper is produced. The children did not seem interested in this information, but they remained excited about examining all the types of paper in the exhibit and in their immediate environment. Each child then chose one type of paper and used it as a drawing surface for crayons and marking pens, a familiar activity for this group. At the teacher's suggestion, the children agreed to bring in a newspaper and one other paper product the next day. Parents were asked to help their children find these items at home and bring them to school. The children brought in paper milk cartons, a paper carnival hat, and greeting cards and added them to the classroom exhibit.

Tearing, crumpling, and folding are typical actions in children's early explorations with newspaper.

In another corner of the room, the teacher had posted large magazine advertisements with photographs of paper products. The class took a walk to a nearby supermarket and observed the large variety of paper products there, trying to find some that matched items in the classroom exhibit. At first, the children focused on items made entirely of paper—newspapers, magazines, grocery bags, writing tablets, and so on. Later, several students noticed that paper was used to wrap other products, such as chewing gum, chocolate, juice, eggs, and laundry detergent.

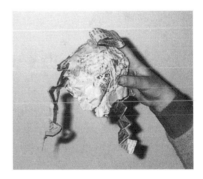

On the day after the field trip, the teacher spread large and small pieces of newspaper all over the tables and floor. She even hung some on the walls and from the ceiling. The teacher told the children to take a piece of newspaper and do anything they wanted with it. Some children pretended to read their newspapers, others threw it in the air, still others wore it on their heads. After a while, many children began to explore the newspaper by transforming it in different ways. As they manipulated the paper, the teacher labeled their actions with comments such as, "Akimi is folding her newspaper" or "I see that Justin is tearing his paper."

At outside time, the teacher and children carried sheets of newspaper to the yard. They created different movement games with the paper—throwing it into the air and catching it; spreading several sheets on the ground and jumping from sheet to sheet; running around and in between the sheets of paper; crumpling the newspaper into balls; rolling the balls and playing catch; tearing the paper and listening to the sounds; squashing the paper into different shapes and making up funny names for the shapes; balancing the newspaper on their heads and trying to walk without letting the paper fall down. As they invented each of these games, children were simultaneously learning about paper's many properties.

In the classroom the next day, each child took another sheet of newspaper. Children worked on the floor or at the tables, alone or in small groups. They continued to explore the newspaper by using only their hands and fingers, tearing the paper and trying to fold it into different shapes. One child commented that it was easier to fold a big shape than a small one, because the paper "was too hard when it got little." Children began attaching labels to some of the things they were making: an arrow, an airplane, a missile, a broom, and a castle. They tried to see if the arrow, the airplane, and the missile would fly. A few children spread their pieces next to one another on the floor and said they were making a paper puzzle.

The teacher and children unrolled a large sheet of white craft paper on the floor. The teacher gave the children glue and suggested they attach their constructions to the craft paper. One girl glued a crumpled ball to the surface, glued torn strips of paper around it, and said she was making an octopus. Another glued an arrow to the backdrop, added a strip of paper around it, and called it a boat. Children glued kites, hats, and many unnamed shapes to the surface. When all the children were done glueing their items, the teacher told them they had made a "relief collage." They pinned the collage to the bulletin board and discussed how they made it.

The next day, the teacher brought out pieces of thin, white paper and gave each child a large sheet and a small sheet. She suggested they try out some of the same things they had done with the newspaper and/or come up with new things to do. Some children began to pleat and twist the paper, making wreaths and bracelets. Others tore the white paper into shapes and said they were skirts, birds, shoes, trees, and a dog's head. One girl created a crown and tore streamers that she glued to the points. She sang as she paraded around the room

Supporting Young Artists

A relief collage of craft paper and newspaper is made using only hands as tools.

wearing her crown. A boy tore long strips of paper, glued the ends to form a circle, looped them around his ears, and declared he had made earrings. As the children used up their sheets of white paper, the teacher set out more so they could continue exploring its properties.

All the children were absorbed in their work, actively problem solving as they tried to make the paper match their intentions. Some children wanted to make the paper stand alone and discovered that folding the paper made it stiffer and allowed it to balance on end. One child declared he had made "the wall of a house" and tore openings for a door and windows. He made a table in front of the wall, applying the same principles of folding and creasing to give the paper enough weight so it would stand. Another child tore paper into shapes of dishes and apples and asked if he could put these on the table. Yet another child

contributed by making chairs, twisting and curving the strips of paper to make comfortable armchairs "like Grandpa sits in." Throughout these explorations, the teacher circulated around the room. She commented on what children were doing,

Children solve structural problems with paper.

called their attention to what their peers were doing, supplied words and labels when children asked, and occasionally posed questions when she was confident they would not distract children from pursuing their own investigations.

2) Enrichment

Children had spent many days exploring these two types of paper, using their hands primarily and solving various problems. The teacher decided they were now ready for an enrichment experience that would allow them to use simple tools and solve more complex problems. She brought out scissors, staplers, tape, rulers, and glue (which they had used before). Then she suggested that those who wanted to could use the newspaper and white paper, as well as the tools, to make something they could wear.

After exploring paper with only their hands, children begin to transform it with tools.

Children spread their papers on the floor. Many announced in advance their intention to make specific items of clothing—hats, crowns, aprons, hoods, skirts, capes, overcoats, pants, belts, and purses. In addition to garments, children created birds with tails, teeth, bracelets, rings, flowers, baskets, and snowmen. Some announced they were making "designs" rather than recognizable objects. And some children working with papers were unconcerned about making anything at all. Throughout their work, children applied the paper techniques they had acquired in the preceding days. They also incorporated the familiar tools, adapting them in new ways with the paper materials. The children wrapped, folded, tore, cut, covered, and measured the paper. Several children decided to decorate their creations and fetched crayons and markers. Many engaged spontaneously in dramatic play as they wore the paper clothing or moved their animals through the air and along the ground.

Following the children's interests and questions, the teacher added more tools and introduced them to new construction techniques.

Some children represent familiar objects; others choose to make designs.

For example, some of the children were interested in making objects of greater volume, so the teacher helped them mix a solution of glue and water to make papier-mâché and showed them how to layer the paper. Other children wanted to experiment with color and design, so she provided them with additional drawing and painting materials. Still others were curious about ways to manipulate and strengthen the paper by hand, so the teacher helped them investigate various techniques for folding, pleating, and weaving the paper into sturdy shapes. Finally, as the children gained in familiarity with the properties of newspaper and plain white paper, the teacher put out an increasing variety of paper—cardboard, construction paper, cellophane, tissue paper, and crepe paper.

The teacher provided further enrichment with books and photographs. She read a book about a "strange bird" and the children interpreted the story with collages. With help from their parents, children brought in boxes and the teacher introduced the idea of dioramas. She brought in slides showing the work of the artist Joseph Cornell, and the children talked about the diorama-like constructions he made inside his "magical boxes." The teacher talked about how this artist incorporated many different types of materials in expressing his ideas and conveying his emotions. She said Cornell and many other artists were interested in reusing and recycling materials in their art. The children talked about how they were recycling the newspapers, magazines, greeting cards, food boxes, and other paper items in their own art. As the teacher enriched the children's knowledge with each of these ideas, the children simultaneously used the growing assortment of papers and tools to make their own strange birds, dioramas, and other creations.

3) Production

Children found the paper so versatile and intriguing that they began making products almost immediately. As noted above, their work with newspaper and plain white paper had resulted in clothing, animals, houses, furniture, flowers, boats, and designs. The discovery of each new type of paper or tool during the enrichment phase led to a preliminary phase of exploration. Soon, however, the children used their cumulative knowledge to create more elaborate objects and structures. They created things for their own sake and also used them in their dramatic play.

A turning point seemed to occur when the teacher introduced cardboard. The rigidity of the material inspired the children to produce more permanent constructions. The size of many of the cardboard boxes alone suggested ideas to the children. They stacked them vertically or aligned them horizontally. They created spaces for moving in and out of and for hiding—houses, tents, huts, shops, and caves. They disassembled the boxes and reassembled them for their structures, measured walls and doors, and used various fastening techniques. In addition to flat pieces of cardboard, the children used heavy paper tubes. The cylinders became tunnels and towers or legs to support the flat pieces. Children crawled into some of the big cylinders and used their bodies to make them roll on the floor. They tried moving alone and in pairs.

A group of children collaborated on making a clothing store. They used cardboard to make the structure and then collected some of the clothing the children had made earlier to sell in their store. Several children became increasingly interested in making more clothing, this time by incorporating the wider variety of types of paper and decorative elements. Because of the children's interest in embellishment, the teacher told them that some stores specialized in

The rigidity of cardboard inspires children to make more permanent structures.

Children make clothing and "accessories" of paper.

"accessories," which she defined as things we use to add decoration to the clothes we wear. The children then began to make belts, bracelets, rings, purses, flowers, pendants, umbrellas, masks, and other decorative items they could wear. They also decided to have a fashion show. Some children modeled the clothing and accessories they made, others sang or played music, and a few decided they would be the photographers who took pictures for the magazines.

Reading the book about the strange bird led to yet another type of production. Children were intrigued by the use of cellophane paper in the book's collages and made their own birds and other flying creatures—butterflies, bees, and so on. As they worked with the cellophane, they held it up repeatedly to the light to see how the overlapping papers created different colors. This led to the creation of mobiles so their artwork could hang in the air and continually catch the light in different ways. The children used yarn,

Inspired by a book about a strange bird, children make mobiles with cellophane and crepe paper.

string, hole punches, tape, and other tools to create their mobiles. They hung them in front of the windows and commented on the changing colors.

After seeing the slides by Joseph Cornell and learning about dioramas, several children chose to make dioramas of their own. The children planned them very carefully and announced that the subjects of their dioramas would be the bottom of the sea, shop windows, and houses. The children made objects out of different kinds of paper, measured things to see if they would fit, and arranged and rearranged the items in the box. Four children collaborated on the underwater diorama. They made fish, weeds, and a sunken treasure boat, included shells from the science area, and collected small pebbles from the school yard. Another group of children worked together on the interior of a house. They cut holes for the doors and windows, made furniture, drew little pictures to hang on the wall, and added small figures of people to represent a family that would live in the house. Yet another group made a bus that required making windows, cutting out wheels, and making passengers. They took the bus into the block area and made roadways and bridges. Then they took turns driving the bus around.

As children made buildings and other structures with sheets of cardboard, boxes, and other paper products, the classroom took on the feel of a village. The teacher explained how architects and urban planners make *maquettes* (small models) before they spend time and money building the real things. She asked them to close their eyes and try to remember the streets, houses, and shops in their own village. The children spoke about the features that made their village special, including the Byzantine tower in the middle of the square and the boats along the seashore. Many of the children decided to create a maquette to represent their village and used all of the materials and tools they had investigated over the preceding weeks. The children talked about who would make the

Children make a maquette (small model) of their village.

different structures in the village. Some of the children made the houses, and some made the shops. One girl made the tower. Other children cut strips for roads, tore blue strips to make the "wavy water," or added boats and fish. The construction of the maquette was the culminating production of the in-depth approach with paper. It allowed the children to draw on all of their experiences and use them to represent something special to them—their home.

4) Reflection

Opportunities were plentiful for the children to remember and reflect on their experiences throughout their in-depth work with paper. In the very beginning, when the children saw the varied display of paper in their classroom, their teacher encouraged them to think about familiar paper products in their homes and communities. The field trips to the yard and the supermarket encouraged them to observe and talk even more about the presence of paper in their everyday lives. On their own, several children had the insight that some products were made entirely of paper, while other types of materials were wrapped in paper.

After the children had explored newspaper for several days and made a relief collage, the teacher facilitated their recall by hanging the collage on the wall. As the children looked at the items they had glued to the surface, they were encouraged to remember what they wanted to do with the paper and how they made the various items. Children remembered tearing, folding, poking, and crumpling the newspaper. The teacher repeated their words and supplied additional words to describe their actions—creasing, twisting, and wrapping. She encouraged the children to pick up fresh sheets of newspaper and compare the unaltered pages with the transformed ones. The children observed that the original sheets were larger, softer, and flatter and that it was easier to read the letters because they weren't "all smooshed up." Later, when the children compared the newspaper to the thin white paper, they commented that the latter was skinnier, had no letters, and did not leave black marks all over their hands when they played with it. However, they reported being able to carry out many of the same activities with both types of paper.

A teacher's interest encourages children to describe what they did with the paper.

Throughout the enrichment phase, children were continually reviewing and talking about their experiences, for example, by sharing the various ways they solved problems to make their cardboard constructions. They talked about how they leaned one piece against another, how they attached the walls of their structures using various fastening devices, and how they had to coordinate their movements when they attempted to roll in pairs inside the giant cardboard cylinders. Looking at books and photographs of artwork made from paper encouraged the children to reflect on the intentions and techniques of other artists. The work of Joseph Cornell, in particular, inspired children to think about the "magical boxes" they could create and to talk about why the themes and contents were meaningful to them.

Creating the maquette was perhaps the ultimate recall experience. Planning and constructing a model of their village helped children to visualize and recall salient features of their daily lives. In addition to thinking about the structures and activities that made their village special to them, children recalled all their experiences with paper. They remembered the properties of different kinds of paper and the techniques they used to transform them. The children had to recall and apply these memories to represent the familiar images of their environment.

Finally, to facilitate recall and review at each stage of the in-depth process, the teacher made sure to display the children's work following each experience. The work was left out for an extended period of time so children could review what they had done and share it with peers and family members. Seeing their own work helped the children remember, describe, and think about their actions and the resulting effects. Seeing the work of others inspired children to try out new ideas—not to copy, but to extend their own investigations. The result was a unique opportunity for young children to acquaint themselves with paper as a versatile medium for artistic expression.

PROGRAM B: SCRAP PAPER

1) Introduction

Program B was implemented in a preschool center located in an urban setting. The purpose of the in-depth program was to introduce children to the recycling of scrap paper as an art material. In addition to being able to invent new ways of using paper, the experience was an opportunity for the children to learn that creation does not always require expensive store-bought materials.

The children in Program B had tried tearing newspapers once a few months earlier, but had not had any other experience with this material. Their initial explorations grew out of a class field trip to the zoo—the children were very interested in animals. The teacher asked parents to help children bring in newspapers, magazines, greeting cards, grocery bags, catalogs, and other unwanted paper items from home. The children enjoyed sorting the materials (into piles of newsprint versus glossy paper, and so on) and seeing the piles of paper grow. When the volume and variety were great enough, the children began looking through the paper for pictures of animals they had seen at the zoo and other animals they were familiar with. Some of the papers had letters as well as pictures. There were pictures of single animals and animal families; some showed only the animals, while others showed the animals in the places where they lived.

After a trip to the zoo, children make a collage of animal pictures on different types of paper.

The next day, children cut out the animals and arranged them on large sheets of construction paper. The teacher told them they were making a collage. The children became aware of the differences between black-and-white images versus those in color and commented on the textures of the different types of paper, from smooth and shiny catalogs to coarser advertising circulars. They paid attention to size, noticing that the newspapers came in large sheets while the greeting cards were small. The children compared all these qualities as they arranged their cut-out animals on the construction paper. Some children wanted to leave spaces between their pictures so each animal would stand out. Other children liked the effect of overlapping the images in the collage. All of the children enjoyed using glue to attach the pictures and complete the collage. With the teacher's help, they hung the collage on the wall and eagerly showed it to their parents at the end of the day and at many drop-off and pick-up times thereafter.

On the following day, the teacher began to tear, fold, and crease some of the newspaper. She suggested that the children take sheets of newspaper and see how they could change them into something different. Children spread out their newspapers on the floor, tables, and

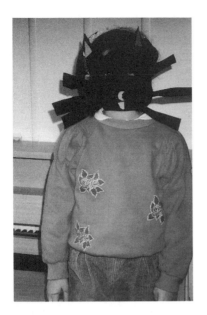

A girl attaches ears and whiskers to her kitty mask.

The teacher extends children's explorations by demonstrating twisting, rolling, and pleating.

chairs. Some looked at the papers and pretended to read them. Others balanced them on their heads or wrapped them around their bodies. Soon the children started to transform the newspaper. They tore it into strips and small pieces. They crumpled, folded, and shredded it. A few children continued with the animal theme, announcing they were making a monkey or dog or tearing strips for the "kitty's whiskers." Some children represented other familiar objects with the newspaper, such as a house or a boat. Most just explored the material without the intention of representing anything.

When the children had been exploring the newspaper for a while, the teacher modeled some other ways to alter its appearance—by twisting, rolling, or pleating. Several children imitated these actions and then proceeded to invent new transformations. The teacher commented on their actions and offered labels to describe their movements and the results. Children supplied their own words and readily talked to the teacher and their peers about what they were doing. The teacher told the children they could work with as many sheets of newspaper as they wanted. Some chose to work repeatedly with one or two sheets, seeing how many different ways they could progressively alter the same piece. Others were excited by the abundance of materials and enjoyed surrounding themselves with this moving and rustling substance.

2) Enrichment

After the children had been introduced to the basic properties of newspaper, the teacher suggested they could use paint, brushes, and other familiar materials with their newspapers. Most of the children chose to paint their paper, using water-soluble paints and large brushes to change its color. As they transformed the newspaper,

Supporting Young Artists

the children noticed that painting on a twisted or crumpled piece of paper resulted in a different effect than did stroking a brush against a flat surface. When the newspaper dried, the children felt it and talked about how the paint made it feel stiffer or gave it bumps. A few children tore their papers into long strips and painted

Children discover the effect of wind on paper streamers.

them different colors. They danced around the room waving their "streamers" behind them.

For those children who seemed particularly interested in color, the teacher made sure there was an ample supply of magazines, catalogs, and similar paper products. The children used these to create flat collages and then relief collages. Many then proceeded to make masks and clothing. Through their own investigations, the children had progressed from making two-dimensional representations to creating in three-dimensional space.

To further extend the children's experiences with recycled paper, the teacher and a group of parents took the children to see a nearby exhibit by the Greek artist Pavlos. This artist uses scrap paper to make clothes, flags, and large architectural installations. The children saw several environmental constructions, including a forest, furniture, clothing, shop windows, and baskets of fruit, all made of recycled paper. They were excited to see so many familiar objects and environments made of the same materials they had been using in the classroom and were encouraged to move around the constructions. The children observed closely and asked many questions of the museum's art educator. They decided that many of the objects looked like toys and games. Back in the classroom, the children created many similar objects inspired by the exhibit. They made environments that they could crawl in and out of, fashioned fanciful toys out of paper, and invented games with them.

The class visits an exhibit by the Greek artist Pavlos, who uses scrap paper to make large installations.

The work of Pavlos inspires children to make structures they can crawl in and out of.

3) Production

Each enrichment experience was accompanied by children's production. After cutting out animal pictures and exploring the properties of different kinds of paper, the children were eager to make their own

Children interested in design make rugs and blankets.

animals. In two- and three-dimensional representations, they made snakes, a baby turtle and a giant turtle, a bird, a butterfly, and a mother cat with lots of kittens. They drew and painted on their constructions, or used other pieces of paper to decorate them. After exploring colored scrap paper, several children became very interested in the elements of design. They cut out strips and shapes and arranged them on a flat surface to make "rugs" and "blankets." The children used paint to add their own colors to these creations.

For other children, working with magazines and catalogs led to an interest in making brightly colored masks and clothing. They used scrap paper to create and decorate their masks, adding other materials (feathers and beads, and so on) for further embellishment. The children who made items of apparel created capes and hats. They used crayons, paint, and markers to add more color and detail. The children wore their masks and clothing as "disguises" and their

Supporting Young Artists

dress-up activities soon led to other dramatic play activities.

Finally, after the visit to the Pavlos exhibit, there was a change in the scale and content of many of the children's productions. In some instances, the works were much larger. These productions had an environmental quality and allowed the children to move freely through the spaces they created. Some children were inspired to extend their work with clothing and started making items they had seen in the exhibit, such as socks and ties. They tried to remember similar articles of clothing worn by family members and decorated their creations accordingly.

After the Pavlos exhibit, children collaborate to produce works on a large scale.

4) Reflection

The teacher in Program B incorporated opportunities for reflection throughout the children's work with paper. For example, when the children initially looked for animal pictures in the papers brought from home, they recalled the animals they had seen at the zoo, as well as other familiar animals. They reflected on the sizes, shapes, and colors of the animals and imitated how the animals walked. They talked about what the animals ate, whether they smelled, and the sounds they made. The children remembered which animals liked to play and which ones just slept or stared from their enclosures. Most of the children decided they preferred being with the real animals instead of just looking at their pictures.

Each time the children created things with paper—animals, clothes, masks, or crawling spaces—the teacher displayed the work for several days thereafter. Having this work in view encouraged the children to discuss their activities, describe the results, and make plans for further investigation and production. Viewing the Pavlos exhibit prompted a great deal of discussion at the museum and the conversations continued afterwards in the classroom. The teacher got special permission to take pictures at the museum exhibit so the children would have a visual representation of the experience. As they worked, some of the children would refer to the pictures to compare their productions with those of the artist. The teacher also took pictures of the children's work to put on the bulletin board and to send home. As a result of these diverse experiences with scrap paper, the children's ideas about how to use this material were forever transformed.

PROGRAM C: HANDMADE PAPER

1) Introduction

Program C was located in a village outside the city where Program B was situated. For this in-depth studio experience, the children's experience with scrap paper was extended to recycling that paper to make more paper. In the past, paper was handmade, but most people today, including most artists, work with manufactured papers. However, the possibilities for achieving unusual textures, blending complex colors, and creating sculptural forms have inspired a growing cadre of fiber artists to elevate handmade paper to an art form, and making and manipulating handmade paper is experiencing renewed interest.

"Basically, papermaking is a process of reducing fibers (strong threads of material) to a pulpy state and then gathering that pulp into a flat sheet" (Wilkinson, 1997, p. 8). Most inexpensive papers like newsprint, napkins, paper towels, and tissues are made by grinding wood pulp and treating it chemically. "By contrast, hand-crafted paper has a soft and rich appearance and doesn't contain as many chemicals as machine-made paper" (Wilkinson, 1997, p. 8).

Papermaking is an easy process and one that young children find intriguing. To make paper, the following materials are needed:

- Scrap paper that is easily dissolved and has not been treated with plastic coatings (newspapers, napkins, paper towels, uncoated paper plates and cups, magazines, and so on)

- Bucket with water

- Plastic basin

- Blender or old electric mixing machine

- Screens or sieves on wood frames (old window screening)

- Trays (to balance the screens on and catch dripping water)

- Sheets of porous material

- Large sheets of plastic to spread on the floor (or work outside)

- Sponges to wipe up spills

- Materials to add color to the paper (cinnamon, coffee, pepper, vegetable dyes, paints, and so on)

- Materials to add texture to the paper (sand, dried leaves, pine needles, thread, confetti, and so on)

The initial phase of Program C was aimed at introducing children to all the ways they and their families use paper. As in Program B, the teacher in Program C had made an exhibit of many types of familiar paper. She asked the children whether they had these types of papers at home and how they were used. Children offered comments such as "My daddy reads the newspaper in the morning" or "My brother cuts out pictures of his favorite singers from the magazine and puts them on the wall over his bed" or "My mommy sees the ads and buys things for the garden." The teacher asked the children what happened when they were done with the papers, and the children talked about ways they were reused, recycled, or just thrown away in the trash.

Some of the children said they wanted to make their own newspaper. They got plain sheets of paper and "wrote" articles and advertisements. A few children drew pictures to represent photographs. One child said a newspaper needed "lines" and got a ruler to mark the columns. The teacher and children tacked the newspaper on the bulletin board and eagerly showed it to the parents. Over the next several days, several of the children made more newspapers. Others decided to explore the papers in the exhibit and did many of the same things with newspapers and magazines that were described in Program B. A few children in Program C scrunched up the paper into balls and invented a catching game with elaborate rules. They remembered many of the rules the next day and continued to modify the rules as the game evolved during the week. On the third day, as the children were tossing the paper balls in the air, the teacher started to play a tambourine. The children began throwing the balls to match the beating of the tambourine. They took turns beating the tambourine while their peers tossed the paper balls to one another, threw them up in the air, and rolled them along the floor and under the furniture.

2) Enrichment

When children had been exploring scrap paper for a couple of weeks, the teacher reintroduced the question about how these papers could be used. Now, in addition to talking about "reading the news" or "learning things," the children said things like "we can make things with paper" or "we can play games." They proceeded to do just that, creating and decorating many objects and environments or continuing to evolve their ball game.

At the end of class each day, the teacher asked the children to help her gather up bits and pieces of leftover paper. The children made a game of it and eagerly collected paper scraps and put them into a large carton. After a couple of days of collecting bits of paper, the teacher asked if any children wanted to tear up larger sheets of paper into little pieces. Many of the children became involved in tearing up the newspapers, magazines, and other scrap paper. They filled several cartons over the next few days. The children enjoyed plunging their hands into the paper bits, making them fly up into the air, spreading them on the floor, rolling in them, and re-gathering them into the cartons.

When enough paper had accumulated, the teacher announced that the next day they were going to make their own paper. To begin, she asked the children to put a pile of paper pieces into a basin, fill a bucket with water, and then pour the water over the paper in the basin. She said they would let the paper "soak" overnight. The next day, the children were fascinated by the pulpy mass in the basin. They noticed how the ink had run out and made the water dark. Using a sieve, the teacher and children drained off the dark water into the bucket. The teacher explained that they could not pour the water down the sink because the bits of paper that got through the sieve might clog up the drain. The children talked about these "itty bits pieces of paper" and emptied the bucket outside. In the next step, the children mixed the remaining paper pulp with a small amount of clean water and put the mixture in the blender. The teacher operated the blender, and as the children watched the blades whirl around, some children began to spin themselves in circles. The pulp was taken out of the blender, put in a basin, and stirred with some additional water.

The children spread large sheets of plastic on the floor. With the teacher's help, the children poured a thin layer of pulp onto a wood-framed screen and rested it on a tray to let the excess water drain out. They covered the pulp with a piece of porous material so it would finish drying slowly. Working alone, in pairs, and in small groups, the children continued to fill screens with thin layers of pulp and set them out to dry. The children checked the screens each day to observe the drying process. Soon, the pulp had dried into a sheet of paper with fine lines impressed by the screening material. Several of the children declared that they had done "magic!"

The children were eager to make more paper. They used the paper they had torn earlier and continued to tear more paper into small pieces. The teacher suggested they could also add color to the water or mix in other matter to change the paper's appearance. The children tried adding various natural and industrial materials. Through experimentation, they learned that natural coloring (such as coffee or spices) produced more subtle colors than paints. They discovered that smaller matter (such as sand, string, or pine needles) worked well, while larger materials (such as pebbles or twigs) did not always "set" in the finished paper. When their handmade paper was ready, some of the children displayed and kept it. Other children chose to use the paper as a starting point for drawing, painting, sculpting, and other activities.

3) Production

In Program C, production began as early as the introduction phase. For example, many of the children worked diligently to make newspapers, adding writing and pictures and ruled lines to represent its components. They also used newspapers to make balls. Although their initial discovery that paper could make a ball was serendipitous, they then deliberately made balls to play the game they invented. As in other programs that worked in depth with paper, the children in Program C also used paper to represent familiar

Children make a puppet theater.

things. They tore, cut, or rolled strips of paper to make umbrellas, canes, and the tails of mice and cats. Some children made hats and aprons and wore them during dramatic play. Children used paper to make baskets with eggs, trees and flowers, animals and people. Later, several children collaborated on more elaborate products. One group created a forest with trees, flowers, butterflies, picnic tables, and tiny ants. Another group of children made puppets and a puppet theater, painted them, and put on a puppet show for their friends.

For this program, of course, the most exciting experience was producing handmade paper. While the process itself was intriguing, many of the children were fascinated by the textural and colorful variations they produced by altering the ingredients. Children tried to reproduce effects they had initially achieved by accident. For example, one child liked the coarse texture produced by adding sand to the water. She altered the amount of sand to produce different degrees of roughness. Other children set out to achieve certain colors, either because they liked the aesthetics of a color or because they intended to use the resulting paper for a particular purpose. One boy added blue so the paper could serve as the water for his boat; another child mixed several shades of green before deciding on the one that would be "just right" for her leaves.

4) Reflection

The children engaged in reflection about paper use and production throughout this program. Initially, they talked about the types of papers they had at home, how they were used, and how they were disposed of. Later, after the children had explored the scrap paper, the teacher revisited these questions with them. This time, the children recalled all the additional ways they had used paper in the classroom, for example, by making familiar objects and playing games.

As children invented the game with the paper balls, they remembered (or tried to remember) rules from one day to the next. If the children forgot a rule or found it was not working, they made up a new one or modified an existing one. The interplay between inventing and applying the rules was consistent. Sometimes, the children's debates about the rules took precedence over playing the game, but the attraction of the paper always drew them back.

The fascination of the papermaking process stimulated a great deal of observation and discussion. In making their own paper, children had to recall all the steps and carry them out in sequence. When they strove for particular color or textural effects, many evaluated the result to see if they had achieved their plan or needed to modify their actions.

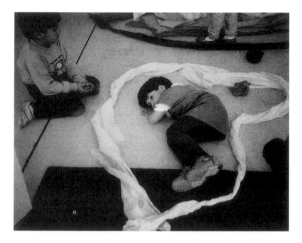

Children use paper to represent the environment and to create the environment itself.

Perhaps because observed changes were so striking in this case—a cycle that went from paper to a mushy mess and back to paper—the children were especially encouraged to reflect on the process of transformation with this art form. Finally, as in all in-depth programs, displaying the children's work prompted them to recall, explain, and discuss their experiences with peers and family members. The act of reflection in turn inspired the children to develop and try out new visual ideas with paper.

Programs A, B, and C all gave young children an opportunity to expand the limits that define the uses of paper. They were able to see paper from new perspectives, observe its transformation, exploit the qualities they discovered accidentally, and use the material in a deliberate fashion to carry out their intentions. The playful manner in which children investigated paper was much like that of adult artists. The aesthetic value of their judgments and products was impressive. The children engaged in problem solving with the material and expressed thoughts and emotions. They explored formal artistic properties such as color, texture, transparency, line, form, rhythm, balance, symmetry, and composition. In the process of exploring this art medium, they also engaged in virtually every other social, emotional, and cognitive key experience. The range of experiences offered by paper's versatility shows clearly the value of in-depth exploration with a single medium. "Many important aesthetic experiences come from continued, deepening involvement with very simple materials. Compositions may be created, not only out of different stuffs, but also out of the different possibilities of one stuff" (Chandler, 1973, p. 90).

9

Plastic Materials

Seventeen-month-old Martin rolls a ball of pink play dough between his hands. He smells it, then licks it. After squeezing the ball of dough, Martin looks at the impressions made by his fingers. He then puts the ball down and reaches for a string of yellow dough that is lying on the table. With one hand at each end, Martin stretches the string of dough. Holding it up to his neck, he looks at Paul, his caregiver, as if to say, "See the necklace I made?" Paul smiles at Martin and says, "Shall we show this to Daddy?" Martin nods, and Paul gently sets the play dough "necklace" on a counter where children's work is displayed for parents to see at drop-off and pick-up time.

At small-group time, the teacher Joyce gives each child a wedge of clay and small plastic toys. Three-year-old Marigold forms a large mound with her clay. She presses in small plastic shapes—a star, a circle, a triangle—and pushes the mound in front of her friend Alice, the four-year-old sitting next to her. Marigold claps her hands and says, "I made a cake!" She begins to sing "Happy birthday to Alice, happy birthday to Alice." Joyce joins in. "I'm going to cut the cake," says Alice as she goes to the house area for a plastic knife. Bringing the knife back to the table, Alice cuts the cake into three pieces. "One for you" (giving a piece to Marigold), "one for you" (giving a piece to Joyce), "and a big one for me because it's my birthday!"

Plastic art materials are malleable substances that can be shaped and formed. The plastic arts are important in early childhood education because they are so tactile. Children can hold the material as they explore its properties and use their own hands as tools. They can transfer the energy from their hands and bodies directly to the materials.

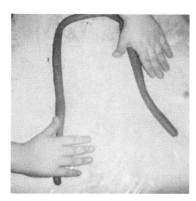

Children transfer energy from their bodies directly to clay and dough.

Plastic materials include clay and dough. (Paper pulp, described in Chapter Eight, can also be molded.) Although young children can use Plasticine and other commercial materials, High/Scope recommends that they work primarily with natural materials. As this chapter on clay and dough will explain, natural materials allow children to directly experience how they are made, how they feel, how they can be transformed, and how they can be used to make artistic statements.

A Brief History of the Use of Clay as an Art Medium

Put simply, clay is mud, the natural product of the geological weathering of the earth's surface. "Clay forms when the finest particles of soil settle out on top of the larger and heavier ones" (Koster, 1999, p. 18). Clay is abundant in our environment, covering much of the earth's surface. Along with being a natural material, clay also can be considered a found material. Often, clay is transported by water and found on the banks of bodies of water. It is inherently ecological, coming from and returning to the earth without destroying other resources or causing pollution. Clay's availability, low cost, and ease of manipulation make it a popular medium. Dug from the moist earth, it is ready to be worked by the artist's hands. "Clay is a deceptively simple material. It keeps forever and improves with age" (Rhodes, 1974, p. xvii).

Clay is one of the earliest materials used to make art. People in different cultures throughout the world have found ways to express themselves through its unique properties. Art and natural history museums are filled with ancient and contemporary objects made of clay: statues,

The medium of clay connects children to the art of their cultures and communities.

figurines, furniture, sarcophagi, jars and jugs, vases, jewelry, cups and bowls, toys, bricks and tiles, cooking pots, and drain pipes. Ceramics made of clay and dating back thousands of years have been discovered in archeological digs. (Rhodes defines ceramics as "the art of making permanent objects of usefulness and/or beauty by the heat treatment of earthy raw materials" [1974, p. xix].) Because it is such a universal medium, clay is an excellent vehicle for connecting children to the arts of their cultures and communities.

As an art medium, clay is extremely versatile. Artifacts of permanence, beauty, and utility—ranging from small, delicate objects to massive architectural forms—can be created with clay. The basic techniques for working with clay have remained unchanged for centuries and are easily re-created in the classroom.

Characteristics of Clay

GENERAL CHARACTERISTICS

The main characteristics of clay are softness, moistness, and extreme plasticity. "Clay comes in many colors, depending on the kind of rock particles and other materials in the soil. There are white clays and red clays and gray and tan clays" (Koster, 1999, p. 18). As a utilitarian medium and as an art medium, clay can be transformed in myriad ways—pounded, flattened, pinched, rolled, coiled, pressed, modeled, engraved, scored, cut, or stamped. It can be shaped by hand, worked on the wheel, or cast in molds. Once shaped, clay can be left raw or dried and fired (baked). Although clay objects are fragile and easily broken, fired clay itself is relatively indestructible. A piece of pottery may break, but "its fragments will remain unchanged for thousands of years even when buried in damp soil or immersed in water" (Rhodes, 1974, p. 15).

Clay shrinks with drying and firing, due to the loss of moisture. It loses between five and eight percent of its volume, depending on the amount of water in the clay, the humidity of the surrounding atmosphere, and the overall size of the object. If clay dries too rapidly, the moisture loss will be uneven and may cause warping or cracking, especially when the object is fired in the kiln. To avoid such deformations, clay should be covered and allowed to dry slowly.

Rhodes (1974) summarizes the *stages of drying and firing clay* as follows:

- When initially worked and still moist, clay is considered *plastic.*

- When shrinkage due to drying is complete, clay is at the *leather-hard stage.* In this state, the clay is firm enough to be picked up without bending or losing its shape.

- When all of the moisture is out of the clay, it is called *greenware* and is ready to be fired in either a gas or electric kiln. (A word of caution: If there is any moisture left in the clay, it may explode in the kiln.)

- After the first firing, when clay is bone dry, it is called *bisqueware.* The kiln must be cooled gradually to prevent the clay from cracking. The clay pots can be left as they are at this point or they can be glazed.

- If the clay is glazed, it goes through a second and hotter firing in the kiln. After a final and slow cooling, the glazed pot is waterproof (nonporous) and complete.

TYPES OF CLAY

Clay can be divided into two broad categories: primary and secondary. According to Rhodes, *primary clays* "have been formed on the site of their parent rocks and have not been transported, either by water, wind, or glacier" (1974, p. 11), while *secondary clay* "has been transported from the site of the original parent rock. Although water is the most common agent of transportation, wind and glaciers may also carry clay" (p. 12).

China clay is a primary clay that is rather scarce in nature. Deposits of this type of clay can be found in Europe, North America, and Asia. China clay is so named because it is used in the making of fine china and pure white porcelain. Secondary clays are finer-textured and highly plastic and are the ones most commonly used in schools. There are several types of secondary clay:

- *Ball clay* and *fire clay* are highly plastic secondary clays that are used in a variety of ceramic products. Large amounts are found in

Kentucky and Tennessee. They are mostly used for manufacturing pots, furnaces, and bricks.

- *Stoneware clay* is a secondary clay that varies in plasticity and color. In its natural state, it is usually a grey or buff color. Stoneware clays become vitreous (glasslike) at 1200–1300 degrees Fahrenheit. This clay is used to make heavy, nonporous pottery.

- *Earthenware, also called common clay,* is the kind most often found in nature. When raw, earthenware is reddish-brown, grey, or greenish, but it can also have a yellow ochre or black-brown color. The color depends on the minerals and other impurities the clay has picked up during transportation. (For example, iron in the clay imparts a reddish color.) When fired in the kiln, earthenware changes color and may end up pink, red, tan, brown, or even black, depending on the content of the clay and the firing process. Earthenware is used to make pottery, as well as bricks and tiling for floors, walls, and roofs.

Earthenware is the best type of clay to use with young children.

Earthenware is the best choice for introducing young children to clay. In fact, clay may be found in the vicinity of the school, especially if the program is located near a flowing body of water, such as a river. The denseness and plasticity of earthenware clay make it easy for children to work with, although in its natural element the presence of sand or rocky fragments may pose problems. Nevertheless, children will enjoy exploring this type of clay in the natural environment. Letting them dig the clay and work with it outside helps children understand the origins of this material.

For art projects in the classroom, schools generally purchase earthenware from ceramics suppliers or art supply catalogs. It comes in blocks or large plastic bags and is inexpensive. Clay purchased from suppliers is still natural, but it has been cleaned and restored to maximum plasticity. In addition, air pockets have been removed so the clay does not need to be "wedged," or kneaded, to remove the air. (Note: Unless the clay will be fired, which is generally not

Store clay in airtight plastic bags to retain moisture.

recommended for young children, air pockets need not be of concern in early childhood programs.) To make sure the children have a positive first experience, teachers should select clay that is neither too moist and sticky nor too dry and firm. Check the consistency by first trying to roll the clay into a coil or press it into a slab. If the clay sticks to the hands and cannot be shaped, it may be too moist and should be slightly dried out before use. If the clay cracks, then it is too dry and needs to be slightly re-moistened. To retain its humidity, clay should be stored in airtight bags, kept in moist cupboards, or placed in plastic bins with tight covers. The moisture of clay can be maintained for long periods of time if it is covered with wet fabric. Keeping a wet sponge in the bag or bin is another effective technique to keep clay from drying out.

Working With Clay

TOOLS AND SUPPLIES

Because of clay's tactile qualities, children should begin by working only with their hands—palms, fingers, fists, fingernails, and knuckles. Direct manipulation will enable children to feel changes in temperature, smoothness, and moisture. They can experience the clay as it progresses from cool to warm in their hands, soft to hard as they work with it, and wet to dry as air acts on it.

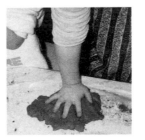

Children begin by exploring clay with their hands.

Once the children have manipulated the clay with all parts of their hands, they can begin to explore it with tools. A wide assortment of objects make effective tools for shaping, cutting, embedding, and creating impressions in clay. These include natural items, such as sticks, stones, shells, and leaves. Children can also use manufactured items, such as rolling pins, plastic eating utensils, kitchen tools, woodworking tools, hair ornaments, clothespins, and buttons. To introduce children to the world of art and convey that children are themselves artists, schools

Supporting Young Artists

Tools for exploring clay include natural and manufactured items.

may also want to purchase a small number of professional modeling tools made of wood, metal, and plastic. Children will often want to decorate their ceramics while they are still moist or paint them when they are dry. For these interests, children should have an ample supply of found materials and tempera paints and brushes. (See pp. 67–69 for more ideas on materials that promote modeling and sculpting.)

Finally, programs will need equipment for storing and working with the clay. As noted above, it is important to have the right containers and environment for keeping the clay moist (plastic bins with airtight covers, plastic sheets, damp cloths, storage cupboards, and so on.) Large sheets of plastic, oilcloth, tablecloths,

Provide ample display space for children's work in clay.

Individual Masonite or Formica boards make it easy to move clay to a drying area.

and tarps can serve as work spaces by covering floors and tables. Children will also need individual surfaces, such as pieces of Masonite or Formica, so they can work with the clay and then transport it to a drying area. Shelves, cupboards, and pedestals can provide space for allowing the covered clay to dry slowly and surfaces for displaying the finished products.

Firing clay

Firing their ceramics in a kiln is not recommended for young children. Letting the work dry is generally sufficient. As noted above, children learn a great deal about the process of transformation just by watching the stages of drying. They can see the clay change in color, hardness, and moisture level. Once the works are dry, children may want to paint theirs and take them home. If the clay objects break, adults may be surprised to discover that children are less upset than expected. In fact, many children seem to enjoy the problem-solving process of figuring out how to glue the pieces back together. Often, however, especially in the early stages of exploration, children do not want to keep what they make. As long as the clay has not been fired, it can be reused. Depending on how dry the clay is, it can be re-moistened by adding water to the storage container, putting wet sponges inside, and/or covering the clay with a damp cloth.

Further, as mentioned earlier, there is a danger in firing clay. Since children's works often dry unevenly or with air pockets, they are

Children can see clay change in color, hardness, and moisture level as it dries. Firing in a kiln is not recommended.

Supporting Young Artists

likely to explode in the kiln. Moreover, even if the clay were suitable for firing, early childhood programs rarely have a kiln available and transporting the work to a kiln off-site is not feasible, given the logistics and possibilities for breakage. In learning about clay, it is nevertheless valuable for children to experience this final step in the production process. A better option than firing the children's work is taking a field trip to a nearby ceramics studio. There the children can see a kiln and learn from a potter about how clay is fired. If possible, the teacher can ask the studio to have ceramics at different stages of firing so the children can see and feel the transformation in the clay.

Young Children and Clay

Despite the pervasiveness of ceramics in past times and cultures, children in today's society have limited opportunities to work with clay. Even in early childhood settings, an emphasis on cleanliness makes adults hesitant to let children fully experience the richness of this tactile medium. Yet when children are allowed to discover clay, their natural affinity for it becomes immediately apparent, as witnessed by the sight of children on the playground digging in the mud, patting mud pies, creating dams with stones, and drawing in the wet earth with sticks. That such a wonderful play material can also be an art medium is a revelation for adults and children alike.

Clay is a wonderful medium for promoting children's growth in virtually every realm of development. For example, active involvement with clay is a powerful affective tool. It enables young children to express their feelings, to work through anger, to radiate joy, and to act out a wide range of other emotions. "The more shapable or unstructured the material, the better to project feelings and ideas" (Cohen et al., 1983, p. 34). The malleability of clay fits this expressive condition. For young children in particular, clay can be emotionally and physically empowering. They can literally mold this amorphous material to their will and see it being transformed under the actions of their hands.

Clay is obviously a medium conducive to promoting large motor development, because working with clay calls forth a great deal of physical energy. Large muscles are engaged in pounding the clay, and children put their entire bodies behind working with the material. Clay also supports fine motor development and eye-hand coordination as children use their fingers and various modeling tools to fashion and

Working with clay develops perceptual-motor and cognitive skills.

decorate their work. The sensory properties of clay—weight, color, temperature, moisture, smell, texture—enhance young children's perceptual awareness.

As a social experience, clay spans the spectrum. Working with clay can be a quiet and private time as children immerse themselves in its sensations. Clay can also be a very sociable medium. Children may accompany their activity with descriptions of their actions and discoveries, or engage in tangential conversations that serve as a pleasant backdrop to the work of their hands.

The inherent ability of clay to transform itself engages children's thought processes. Cognitive constructs in spatial relations, temporal relations, classification, seriation, and so on are made concrete as children work with a mass of clay and see its appearance alter over time. There are rich opportunities for language development as children and adults converse about these changing states.

Clay lends itself to working individually or in groups.

Finally, clay as a medium makes a significant contribution to young children's aesthetic development. Like sculptors, they deal with issues of form and space when they model in three dimensions with clay. Opportunities to embellish the surface of the clay also engage them in principles of two-dimensional design. Clay provides a vehicle for connecting children to the art world of today as well as the artifacts of other times and cultures. They see that something can be both functional and visually gratifying. In the in-depth programs described in the rest of this chapter, children have an opportunity to discover all these properties of clay and its significance in their daily lives.

Supporting Young Artists

The In-Depth Studio Approach With Clay

In the following pages, two programs using an in-depth studio approach to working with clay are described. The first program began with children digging in the earth in their own school yard. The second program included a trip to the beach to observe imprints in the mud and wet sand. In both programs, the children visited a ceramics studio for a firsthand look at the process of preparing and working with clay. Throughout these experiences, the children were actively engaged in a cycle of introduction, enrichment, production, and reflection with clay.

For additional examples of the in-depth studio approach with plastic materials, see the videotapes *Supporting Young Artists: Exploring and Creating With Clay* and *Supporting Young Artists: Exploring and Creating With Dough* (Trimis, 2000a, 2000b).

PROGRAM A: SCHOOL-YARD MUD

1) Introduction

Program A was located in an urban area. The experience with plastic arts for children in this program was very limited, although they had worked with drawing and painting materials and had made some paper collages. The children were introduced to clay in the school's large yard. They carried buckets and shovels into the yard, began to dig in the earth, and mixed the earth with water to make mud. They varied the amount of water so they could experience different consistencies of mud. Initially, the children patted the mud into pies and cakes. Then they collected other natural materials from the yard, such as pebbles, pieces of wood, leaves, grass, and twigs. They added these decorative elements to the mud pies and then began to make more elaborate mud structures—castles and bridges.

Children dig clay in the school yard and combine it with other natural materials.

The next day, the teacher suggested that the children explore the creamy qualities of mud to see if they could use it like finger paint. She unrolled a long piece of white butcher paper on the floor. The children mixed mud with a large amount of water and used their hands (palms, fingers, knuckles, and so on) to paint with mud on the paper. There was a great deal of discussion as children compared their actions and effects with those of their peers. Drawing on their earlier collage experience, some of the children added the natural materials they had gathered the previous day to make a collage on the butcher paper. When the collage was completed, the teacher and the children hung it on the wall and eagerly shared it with family members who came to pick the children up at the end of the day.

Children finger-paint with a creamy paste made of clay.

Because of the soil composition and prevalence of rocks, the school-yard earth was not suitable for making clay. However, the teacher showed the children a videotape of clay being made from earth and said she would bring in clay the next day so they could begin working with it. On the following day, the teacher presented the children with a large block of earthenware clay. The children took lumps of clay and worked individually on Masonite boards. They began to explore the clay with their hands—fingers, palms, knuckles, and fists—and spontaneously compared its texture with that of the school-yard mud. The teacher worked alongside the children, imitating their actions and occasionally modeling new techniques. The children tried a wide variety of manipulations with their hands, including patting, pressing, rolling, bending, coiling, cutting, squeezing, pinching, poking, and stretching the clay. They worked individually, but chatted animatedly with peers in their small group. After a while, the children started to model

Children decorate clay with leaves, pebbles, and twigs.

their clay into forms, making coils and stick figures. Some of the children decorated their figures with the pebbles, sticks, and other natural materials they had collected in the yard. Using the Masonite boards, the children carried their work to empty shelves the teacher had set up near the doorway for drying and displaying their work.

The teacher and children also collected some of the leftover clay and put it in water overnight. On the following day, the children were surprised to discover how the clay had absorbed so much water and become very liquid. The teacher told them that clay of this consistency was called *slip.* The children were eager to put their hands into the slip and found that it was like the very wet mud they had mixed in their school yard. Remembering the earlier experience, the children were eager to draw and paint with the slip. They got sheets of white butcher paper, dipped their fingers in the slip, and began to draw. Some of the children decided to paint with brushes on colored construction paper. They spread their papers on tables and across the floor. Many of them took their papers and

Children use brushes to paint with watery clay called "slip."

slip into the yard at outside time to continue their activities. Some children drew familiar figures, such as people, houses, animals, and flowers. Others made designs. Some used only the slip, while others incorporated natural materials into their work.

2) Enrichment

A week after the children had begun to work with clay, the teacher arranged a visit to a local potter's workshop. The potter began by showing the children how he stored the clay and by talking about the importance of keeping it moist. The children shared with the potter their own adventures mixing earth and clay with water. Next, the potter showed the children how he prepared the clay, wedging it to knock out all the air bubbles. The children were eager to try wedging the clay themselves and enjoyed testing their strength as they pushed and pounded the clay. After showing them how to handbuild with the clay, the potter gave each child a lump of clay to do the same. ("Handbuild" means manipulating clay by hand as opposed to throwing it on a wheel or putting it in a mold. Ceramics made this way are called "handbuilt.")

After the children had tried handbuilding, the potter took them into another room and made a large vase on the potter's wheel. The children tried to make the wheel turn by themselves, but discovered it was too heavy. They much preferred handbuilding! All over the studio were racks holding pots at different stages of drying and firing. The children looked inside a big kiln, which the potter was filling with pots for a firing the next day, while the potter explained how he fired his pots twice, once before and once after glazing. The children were able to look at and touch the ceramics at each point of the process. With encouragement from the teacher and the potter, the children compared the temperature, moisture, texture, and color of the pots in their different stages of production. They were full of questions about the heat of the kiln and how the potter mixed and applied his glazes.

A local potter demonstrates a technique called "handbuilding."

Children create a variety of figures in the potter's studio.

After the children toured the studio, the potter sat them around his large table and gave each child a big lump of clay. The children had a wonderful time working with the clay, without having to worry about making a mess. They created human figures, houses, trees, coil pots, boats, cups, plates, and animals. Some of the children modeled vases and other shapes that were reminiscent of those they had seen in the potter's studio. The children carefully carried their creations to the potter's racks. The potter told them that after the pots dried, he would try to fire them in his kiln and bring them to the school the following week. Before the children left, he gave them a large bag of clay to take back to their classroom. In the following days, the children continued to work with this clay.

Families bring ceramics from home to create an exhibit in the classroom.

Children visit an archaeological museum where the docent answers their questions.

To further enrich the children's experience, the teacher took them on a walk around the school building to identify all the items made of clay. The children found many ceramic objects, including tiles on the bathroom floor, bowls in the kitchen, flower pots in the entryway, bricks on the front walk, and picture frames in the director's office. The teacher asked the children to bring ceramic items from home to school, with help from their parents. The next day, the children brought in an assortment of decorative and functional items and created an exhibit.

The teacher put up several posters showing ceramics from museum exhibits, with photographs that featured both ancient and contemporary pottery. She told the children that in three days they would visit a nearby archeological museum to see earthenware collections from people who used to live in their city a very long time ago. At snack time, they discussed what a museum was like. Several of the children had visited museums with their families and talked about how they would be able to "look but not touch" the exhibits. They also said everyone had to be very quiet. But the teacher explained she had arranged a special visit with a docent from the museum and that the children would be free to ask as many questions as they wanted and even touch copies of some of the artworks present.

The teacher brought in books with photographs of the types of ceramics the children would see at the museum. In the days leading up to the museum visit, the children enjoyed looking at the books and comparing the pots to the ones they were making. At the museum, the children were eager to look at the ceramics on

Children read books with illustrations of the clay objects they saw at the museum.

display. They discovered huge vessels with elaborate paintings and carvings. The children were delighted to find not only functional pots but also ceremonial figurines, miniature carriages, lanterns, and even toys made of clay. They were full of questions about how the pots were made and how they were used. The museum docent answered all their questions and was clearly pleased with the students' interest and enthusiasm.

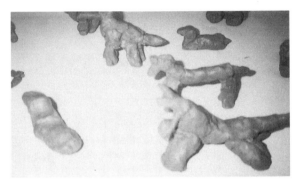

After visits to the studio and museum, children create elaborate human and animal figures.

3) Production

Production had actually been occurring at almost every step of the in-depth studio experience. However, inspired by their visit to the museum and the variety of clay objects they saw, the children seemed to enter an even more intense phase of making clay objects. They incorporated all of the techniques they had learned so far to make bowls, baskets, human and animal figures, vehicles, flowers, and designs. The children used slip to join together the pieces of their constructions. Several groups of children decided to collaborate to build multi-part pieces. One group made a forest, another made a zoo, still another a collection of toys. The children made up stories and acted out various role-plays with their ceramic creations. They placed their works on racks to dry. After the constructions were dry, some of the children chose to paint them.

4) Reflection

As with production, reflection was an ongoing process in the children's experiences with clay. During their introduction to mud in the school yard and clay in the classroom, the children constantly made observa-

Supporting Young Artists

tions about the qualities of the material. The teacher encouraged this process by asking open-ended questions and inviting the children to remember and compare their experiences with the material at different stages. After the visit to the potter's studio and the museum, there were many discussions about what the children had seen and how they were going to make similar objects themselves back in the classroom. The

Teachers encourage reflection and appreciation by displaying the work of students and artists side by side.

teacher provided ample space for the children to dry and display their wares. Having their pots in such a visible location inspired constant observation and discussion. Parents were also intrigued by the growing collection of pots and expressed surprise and delight each day at what they saw.

The teacher helped the children become aware that they encountered clay in their everyday home and school environments. In addition, the children saw the ancient ceramics produced in and around their city. From this exposure, plus their own hands-on experiences, the children began to develop a rich sense of this medium's versatility and prevalence in their lives.

PROGRAM B: A TRIP TO THE SEA

1) Introduction

Program B was located in a small city near the sea. In the introductory stage, the children visited a ceramics studio to see how the clay was stored, prepared, and shaped. The children were able to see a variety of artistic styles by watching the three potters who worked in this studio. One potter used the wheel to throw pots, and the others did primarily handbuilt work. Some of the pots were plain, and others were

Children begin exploring clay with their hands—poking, pinching, and squeezing.

highly decorated. Two ceramicists made household items and used complex glazes and decoration. The other one specialized in urns and sculptures for the garden, many of which were done on a large scale. The children left the studio with a large bag of clay for their classroom. They stored the clay in big bins with tight lids so it would stay moist. There was much talk about all the things the children planned to make with the clay when they returned to school in the morning.

The next day, the teacher and children spread sheets of plastic on the tables and began to explore the clay, using only their hands. They tore off pieces of clay and flattened, rolled, pinched, poked, and pressed it. The children made coils, flat figures, and small bowls. They tried using different parts of their hands—fingertips, fingernails, palms, knuckles, fists—to see what different types of impressions they could leave in the clay's surface. The teacher imitated their actions and introduced new ones for them to try. The children created bridges, flowers, and birds.

On the following day, the children tried stretching and rolling their clay. After using their hands, they experimented with wooden dowels, plastic bottles, rolling pins made of paper-towel tubes covered in foil. They observed that different types of rolling devices left different impressions in the clay. Gradually, the children explored other homemade tools. They tried using plastic eating utensils, hair ornaments, toothpicks, beads and buttons, and hardware fasteners (nuts, screws, bolts). As the children explored the visual effects of these various tools, the teacher explained that they were making "relief" decorations. Several children became intrigued with the process of making coils and wanted to see how high they could stack them. The teacher showed them how to make slip by adding water to the clay and using it to smooth the connections and join the coils. The children observed that the slip was creamy in texture and that it acted like glue to hold the pieces of clay together.

Children create familiar things from their environment, such as bridges, flowers, and birds.

Children experiment with foil-covered paper-towel tubes, plastic utensils, wooden sticks, and hair curlers.

The children carried their creations to a shelf to dry. The teacher explained that if the clay dried too quickly, it would crack and pieces of their sculptures, such as the handle on a cup or the arms on a figure, might fall off. The teacher told the children that they would need to cover the clay so it would dry more slowly and asked them what they wanted to use for a cover. The children remembered the large sheets of transparent plastic that covered the pots at the ceramics studio. They suggested that the plastic sheeting they spread to protect the tables in the classroom would also work well as a cover while their creations dried. Working together, the children draped large sheets of plastic over their clay forms to regulate the drying process.

2) Enrichment

The teacher enriched the children's clay experience by helping them set up a ceramics exhibit in the classroom. She brought in books, post cards, and posters showing ancient and contemporary pottery from the local area. The teacher had collected these materials from displays at nearby museums. She asked the children if in their homes they had any pots like those in the pictures. When the children recalled many familiar items, the teacher asked their parents if they would be willing to loan some pots to the classroom for the exhibit. The parents were happy to contribute clay items from home, and many also brought in additional books, magazines, and photographs. Over the course of several weeks, the classroom exhibit continued to grow. It was a favorite place for children and families to congregate at drop-off and pick-up times.

A few weeks into the school year, the teacher suggested a trip to the nearby beach. Here the children observed imprints in the wet

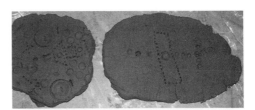

At the beach, children observe imprints in the sand and collect shells and pebbles.

Children make engravings and decorate reliefs with materials they collected at the beach.

sand—impressions made by footprints, seaweed, and shells. Using bags and boxes they had brought from school, the children collected pebbles, sticks, shells, and other natural objects to use as decorations in their own work. While at the beach, the teacher also called the children's attention to the sound of the waves and the temperature and smell of the air. Back in the classroom, the teacher put on a tape of music that evoked the sea, and the children spread their collections on the tables. They rolled the clay into balls and slabs and used the items from the beach to shape and decorate the clay. They engraved with sticks and made mosaics with shells and pebbles. They made flowers, handbags, hats, houses, and designs.

The following day, the teacher again spread plastic on the tables. The children brought out their treasures from the beach and the tools they had used in their initial explorations. The teacher further enriched their collection of tools by adding combs, clothes pins, spools, bottle caps, and other household items. The children worked individually, in pairs, or in small groups. They tore lumps of clay with their hands or cut slabs with knives and proceeded to make imprints with all their natural and manufactured found materials. After the children had been working for a while, the teacher again put on some music. Several children began moving their tools along with the music or announced they were making images of the sea and the beach. Others created gardens or made decorated tiles. They let their work dry slowly and added it to the classroom exhibit.

A tire tread in mud inspires children to make their own impressions in clay.

3) Production

As they became more adept at working with the clay, the children became interested in making increasingly larger creations. The teacher set out coffee cans, boxes, and empty plastic food containers and suggested the children try to cover these shapes with coils and slabs. The children applied these basic techniques, which they had practiced on a smaller scale, to covering the large shapes and making free-standing forms. Several children made big houses with slab walls. They cut out doors and windows and added balconies. One girl decided her building looked like a church and made a cross on the roof. Several others followed her lead and soon there were five churches on the shelf. Another group of children coiled clay around mixing bowls to create a set of

Further experiments include building with coils and draping slabs over boxes and bowls.

giant caves. Some children thought the mounds looked like turtles. Throughout these productive activities, the children increased the scale and complexity of their work. In the process, they solved many problems and made new discoveries about the properties of clay.

Several children decided they wanted to paint these large-scale structures. They talked about how long the clay should dry before being painted and what type of paint to use—finger paint or tempera. The children felt the clay every day to determine if it was dry enough. They tried out different types of paint on clay samples and decided the tempera paint would work best. Some children who had collaborated on a structure had disagreements about what paint colors to use, but with the teacher acting as mediator, the children solved this problem. Each child got to paint a wall of the house in a color of his or her choice. They could also add whatever decorations they wanted. The finished houses, churches, caves, and other buildings were added to the ceramics display. After seeing the display, a few children also chose to paint representations of their structures on paper. They added details, such as grass and flowers and trees, to provide a setting for the houses in their paintings.

Slabs lead to large free-standing structures. A girl decides her building looks like a church and adds a cross on top.

Meanwhile, other children were more interested in continuing to use the clay itself as a two-dimensional medium. The same group of children also enjoyed listening to music and painting with the clay. Over a period of two days, these children listened to tapes with sea sounds and melodies and made a large mural with images and designs about the sea. The sea was a prominent feature in their city and provided employment and recreational activities for their

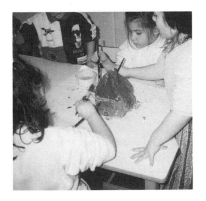

Children paint their clay buildings and represent them on paper. They add details such as people, a sun, and flowers.

families. The children were able to represent this pervasive element in their lives through their art. In addition to creating visual representations, the children invented songs and dances, pretending to be crashing waves and floating boats.

4) Reflection

As with other programs, the children continually reflected on their experiences with clay. On their way back to the school after visiting the ceramics studio, the children discussed what they had seen and what they would make with the clay the potters gave them. As they investigated the clay with their hands, natural objects, and manufactured tools, the children commented on their actions and the effects they were producing. The teacher supplied additional vocabulary words to help them describe and think about the process and products of working with clay. She took pictures so the children could see what they had done and describe their actions to one another.

Finished items made by the children were added to the growing display of ceramics from home. This exhibit was enriched by books, posters, post cards, and magazine photographs of ceramics that the children enjoyed looking at and talking about. Pictures of the class field trips, as well as photographs of the children at work, were also included in the display. The children eagerly showed their work, the photographic documentation, and the background information to

Displays encourage children to remember and reflect on their work with clay.

parents and visitors. They recalled how they made the items on display. They reported how they collected the materials and arranged everything on the shelves. The children constantly looked at the display and talked about how to amplify and enhance it.

Problem-solving with the clay also presented many opportunities for reflection. For example, the children tried different methods to layer coils and attach representational and decorative pieces to the figurines they created. They evaluated each step of the trial-and-error process to see if their solutions were effective. Eventually, they discovered a promising technique for re-wetting the clay with slip and then smoothing the connections with their fingers. As the children sculpted larger forms over boxes and bowls, they encountered a new set of problems to be solved. After rolling slabs to make walls, the children discovered it was easier to attach the joints if they collaborated—one child holding the pieces in place while another applied the slip and connected them. They also problem-solved ways to remove the clay from the supporting shape without the work coming apart. As their constructions became even more elaborate, the children realized they had to measure so that parts would fit together or fit inside one another. They developed measuring strategies that involved their hands, rulers, and stand-in objects.

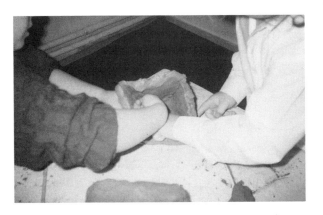

Joining walls is easier when friends work together.

All of these problem scenarios—joining, removing, fitting—prompted children to think about possible solutions. Each time a new problem arose, they remembered how they had solved similar problems. The children applied the same procedures to see if they would work in the current situation. When necessary, they modified their techniques to meet different demands. They learned a great deal about clay and its properties. In the process, they also developed their reasoning abilities and felt a sense of accomplishment about the resulting artistry.

A Brief History of the Use of Dough as an Art Medium

Dough is a natural material used as a foodstuff throughout the world. While it is usually produced commercially, dough is still homemade in many parts of the world. Most people consume dough in some form every day—pasta, bread and rolls, cakes and pastries, and other baked goods. Yet in many places throughout the world, dough has also been developed as a craft. It is an inexpensive medium, making it a suitable venue for artistic expression even in cultures with limited resources. On holidays and festive occasions, dough is used to make elaborate and beautiful creations that are edible and/or decorative.

Dough is a natural material used in many foods.

Dough has also been used to make toys, dolls, and other small sculptural objects. It is growing as a popular medium for jewelry, either alone or as a base for embedding beads and other decorative items. A small number of artists have begun using dough to create larger sculptures. They take advantage of the medium's inherent flexibility, the changeability of its shape and color, and its amenableness to surface design. Some artists use dough as their medium to make an artistic or political statement. They encourage viewers to consume their sculptures as a way of emphasizing the impermanence of art, thus taunting a market that they perceive inflates the worth of

Dough's flexibility lends itself to shaping and surface design.

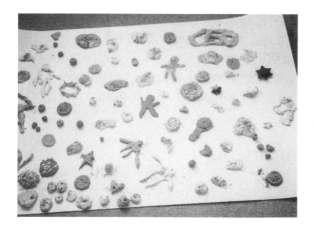

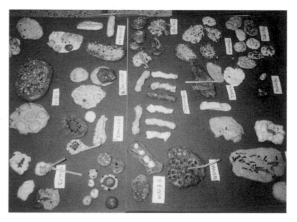

questionable art artificially while leaving many artists to starve, their output unrecognized. Dough can thus be both a playful and a serious art medium.

Characteristics of Dough

Dough is a food product made by mixing water and flour from wheat or other grains. Other ingredients, such as salt, sugar, eggs, flavorings, or yeast may also be added. In modern society, children are becoming less familiar with dough. They see finished products made of dough in bakeries, pastry shops, and general food markets, but are unaware of the raw ingredients involved or how dough is kneaded and formed. Dough can be prepared easily at home or in early childhood settings to give children a better understanding of where these products originate. Of course, preparing the dough by themselves also enables children to experience dough as a potential art medium.

Dough is a very sensual medium. It has color, volume, shape, texture, smell, and taste, and is considered a plastic art because of it

A boy explores dough's malleability with a toy drill.

malleability. Due to its softness, dough is particularly easy for children to handle and easily mixed with other materials, such as sand or grass, to change its texture. Dough's softness also means that it can be embedded and decorated with other materials—natural materials like nuts, shells, pebbles, leaves, twigs, and pine cones, and manufactured items like yarn, ribbons, beads, and buttons. Dough is a neutral color that can vary with the type of flour and liquid used. The color can be changed readily by mixing in other ingredients, including natural colors such as spices (cinnamon, mustard powder, or red and black pepper) and other foodstuffs (coffee, cocoa, or vegetable dyes), as well as chemical colorings (paints and commercial dyes).

Young Children and Dough

Many early childhood programs buy ready-made dough because it is convenient. However, working with commercial dough deprives children of the opportunity to see how this material is created and transformed. Also, commercial dough usually comes in only one texture and a limited range of bright colors. In contrast, making their own dough allows children to experiment with and control the texture and color of the medium, allowing them to produce a much wider range of effects.

Making dough offers more opportunities to discover its properties than buying it ready-made.

Mixing dough and using it as an art medium provides young children with a multitude of sensory, cognitive, and aesthetic experiences. The process of mixing and kneading helps them develop large and small muscles. Their physical energy is transmitted directly to the dough and acts to change its consistency and its shape. Working with dough also presents many opportunities for learning. Children experience the process of measuring and mixing ingredients, and they see the dough transformed when they add color. They observe another transformation when they watch and feel the dough dry. All of these experiences contribute to their concept formation about the physical world.

As emphasized above, working with dough is an inherently sensory experience. Children can feel the texture of the dough against their skin, smell and taste the ingredients, and sense its warmth as they roll it between their hands. Because dough and dough products are often associated with holiday celebrations, this medium is wonderful for establishing ties between the school and children's homes and

Mixing dough provides key experiences in measurement and social interaction.

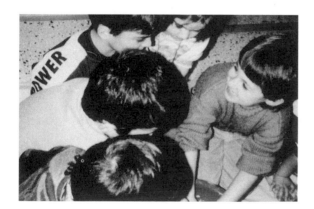

Children associate dough with holiday celebrations at home.

Dough helps children appreciate the aesthetics of sculpture and surface design.

communities. Dough is a medium likely to show up at local craft shows and artisans' markets, where children can see how this familiar substance is used as both a foodstuff and as an art medium by family members and neighbors.

Finally, dough provides opportunities for aesthetic development. It is an excellent medium for introducing young children to the process of sculpting and modeling. They are likely to have more control over dough than over any other plastic material. And they can easily represent the images in their minds through the actions of their hands. Dough also contributes to the development of two-dimensional concepts and skills in the visual arts. Because the surface of dough is so receptive to making impressions, it is an excellent medium for exploring decoration and design. In sum, by using dough as an art medium, children can begin to form aesthetic judgments about size and shape, color, and embellishment.

The In-Depth Studio Approach With Dough

The rest of this chapter describes an in-depth studio approach with dough used in one early childhood program. The children in this program had many opportunities to create and manipulate dough, to see dough used in their communities, and to connect dough with familiar cultural events. The introduction, enrichment, production, and reflection stages intertwined to give children a rich experience with this medium as a sculptural and decorative art form.

Supporting Young Artists

PROGRAM C: A NEW USE FOR AN OLD MATERIAL

1) Introduction

Program C was located in a city. While most of the children knew that dough was used to make bread, none of them had worked with dough directly as either a foodstuff or an art medium. In the introductory stage, the teacher and children talked about dough as they ate bread and other dough products at snack time. They also decided to create an exhibit about wheat, the main raw ingredient of dough. The teacher brought in posters and photographs about wheat and asked the children and their families to add more wheat-related items. With the eager cooperation of their parents, the children brought in wheat stalks, barley grains, corn kernels, and various types of flour and meal.

While the classroom exhibit continued to grow, the teacher told the children that they would be making their own dough. Together, they spread a large sheet of plastic on the floor. The children sat on the floor and divided into small groups. Each group had a plastic basin, a bag of flour, a cup of salt, and a pitcher of water. They put these ingredients in the basin and tried to make a dough that was malleable, but not too soft. The

Children learn about the origin of dough by reading illustrated books and examining stalks and kernels of grain.

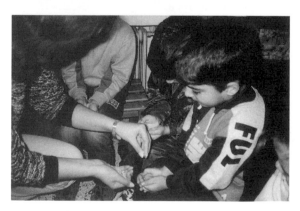

children enjoyed pouring in the ingredients and mixing the dough. They kneaded the dough with their fists and palms, pushing and pulling it to feel its consistency change. The children smelled and tasted small bits of dough. Using only their hands, they rolled, pinched, squeezed, twisted, poked, cut, flattened, and coiled the dough—the same types of manipulations that children in Programs A and B used when exploring clay. The children rolled the dough into long strands and then used these strips to "draw" shapes on the floor and table, making a variety of shapes and designs.

Because dough is so easy to manipulate, children quickly progress from flattening and rolling to making shapes and designs.

2) Enrichment

After the children had a few days of firsthand experience with dough, the class went on a field trip to a bakery shop. Here the children observed how flour was turned into dough by using big machines. They watched the dough being kneaded and shaped into loaves of bread and then baked in huge ovens. A few days later they visited a pastry shop where they saw bakers creating a variety of cakes and cookies, each elaborately decorated. The children talked about their experiences at the bakery and the pastry shop. After these visits, they used chalk and pastels to draw pictures of breads and cookies on white and colored paper. The children decorated their pictures and made plans to re-create their ideas by mixing up a new batch of dough. They were very eager to play cooks and bakers.

At this point, the teacher brought in different natural materials so the children could color their dough. They mixed in coffee, cocoa, cinnamon, and other spices. They added food dyes in primary colors. To create more intense colors, the children mixed finger paint into the

Supporting Young Artists

Children re-create the experience at the bakery by making their own fancy breads and pastries.

On a field trip to the bakery, children see the dough mixer and braided breads ready for the oven.

dough. The teacher also provided various tools the children could use to manipulate the dough, make impressions in it, or add decorations— plastic eating utensils and other cooking tools, as well as natural and manufactured objects.

The teacher and children continued to add to the exhibit on wheat and dough, enriching it with photographs from their field trips and related books and stories. At another time, after reading the story *Rapunzel,* the children decided to represent this fairy tale with dough. They divided into groups, with one group making the castle and another making the characters—a witch, Rapunzel, and the prince. Others contributed trees, flowers, and birds to the fantasy set. They discovered that it was difficult to make larger structures that could stand because the dough was so soft. With the teacher's help, however, they problem-solved and discovered that by using boxes and other sturdy objects as supports, they could make their dough creations stand.

Several days later, the teacher, children, and parents took a short walk near the center to look at the shop windows being decorated for the approaching winter holidays. They saw holiday breads and cookies, tree decorations, toys, and other gifts. The teacher explained that in some countries, people also decorated breads for wedding celebrations and made other decorative items out of dough, such as jewelry, plaques, hanging

Children mix natural colorings and finger paints into the dough.

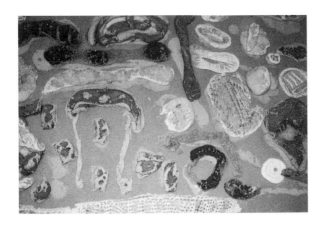

Children create their own designs after seeing store windows decorated for the holidays.

sculptures, and statues. The children returned to the classroom eager to make similar decorative items by using dough, colorings, and found materials.

3) Production

As noted above, the children's experiments and field trips all inspired them to make various products with the dough. Following their trips to the bakery and pastry shop, the children made a wide variety of foods and baked goods. They filled paper plates with familiar foods: fruits and salads, vegetables, meatballs, sausages, hamburgers, eggs, pasta, pies, and cakes. They decorated their work with nuts and seeds. They used kitchen tools such as a garlic press and pastry cones to make squiggles and flowers with the dough. The children decided to have a party with all the food and invited the teachers, children, and administrative staff of the center to join them in the feast. Many parents came, too. The children "wrote" invitations, delivered them to the other classrooms and offices, and made place settings by decorating construction paper and folding napkins. All the children and their guests pretended to eat the food and exclaimed

The children model foods and invite parents and everyone at the center to a party. They arrange their creations in an exhibit.

over how wonderful it tasted. After the party, the children arranged all their food creations in an exhibit.

The children used dough to make many other items from their everyday lives and from the stories they loved. They created houses, birds, flowers, animals, clothing, and jewelry out of dough. They made Rapunzel's castle and the characters from the fairy tale. After looking in the shop windows, the children made holiday and wedding breads, hanging toys, picture and mirror frames, boxes, and jewelry. They decorated these objects with stars, angels, and flowers made of dough. They also used objects such as beads, shells, and ribbons to decorate their work. The children placed their work in trays and spread it on shelves to dry.

The next day, a few parents brought in small bare trees. Once their dough creations had dried, the children hung them on the branches of the trees. Some children were interested in making larger hanging items so the teacher brought in photographs of mobiles. Several children made mobiles out of dough and hung them in different places in the classroom—from clothing hooks, from lamp stands, and from the handles of the storage cabinets. The room took on a festive look that was similar to what the children were experiencing in their own homes as family preparations for the holiday season intensified.

4) Reflection

Opportunities for reflection occurred throughout the children's experiences. For example, in their initial exploration with mixing dough, the children talked about its texture and how they had to vary the amounts of the ingredients to make a dough they could mold with

Children decorate the branches of a tree brought in by their parents and make holiday mobiles.

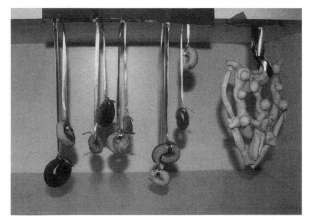

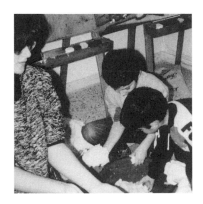

A teacher encourages children to reflect during their initial experiences mixing and exploring dough.

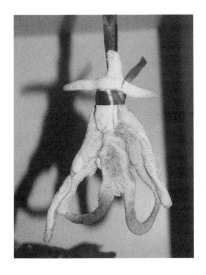

Children solve problems such as how to hang their dough mobiles.

their hands. Each time they mixed a new batch of dough, they had to remember the steps of the process and the effective proportions of ingredients. The children kept up a running dialogue as they used their hands and various tools to explore the properties of the dough. They compared the visual effects of these efforts. Through their actions and observations, the children became aware of their capacity for transforming the dough by using other natural materials and found manufactured objects.

After their visits to the bakery and pastry shop, the children talked about how the dough was mixed and baked in big machines and ovens. They recalled the heat of the ovens and how they had to stand far back from the oven doors. The children remembered the wonderful smells in both places. They recalled how the breads were twisted into interesting shapes and sprinkled with seeds. They talked about the different colors and styles for decorating the cakes and cookies and represented these variations in their own plans and drawings. At each place, the children received free samples. They talked a great deal about how good these products made of dough tasted.

In making larger dough structures, such as Rapunzel's castle, the children had to problem-solve how to make a soft substance more rigid. With help from the teacher, they figured out that they could use boxes, plastic bottles, and cardboard rolls to provide a structure underneath the dough. In making tree decorations and mobiles, the children problem-solved how to hang their creations. They either designed their dough pieces to include hooking devices or they attached ribbons and other materials that they could use for hanging. Working with dough thus presented many challenges that the children were interested in solving to carry out their plans and intentions.

As in the other in-depth programs described in this book, the children's work-in-progress and finished work was always displayed. These exhibits of both the process and products of their investigations

Displaying the finished work encourages children to reflect on their experiences.

helped children to recall what they saw and did. The displays also prompted many conversations among the children and between the children and adults—teachers, parents, and visitors to the classroom. In the process of exploring dough and its myriad uses, the children ventured out into their communities, collaborated with peers in the classroom, and solved many physical and aesthetic problems. The entire experience gave children an appreciation for a familiar material that they never knew could be a medium for art.

Glossary of Art Vocabulary Words[1]

This glossary of art vocabulary words will help adults familiarize themselves with the terms used by artists and critics. In simpler language, adults can include the ideas behind these definitions in their discussions with young children. As conversations about art become part of the everyday classroom experience, adults may introduce some of these actual words to young children to expand their language for talking about art.

abstract art. Art that is not realistic or recognizable as actual objects and events (also called non-objective or non-representational art); emphasizes formal elements instead of depiction. Opposite of figurative art.

aesthetics. The branch of philosophy that considers the question "What is art?"

architecture. A unifying method or style of building.

background. The area of an artwork that appears to be behind other objects or farther away from the viewer. Opposite of foreground.

canvas. A heavy cloth (made of hemp, linen, flax, or cotton duck) stretched on a wooden frame and used as a surface for painting.

clay. A natural earthy material that is plastic (capable of being shaped or formed) when wet.

collage. An artistic composition of materials and objects attached to a surface.

color. Property caused by different qualities of the light reflected or emitted by objects.

> *hue*—The name of a color.

> *primary*—Red, yellow, and blue; pure color.

> *secondary*—Orange, green, and violet (made from combining two primary colors); mixed color.

> *complementary*—Colors that are opposite one another on the color wheel: red-green, blue-orange, and yellow-violet.

> *intensity*—Brightness or dullness of color. Also called saturation.

> *value*—Lightness and darkness of color.

> *shade or tone*—The darkness of a color; may be achieved by adding black. Opposite of tint.

> *tint*—The lightness of a color; may be achieved by adding white. Opposite of shade or tone.

> *temperature*—Quality associated with different hues; colors at the blue end of the spectrum are cool and those at the red end are warm.

> *relationship*—How colors change when they are mixed or put next to one another.

conceptual art. Art that focuses on ideas as well as images.

criticism. The analysis of the formal or expressive properties of an artwork.

design. The planned arrangement of elements and principles in an artwork.

> *design elements*—Line, form, space, texture, shape, color. Also called formal elements.

[1]Adapted from Marshall, 1999

design principles—The way in which the elements of art are organized in a composition, including balance, symmetry, movement, repetition, alternation, unity, variation, and emphasis.

figurative art. Art that depicts objects and events (also called representational art); emphasizes realism or subject matter. Opposite of abstract art.

foreground. The area that appears to be closest to the viewer. Opposite of background.

form or shape. External shape, outline, or contour of a two- or three-dimensional object.

> **size**—Continuum from small to large; perception of size affected by color, placement, and surrounding objects.
>
> **geometrics**—Named (recognizable geometric shape) or unnamed.
>
> **other qualities**—Open or closed, regular or irregular, empty or full (solid), separated or connected, isolated or enclosed, independent or overlapping.

fresco. Italian for "fresh"; a wall-painting technique in which water-based paints are mixed with lime water and applied on wet plaster.

functional. Referring to how an artwork is used rather than how it appears.

gouache. A method of painting using opaque water colors mixed with white powder or chalk along with gum arabic or honey.

impasto. The technique of applying dense amounts of paint by brush, knife, or hand to form a textured, low-relief surface.

kiln. An oven or furnace used to fire clay (ceramic) products; firing in a kiln dries and hardens the clay.

line. A mark used to define a shape or represent a contour; any of the marks that make up the formal design of a picture.

> **kind**—Straight, curved, or a combination.
>
> **length**—How long the line is.
>
> **beginning/end**—Where the line starts and finishes.
>
> **direction**—Where the line moves up and down, side to side, or diagonally; whether the line follows one path or changes direction.
>
> **other qualities**—Width, steadiness, heaviness.
>
> **relationship**—How lines appear relative to other lines (separate, intertwined, parallel, crossed).

medium. Material(s) used to create an image (plural: media); mixed media is the use of different media in the same artwork.

minimalism. A style of art that uses the least amount of formal elements; reduces images and ideas to their simplest forms, shapes, and colors.

mosaic. The technique of embedding pebbles, stones, glass, tesserae (small squares of stone or glass) and so on in the surface of stucco or plaster.

motif. A dominant theme, pattern, or idea in an artwork; motifs are often repeated.

mural. Any painting or other decoration made directly on a wall or ceiling.

oil paint. Pigment bound in oil (usually linseed oil).

palette. A holder or surface for mixing paint colors; also refers to the range of colors chosen by an artist and included in an artwork.

performance art. Artwork that combines visual arts with other artistic media, including music, theater, dance; often includes audience participation and may

Glossary of Art Vocabulary Words

therefore change from one performance to the next.

pigment. The coloring agent, in powdered or other form, used in painting and drawing media.

pop art. Art that includes everyday and common objects from life (such as food, tools, media stars, cartoons); focuses on mass culture and advertising.

portfolio. An artist's body of finished work or a representative sample of that work.

relief. The projection of figures or forms from a flat background; may be low relief or high relief.

reproduction. A copy of an artwork such as a photograph in a book, post card, or slide.

sculpture. Three-dimensional representations, forms, and figures that have been carved, cut, hewn, cast, and/or molded.

space. The way objects fill the artwork and the distances between them.

> *positive space*—The area occupied by the object.

> *negative space*—The area left unoccupied.

> *other qualities*—Crowded or sparse, open or restricted, bounded or unbounded, inclusive or exclusive, solid or permeable.

still life. Representation of inanimate (non-moving) objects such as flowers, fruit, books.

support. Surface used for drawing and painting, such as paper, canvas, or wood.

symbol. Lines, shapes, and colors used to represent something else.

technique. A specific procedure or set of procedures used to create artwork.

tempera paint. Paint made from powdered pigments mixed with water and egg yolk.

texture. Surface characteristic(s) of an artwork.

> *actual or implied*—texture may be inherent in the object or visually suggested.

> *other qualities*—soft or hard, rough or smooth, regular or irregular, reflective or absorptive, shiny or dull (matte).

three-dimensional. Artwork that has height and width and depth and occupies all dimensions of space (see two-dimensional).

two-dimensional. Artwork that has height and width and occupies only the surface space (see three-dimensional).

watercolor paint. Pigment bound in water.

weaving. The interlacing of threads on a loom to make fabric; the fabric so made.

> *warp*—The fixed threads on a loom, usually vertical.

> *weft*—The filler threads on a loom, usually horizontal.

work-in-progress. An artwork that is not yet finished.

References

Arnheim, R. (1974). *Art and visual perception: A psychology of the creative eye.* Los Angeles: University of California Press.

Arnheim, R. (1989). *Thoughts on art education.* Los Angeles: The Getty Center for Education in the Arts.

Arts Education Partnership. (1998). *Young children and the arts: Making creative connections—A report of the Task Force on Children's Learning and the Arts: Birth to Age Eight.* Washington, DC: Author.

Baker, D. W. (1990, July–August). The visual arts in early childhood education. *Design for Arts in Education, 91*(6), 21–25.

Baker, D. W. (1992, September). *Toward a sensible education: Inquiring into the role of the visual arts in early education.* Keynote address presented at Making Meaning Through Art: Art in Early Childhood Education Symposium, University of Illinois at Urbana-Champaign.

Barkan, M. (1966). Transitions in art education: Changing conceptions of curriculum content and teaching. In E. W. Eisner & D. W. Ecker (Eds.), *Readings in art education* (pp. 429–430). Boston: Xerox College Publishing.

Barnes, R. (1987). *Teaching art to young children 4 to 9.* Boston: Allen and Unwin.

Barsotti, A., Dahlberg, G., Gothson, H., & Asen, G. (1993, September). *Early childhood education in a changing world: A practice-oriented research project.* Paper presented at the Third European Conference on the Quality of Early Childhood Education, Kriopigi, Chalkidiki, Greece.

Beittel, K. R., & Mattil, E. L. (1966). The effect of a "depth" versus a "breadth" method of art instruction at the ninth-grade level. In E. W. Eisner & D. W. Ecker (Eds.), *Readings in art education* (pp. 246–258). Boston: Xerox College Publishing.

Bell, L. A. (1982). *Proto-paper in making paper.* New York: American Craft Museum.

Blandy, D., Congdon, K. G., & Krug, D. H. (1998). Art, ecological restoration, and art education. *Studies in Art Education, 39*(3), 230–243.

Bowman, B., Donovan, M. S., & Burns, M. S. (Eds.). (2000). *Eager to learn: Educating our preschoolers.* Washington, DC: National Academy Press.

Bredekamp, S. (Ed.). (1987). *Developmentally appropriate practice in early childhood programs serving children from birth through age 8, expanded edition.* Washington, DC: National Association for the Education of Young Children.

Bredekamp, S., & Copple, C. (Eds.). (1997). *Developmentally appropriate practice in early childhood programs, revised edition.* Washington, DC: National Association for the Education of Young Children.

Brittain, W. L. (1979). *Creativity, art, and the young child.* New York: Macmillan Publishing Co.

Burton, J. M. (1980, September). Beginnings of artistic language. *School Arts, 80*(1), 6–12.

Burton, J., Horowitz, R., & Abeles, H. (1999). Learning in and through the arts: Curriculum implications. In E. B. Fiske (Ed.), *Champions of change: The impact of the arts on learning* (pp. 35–46). Washington, DC: Arts Education Partnership and The President's Committee on the Arts and Humanities.

Catterall, J. S., Chapleau, R., & Iwanga, J. (1999). Involvement in the arts and human development. In E. B. Fiske (Ed.), *Champions of change: The impact of the arts on learning* (pp. 47–62). Washington, DC: Arts Education Partnership and The President's Committee on the Arts and Humanities.

Cembalest, R. (1991). The ecological art explosion. *ArtNews, 90*(6), 96–106.

Cerny, C., & Seriff, S. (1996). *Recycled re-seen: Folk art from the global scrap heap.* New York: Harry N. Abrams.

Chandler, R. (1973). *Art for teachers of children.* Columbus, Ohio: Merrill Publishing Co.

Clemens, S. G. (1991). Art in the classroom: Making every day special. *Young Children, 46*(2), 4–11.

Cohen, D. H., Stern, V., & Balaban, N. (1983). *Recording the behavior of young children.* New York: Teachers College Press.

Colbert, C. B. (1995). Developmentally appropriate practice in early art education. In C. M. Thompson (Ed.), *The visual arts and early childhood learning* (pp. 35–39). Reston, VA: National Art Education Association.

Colbert, C., & Taunton, M. (1992). *Developmentally appropriate practices for the visual arts education of young children.* NAEA Briefing Paper. Reston, VA: National Art Education Association.

Cole, E. S., & Schaefer, C. (1990). Can young children be art critics? *Young Children, 45*(2), 33–38.

Deasy, R. J., & Fulbright, H. M. (1999, November). The arts advantage. *American School Board Journal, 186*(11), 32–36.

Dobbs, S. M. (1998). *Learning in and through art.* Los Angeles: The Getty Education Institute for the Arts.

Edwards, C., Gandini, L., & Forman, G. (Eds.). (1998). *The hundred languages of children: The Reggio Emilia approach—Advanced reflections* (2nd ed.). Greenwich, CT: Ablex.

Eisner, E. W. (1972). *Educating artistic vision.* New York: Macmillan Publishing Co.

Eisner, E. W. (1987). The role of discipline-based art education in America's schools. *Art Education, 40*(5), 6–26.

Engel, B. S. (1995). *Considering children's art: Why and how to value their work.* Washington, DC: National Association for the Education of Young Children.

Epstein, A. S. (1993). *Training for quality: Improving early childhood programs through systematic inservice training.* Ypsilanti, MI: High/Scope Press.

Epstein, A. S. (2001). Thinking about art: Encouraging art appreciation in early childhood settings. *Young Children, 56*(3), 38–43.

Epstein, A. S., Schweinhart, L. J., & McAdoo, L. (1996). *Models of early childhood education.* Ypsilanti, MI: High/Scope Press.

Feeney, S., & Moravcik, E. (1987). A thing of beauty: Aesthetic development in young children. *Young Children, 42*(6), 6–15.

Fiske, E. B. (Ed.). (1999). *Champions of change: The impact of the arts on learning.* Washington, DC: Arts Education Partnership and The President's Committee on the Arts and Humanities.

Frangos, C. (1993). A child development centre based on the world of work and everyday life: A case of quality education provision for 2.5–5 year old children. *European Early Childhood Education Research Journal, 1*(1), 41–52.

Gair, A. (1995). *Artist's manual: A complete guide to painting and drawing materials and techniques.* San Francisco: Chronicle Books.

Gaitskell, C. D., & Hurwitz, A. (1975). *Children and their art.* New York: Harcourt Brace Jovanovich.

Gardner, H. (1970). Children's sensitivity to painting styles. *Child Development, 41*(2), 813–821.

Gardner, H. (1978). Critical judgment: A developmental study. *Journal of Aesthetic Education, 9*(2), 60–77.

Gardner, H. (1982). *Art, mind, and brain: A cognitive approach to creativity.* New York: Basic Books.

Gardner, H. (1988, Spring). Toward more effective arts education. *Journal of Aesthetic Education, 22*(1), 162–168.

Gardner, H. (1990). *Art education and human development.* Los Angeles: The Getty Center for Education in the Arts.

Glaubinger, J. (1986). *Paper now.* Bloomington, IN: Indiana University Press.

Goldschmied, E., & Jackson, S. (1994). *People under three: Young children in day care.* New York: Routledge.

Golomb, C. (1974). *Young children's sculpture and drawing: A study in representational development.* Cambridge, MA: Harvard University Press.

Golomb, C. (1992). *The child's creation of a pictorial world.* Berkeley, CA: University of California Press.

Greer, W. D. (1984). Discipline-based art education: Approaching art as a subject of study. *Studies in Art Education, 25*(4), 212–218.

Hardiman, G., & Zernich, T. (1980). Some considerations of Piaget's cognitive-structuralist theory and children's artistic development. *Studies in Art Education, 21*(3), 10–18.

Hardiman, G., & Zernich, T. (1985). Discrimination of styles in painting: A developmental study. *Studies in Art Education, 26*(3), 157–162.

Healy, J. M. (1994). *Your child's growing mind: A practical guide to brain development and learning from birth to adolescence.* New York: Doubleday.

Heath, S. B. (1998, November 18). Study finds participation in the arts has academic benefits for young people. *San Francisco Chronicle,* A19.

High/Scope Educational Research Foundation. (2000). *High/Scope preschool key experiences: Creative representation* [videotape and booklet]. Ypsilanti, MI: High/Scope Press.

Hohmann, M. (1996, November–December). Supporting children's development in drawing and painting. *High/Scope Extensions, 11*(3), 1–5.

Hohmann, M., & Weikart, D. P. (2002). *Educating young children: Active learning practices for preschool and child care programs.* (2nd ed.). Ypsilanti, MI: High/Scope Press.

Katz, L. (1998). What can we learn from Reggio Emilia? In C. Edwards, L. Gandini, & G. Forman (Eds.), *The hundred languages of children: The Reggio Emilia approach—Advanced reflections* (2nd ed., pp. 27–45). Greenwich, CT: Ablex.

Kerlavage, M. S. (1995). A bunch of naked ladies and a tiger: Children's responses to adult works of art. In C. M. Thompson (Ed.), *The visual arts and early childhood learning* (pp. 56–62). Reston, VA: National Art Education Association.

Kiester, G. J. (1985, October). Total education: Arts balance the analytical with the aesthetic. *Music Educators Journal, 34*(10), 24–27.

Kindler, A. M. (1995). Significance of adult input in early childhood artistic development. In C. M. Thompson (Ed.), *The visual arts and early childhood learning* (pp. 1–5). Reston, VA: National Art Education Association.

Kolodziej, S. (1995). The Picture Museum: Creating a photography museum with children. In C. M. Thompson (Ed.), *The visual arts and early childhood learning* (pp. 52–55). Reston, VA: National Art Education Association.

Koster, J. B. (1999, March). Clay for little fingers. *Young Children, 54*(2), 18–22.

Lasky, L., & Mukerji-Bergeson, R. (1980). *Art: Basic for young children.* Washington, DC: National Association for the Education of Young Children.

Linderman, E. W., & Herberholz, D. W. (1979). *Developing artistic and perceptual awareness.* New York: William C. Brown Co. Publishers.

Lindstrom, M. (1974). *Children's art.* Berkeley, CA: University of California Press.

Longley, L. (Ed.). (2000). *Gaining the arts advantage: Lessons from school districts that value arts education.* Washington, DC: The President's Committee on the Arts and Humanities.

Lowenfeld, V., & Brittain, W. (1987). *Creative and mental growth.* New York: Macmillan Publishing Co.

Lund, P., & Osborne, S. (1995). Birthdays, children, and art: Museums as meaningful places for young children. In C. M. Thompson (Ed.), *The visual arts and early childhood learning* (pp. 49–51). Reston, VA: National Art Education Association.

Luoma, J. R. (1998, March–April). The magic of paper. *Georama-Experiment, 24*(2), 150–175.

Malaguzzi, L. (1987). *The hundred languages of children.* Reggio Emilia, Italy: A.C.M.

Malaguzzi, L. (1998). History, ideas, and basic philosophy of Reggio Emilia: An interview with Lella Gandini. In C. Edwards, L. Gandini, & G. Forman (Eds.), *The hundred languages of children: The Reggio Emilia approach—Advanced reflections* (2nd ed., pp. 49–97). Greenwich, CT: Ablex.

Marshall, B. (1999, Summer). Art vocabulary for adult understanding. *High/Scope Supporting Young Artists Workshop, Participant Guide.* Ypsilanti, Michigan: High/Scope Press.

Meredieu, F. (1981). *Le dessin d'enfant.* Paris: Editions Universitaires.

Mitchell, F. (1995). Art education and children's literature: An interdisciplinary approach for preschool children. In C. M. Thompson (Ed.), *The visual arts and early childhood learning* (pp. 84–87). Reston, VA: National Art Education Association.

Morris, M. (Ed.). (1981). *The American Heritage Dictionary of the English Language.* Boston: Houghton Mifflin Company.

National Art Education Association. (1982). *Quality goals statement.* Washington, DC: Author.

National Education Goals Panel. (1994). *Goals 2000: Educate America Act.* Washington, DC: U.S. Government Printing Office.

National Endowment for the Arts. (1988). *Toward civilization: A report on arts education.* Washington, DC: U.S. Government Printing Office.

New, R. (1998). Theory and praxis in Reggio Emilia: They know what they are doing and why. In C. Edwards, L. Gandini, & G. Forman (Eds.), *The hundred languages of children: The Reggio Emilia approach—Advanced reflections* (2nd ed., pp. 261–284). Greenwich, CT: Ablex.

Newton, C. (1995). Language and learning about art. In C. M. Thompson (Ed.), *The visual arts and early childhood learning* (pp. 80–83). Reston, VA: National Art Education Association.

Oreck, B., Baum, S., & McCartney, H. (1999). Artistic talent development for urban youth: The promise and the challenge. In E. B. Fiske (Ed.), *Champions of change: The impact of the arts on learning* (pp. 63–78). Washington, DC: Arts Education Partnership and The President's Committee on the Arts and Humanities.

Parsons, M. (1987). *How we understand art: A cognitive development account of aesthetic experience.* Cambridge, UK: Cambridge University Press.

Perkins, D. N. (1994). *The intelligent eye: Learning to think by looking at art.* Los Angeles: The Getty Education Institute for the Arts.

Piaget, J. (1951). *Play, dreams, and imitation in childhood.* New York: Norton.

Piscitelli, B. (1988). Preschoolers and parents as artists and art appreciators. *Art Education, 41*(5), 48–55.

Post, J., & Hohmann, M. (2000). *Tender care and early learning: Supporting infants and toddlers in child care settings.* Ypsilanti, MI: High/Scope Press.

Rhodes, D. (1974). *Clay and glazes for the potter.* Philadelphia: Chilton Book Co.

Rosenblatt, E., & Winner, E. (1988, Spring). The art of children's drawing. *Journal of Aesthetic Education, 22*(1), 8–17.

Schiller, M. (1995, March). An emergent art curriculum that fosters understanding. *Young Children, 50*(3), 33–38.

Schweinhart, L. J., Barnes, H. V., & Weikart, D. P. (with Barnett, W. S., & Epstein, A. S.). (1993). *Significant benefits: The High/Scope Perry Preschool Study through age 27.* Ypsilanti, MI: High/Scope Press.

Schweinhart, L. J. & Weikart, D. P. (1997) *Lasting differences: The High/Scope Preschool Curriculum Comparison Study through age 23.* Ypsilanti, MI: High/Scope Press.

Seefeldt, C. (1987). The visual arts. In C. Seefeldt (Ed.), *The early childhood curriculum: A review of the current research* (pp. 183–210). New York: Teachers College Press.

Seefeldt, C. (1995, March). Art—A serious work. *Young Children, 50*(3), 39–45.

Shannon, F. (1997). *The art and craft of paper.* San Francisco: Chronicle Books.

Smith, N. R. (with Fucigna, C., Kennedy, M., & Lord, L.). (1993). *Experience and art: Teaching children to paint* (2nd ed.). New York: Teachers College Press.

Smith, P. (1982). *Introduction to making paper.* New York: American Craft Museum.

Susi, F. D. (1999). *The potential of written reflection by art students: NAEA advisory.* Reston, VA: National Art Education Association.

Szekely, G. (1988). *Encouraging creativity in art lessons.* New York: Teachers College Press.

Szekely, G. (1991). *From play to art.* Portsmouth, NH: Heinemann.

Szyba, C. M. (1999, January). Why do some teachers resist offering appropriate, open-ended art activities for young children? *Young Children, 54*(1), 16–20.

Tarr, P. (1995). Preschool children's socialization through art experiences. In C. M. Thompson (Ed.), *The visual arts and early childhood learning* (pp. 23–27). Reston, VA: National Art Education Association.

Thompson, C. G. (1992). *Recycled papers.* Cambridge, MA: The MIT Press.

Thompson, C. M. (1995). The visual arts and early childhood learning: Changing contexts and concepts. In C. M. Thompson (Ed.), *The visual arts and early childhood learning* (pp. 1–5). Reston, VA: National Art Education Association.

Tompkins, M. (1996a). A partnership with young artists. In N. A. Brickman (Ed.). *Supporting young learners 2* (pp. 187–192). Ypsilanti, MI: High/Scope Press.

Tompkins, M. (1996b). Developing a creative art area. In N. A. Brickman (Ed.). *Supporting young learners 2* (pp. 127–132). Ypsilanti, MI: High/Scope Press.

Trimis, E. (1996a). The development of the visual arts language through developmental programs: The case of drawing and painting of young children. *Ikastiki Pedia, 12,* 108–112.

Trimis, E. (1996b). *Supporting young artists: Exploring and creating with drawing and painting* [Videotape]. Ypsilanti, MI: High/Scope Press.

Trimis, E. (1997). *Supporting young artists: Exploring and creating with paper* [Videotape]. Ypsilanti, MI: High/Scope Press.

Trimis, E. (2000a). *Supporting young artists: Exploring and creating with clay* [Videotape]. Ypsilanti, MI: High/Scope Press.

Trimis, E. (2000b). *Supporting young artists: Exploring and creating with dough* [Videotape]. Ypsilanti, MI: High/Scope Press.

Trimis, E., & Manavopoulos, K. (2001). Promoting the creative abilities of young children through a visual arts program with seemingly scrap materials. *Research in the preschool years* (Vol. 1, pp. 215–231). Athens, Greece: Dardanos.

U. S. Department of Education. (1994). *National standards for arts education: What every young American should know and be able to do in the arts.* Washington, DC: U.S. Government Printing Office.

Vygotsky, L. S. (1978). *Mind in society.* Cambridge, MA: Harvard University Press.

Warash, B. G., & Saab, J. F. (1999). Exploring the visual arts with young children. *Dimensions of Early Childhood, 27*(1), 11–15.

Whitford, F. (1984). *Bauhaus.* London: Thames and Hudson.

Wilkinson, B. (1997). *Papermaking.* Salt Lake City, UT: Gibbs Smith Publisher.

Wright, M. (1995). *An introduction to mixed media.* London: Dorling Kindersley (in association with the Royal Academy of Arts).

Zurmuehlen, M., & Kantner, L. (1995). The narrative quality of young children's art. In C. M. Thompson (Ed.), *The visual arts and early childhood learning* (pp. 6–9). Reston, VA: National Art Education Association.

Index

ABOUT THE AUTHORS

Ann S. Epstein is Director of the Early Childhood Division at the High/Scope Educational Research Foundation, where she has worked since 1975. She has a Ph.D. in developmental psychology and an MFA in visual arts with an emphasis on drawing and textiles. Dr. Epstein develops curriculum materials, leads a team of early childhood specialists who train teachers and caregivers, supervises implementation of the NAEYC-accredited High/Scope Demonstration Preschool, evaluates the effectiveness of early childhood programs and staff development initiatives, and serves as a consulting editor on professional journals. She has published many books and articles on early childhood education for a variety of audiences, including program administrators, practitioners, researchers, policymakers, and parents. Her writings on early art education have appeared in *Young Children,* and she has conducted workshops on the development of the visual arts at the annual conference of the National Association for the Education of Young Children. Dr. Epstein is also a studio artist whose artwork has been exhibited in many shows and galleries throughout the country. She has received numerous awards and commissions, and her work has been recognized by the Michigan Council for the Arts.

Eli Trimis is Assistant Professor in the School of Early Childhood Education Sciences at Aristotle University of Thessaloniki, Greece, where she has worked since 1988. She also teaches art education in the School of Primary Education Sciences at the University of Cyprus in Lefkosia, Cyprus. She has a Ph.D. in art education and a BFA in visual arts. Dr. Trimis has specialized in art education for preschool and preadolescent children since 1972. She has developed curriculum materials and has conducted workshops in visual arts at the High/Scope Educational Research Foundation's annual conferences. She is the author of a series of videos and booklets titled *Supporting Young Artists,* which was published by High/Scope Press. An authority on children's art, Dr. Trimis has been published in early childhood education and art magazines, has advised numerous schools and organizations, and was actively involved in the Melina Mercouri Project for the Arts funded by the Ministry of Education-Ministry of Culture in Greece. She has had several solo and group exhibits in Greece and the United States, and the artwork of her students has been shown in exhibits in Greece and Cyprus.